P9-DXM-267

DATE DUE

AP 17 '04			

DEMCO 38-296

DAWN AFTER DARK

Dawn After Dark

by René Huyghe and Daisaku Ikeda

translated by Richard L. Gage

New York · WEATHERHILL · *Tokyo*

MAR '93

Riverside Community College
Library
4800 Magnolia Avenue
Riverside, California 92506

First Edition, 1991

Published by Weatherhill, Inc., New York, with editorial offices at
Tanko-Weatherhill, Inc., 8–3 Nibancho, Chiyoda-ku, Tokyo 102,
Japan. Copyright © 1980, 1981, 1991 by René Huyghe and Daisaku
Ikeda; all rights reserved. Printed in Japan.

Library of Congress Cataloging in Publication Data: Ikeda, Daisaku. / [Nuit
appelle l'aurore. English] / Dawn after dark / by René Huyghe and Daisaku
Ikeda; translated by Richard L. Gage.—1st ed. / p.   cm. / Translation of:
Yami wa akatsuki o motomete (Japanese ed. of La nuit appelle l'aurore). /
ISBN 0–8348–0238–4 / 1. Civilization, Modern—1950–   / I. Huyghe, René.
II. Title. / CB428.I3813   1991 / 909.82—dc20 / 90–29330 CIP

Contents

Introduction

by René Huyghe

At no time in history has humanity faced problems on a scale as vast as that confronting us now. Since the nineteenth century, extended historical knowledge has led lucid human minds to transcend immediate time and see our own epoch as part of a continuous development of thousands of years. Today, international connections and mass-media information compel us to think in global terms.

Hitherto, for millennia, more or less extended groups of human beings have had no interest in knowing anything but their own needs, appetites, customs, and beliefs. The beliefs of others they ignored or rejected, while attempting to enforce their own wherever they went.

Although suppressing quarrels among their own adherent nations, religions have had no compunctions about denying each other, thus engendering new conflicts and struggles that sometimes grew into holy wars. For instance, Christianity and Islam opposed each other bitterly while being riven by internal sectarian strife.

In our time, an even more universal awareness is emerging. Political, national, economic, and military conflicts occurring all over the world confront us with a general notion of a world crisis and draw us toward that very destiny. We are coming to perceive the unique nature and importance of this crisis, which will affect the future of all inhabitants of the Earth.

It is essential for us to examine the characteristics, causes, and effects of our crisis and the reforms humanity must make to avert it. The best way to obtain an overall view is, surely, to bring together and compare ways of thought from opposite sides of the world: ways of thought characterized by distinct traditions, cultures, and religions; ways of thought as different as those of the East and the West. The comparisons must, however, be made objectively. The desire to undertake such a project was the source of the present dialogue, which was proposed by Mr. Daisaku Ikeda.

Mr. Ikeda is the honorary president of Soka Gakkai, a Buddhist lay organization with six million active members in Japan, and president of Soka Gakkai International, which has ten thousand members in Europe. The heir and proponent of a lofty spiritual tradition, he is acutely aware of the problems of the modern world. In connection with contemporary issues, he has conferred with such people as Henry Kissinger, Alexei Kosygin, and Zhou Enlai and is, therefore, eminently qualified to compare the problems of today with the legacy and spirituality of the past.

The first of the numerous written dialogues he has conducted with representative Western thinkers was *Choose Life*, conversations between Mr. Ikeda and the great English historian Arnold J. Toynbee. The first edition of this, Mr. Toynbee's last book, appeared in 1976. Then, Mr. Ikeda directed his attention to France and Andre Malraux, whose death prevented their project for a written dialogue from being completed. The present volume is the outcome of what was at the time an ongoing effort involving Mr. Ikeda and me.

Next, Mr. Ikeda turned to Italy, where he compared ideas with the late Dr. Aurelio Peccei, president of the Club of Rome, a vital center of reflection on remedies for the increasing imbalance in modern civilization.

In only a few years, this imbalance has become so apparent, that the idea of a general crisis in our civilization has become widely accepted. After unhesitatingly glorifying the progress that has accompanied developments in the sciences for over a century, people in the West have been forced to concede the existence of a crisis. The hymn to progress is fading and giving way to a mounting inquietude, nourished by disappointment with the present and apprehension about the future.

For decades, isolated voices warning of impending crisis were met with skepticism. Gradually, however, the crisis has become evident and its ravages extensive. At first, its greatest effect was on the economy. Later, it came to influence morals and philosophy and, ultimately, extended to all facets of civilization.

The wave of progress has been succeeded by an ebb tide of anxiety that threatens to affect the younger generations first. Attitudes worldwide are being dominated by traits totally different from those that prevailed at the beginning of the twentieth century. In the past, the continents remained isolated in their own traditions and problems. Periodic contacts among them led only to superficial curiosity or confrontations. Europe thus passed from a period of interest in exotic aspects of distant lands to one of colonial aspirations.

Today, however, those peoples who previously managed to preserve spiritual autonomy and so maintain their ways of thinking and living, are also falling into the cauldron of economic communality and modern technology. At first, in an attempt to catch up with apparent advances in Europe and America, these peoples adapted their moral codes in imitation and adaptation of the rationalistic and mechanistic Western ways of life. But the more such imitation satisfied their hunger for progress, the more they realized the price they were paying for what was merely superficial advantages. They, too, found themselves in a general state of crisis.

Common experience teaches such people the relative value of what they have lost. They discover that, in striving to satisfy material needs, they have created within themselves a void, a gulf, into which plunges their spiritual sustenance. They are confronted with the choice of Matter or the Spirit. The profound revolution against the shah of Iran, who strove to march his nation quick-step to Westernization, illustrates an outcome of this situation.

Behind the analyses of economists, politicians, sociologists, and psychologists can be heard, as if from the wings, the confused noises of crisis, together with a loud, collective voice from the inner depths of humanity, the source of the soul and of everything sacred, growling in the face of threats and lamenting the loss of exaltation.

Many analyses either underplay the crisis or misrepresent it by interpreting it too narrowly or on the basis of preconceived theories. Instead, we must recognize the magnitude and truth of the matter. That is what we have tried to do in this book.

The diversity of people with whom he has held dialogues enables Mr. Ikeda to pursue his quest in numerous directions and to address the crisis in various lights. The prominence in this dialogue of art, my principal field of study, might have been no more than a concession to the specialty of a participant, but it is, actually, more.

By its nature and function, art depends on the faculties most seriously threatened by our rational, objective, and communal civilization. These faculties, the restoration of which is essential to the re-establishment of human equilibrium, include intuition, creative imagination, sensitivity, personality, and subjective and qualitative perception.

The persistent, if tacit, presence of art prevents our analysis from traveling down paths into which our era is readily tempted and which reflect prevailing obsessions: with economy, sociology, and politics. Perhaps, too, the pervading presence of art allows access to the heart of the main problem. This is both my hope and my conviction.

It was essential to impose guidelines on the dialogue, which might otherwise have tended to ramble. The first part begins with an exposition of the nature of the crisis in which the world founders more deeply every day. It picks up material evidence manifest in economics, the field with which this epoch is most strongly obsessed, but finds the gravest aspect of the situation to be the moral crisis, which is the true source of internal rupture.

The second part of the dialogue describes the origins of current evils in historical perspective, showing how they coincide with the latest of the great mutations to which civilization has intermittently been submitted.

The third part tries to define the change occurring in humanity and the modifications it will cause in human nature, which has been cut off from some of its essential, though progressively atrophying, resources. There is also an attempt to discover the nature and location of the counterweight that can return humanity to the equilibrium of which we sense ourselves to be so dangerously dispossessed.

The last two parts of the dialogue are devoted to outlining remedies for the problem. The second covers the major resources that can, and ought to, be evoked from human beings and that are uniquely human attributes. One of the resources is art, another is religion; they are linked by a sense of the sacred.

In the face of the problems posed by the modern crisis, dogmatism must be avoided, since its rationale is too dangerous to permit mere circumvention or denunciation.

In this connection, a dialogue has the advantage of comparing two distinct, but converging, ways of thinking. In this instance, the standpoints of the participants are distinct, representing the traditions of the East and West, yet convergent, since they tend to a similar conclusion although they follow radically different paths.

The conclusion then draws its forcefulness from the duality from which it arises.

Introduction

by Daisaku Ikeda

The crisis modern humanity faces is not imposed from without. It is as if, in the name of selfish advantage, dwellers were destroying their own house by fighting for furnishings, ripping out ceilings, tearing up floors, and pulling down pillars. Conflicts of emotion and interest engender hatred inspiring these dwellers to devise and store weapons powerful enough to blow the whole house away. Madness is the only way to describe a situation in which people in a cramped, frail building threaten each other with bombs of tremendous destructive force. But such is the world crisis today, as the environment is being polluted, natural resources are being exhausted, and all humanity lives under the threat of war.

The solution to the situation is clear. Since the barren world of death lies beyond, attempting to flee is senseless. Instead, we must fundamentally alter our way of thinking and living, so that we can all live together in amity and happiness. Instead of struggling to attain selfish ends, we must work to make our house a pleasant and safe place in which to live. Instead of hating, we must love, protect, and assist each other.

My major concern is exploring ways in which religion can assist in bringing about the necessary changes in ways of thinking and living.

In spite of quarrels at the lower echelons, early Christianity and Islam generally strove to unite peoples who had been in constant conflict, and to realize a world united by strong spiritual bonds. But belief by each in the absolute nature of their God led to growing intolerance. As time went on, theological complications aggravated disputes over heresy that, ultimately, led to bloodbaths. I am convinced, however, that, even during these bloody times, some Christians and some Muslims remained true to the fundamental spirit of their faiths and cried out for peace through God's love.

Buddhism, in which I believe, advocates compassion for all things and is generally tolerant of other religions. Peace has usually characterized the political rule of devout Buddhists. But not all Buddhists are confirmed pacifists. In the past, temples have trained warrior priests, who posed great threats to the authorities. And, in Southeast Asia, Buddhists, who are under the precept not to take life, have carried out cruel massacres.

Obviously, choice of religion alone is no guarantee of peace. Each religion has its own doctrine and, with different doctrines come different results in the management of society and in people's daily life. The important thing is how people put religious teachings into practice, because diversity in practice means that while some followers of a religion may be bellicose, others will be thoroughly peace-loving.

Nonetheless, Buddhism has, on the whole, proved outstandingly pacific in approach. In this dialogue, I offer my explanation of this characteristic for the criticism of René Huyghe and the reader.

The great Japanese Buddhist priest Nichiren Daishonin (1222-82), the founder of the school of Buddhist philosophy that I revere, devoted profound thought to the sufferings war causes humanity and to the search for a key to peace. After reading all the Buddhist scriptures and reflecting on the issue, he came to the conclusion that mistaken religious faith leads to war and is the source of social calamity, and that correct religious faith is an issue of paramount importance.

Nichiren Daishonin has often been criticized by those under the mistaken impression that he was self-righteously trying to force his religion on the Japanese authorities of his day. Sometimes, this criticism has even been directed at him by those claiming to practice his teachings.

But an unbiased reading of his writings clearly reveals the error of such a view. A true religion cannot be imposed from without, but must be nurtured in the mind of an individual, and Nichiren Daishonin sought a faith dependent on just such individual free will.

Consequently, in his faith there can be no thought of using power or force to reject or enforce religion, belief in which is always a matter of conscious selection. This interpretation is based on the principle of a revolution of human life force, which is the core of the Buddhism of Nichiren Daishonin.

Buddhism interprets desires, hatred, anger, and so on as the weak aspects of life and the bodhisattva ideal of altruistic service in the name of the happiness of others as its strong aspect. The state of perfection beyond that of the bodhisattva is the Buddha condition. Quite different from the biological approach, the Buddhist interpretation of life is linked to ethics and psychology.

My purpose in going briefly into these topics is to outline the Buddhist background against which I, as a practicing Buddhist, engage in dialogues of this kind and make various other efforts in an attempt to examine and suggest solutions for the problems confronting the world today. This is certainly in keeping with the spiritual basis of Buddhism, which constantly confronts life suffering. Gautama Siddhartha, the founder of Buddhism, gave up secular life for that of religious discipline in the hope of solving the problems caused by suffering. And Nichiren Daishonin's life was a continuous struggle with human suffering.

I am, of course, not trying to draw a comparison between myself, a perfectly ordinary mortal, and these great people. I cannot discover truths or pioneer the way, but can merely direct people's gaze toward the beacons these outstanding leaders illuminated.

As is also true in other religions, the words of the great Buddhists of the past, though fresh and alive at the time of their initial utterance, sound a little old-fashioned to modern ears. But their truth remains, just as gold, no matter how dust covered, remains gold.

Similarly, as the dust must be wiped away to reveal the gold beneath, so also must the fixed ideas and prejudices, that have come to conceal the truth of the founders' words, be eliminated to convince people today of their great value.

Of course, I must make every effort to ensure that my own comments and explanations do not merely add to the obscuring dust. Awareness of this danger and a desire to avoid it are one of the reasons that I hit upon the idea of moving out of the world of Buddhism to conduct dialogues with intellectuals and thinkers from the West.

The late Arnold J. Toynbee, one of the most outstanding historians of the twentieth century, was my first dialogue partner. The great power of reflection that enabled him to interpret human civilization, in sweeping historical terms, provided an excellent mirror in which I could verify my own thoughts.

René Huyghe, in addition to being one of the leading art specialists and critics in France today, is, as his numerous written works reveal, a profound observer of the human soul, from which works of art are born. I was especially impressed to find in his *Dialogue avec le Visible* (Dialogue With the Visible) a passage expressing ideas in close agreement with the Buddhist principle that life is divided into Ten States.

Mr. Huyghe is a cultivated European intellectual and I am an Oriental practitioner of the teachings of Buddhism. Our dialogue is not, therefore, a discussion between two scholars. I shall be happy if the reader simply approaches it as a dialogue between two souls attempting to shed light on each other. I am especially grateful that, in the lucid mirror of Mr. Huyghe's thoughts, I have been given yet another chance to examine my own mind.

PART ONE

The Contemporary Crisis

IKEDA: In attempts to characterize it, many scientists, thinkers, and others view the contemporary age as a time in which our civilization is fated to undergo a great and inevitable change. Undeniably, the West has created the current crisis, which has emerged from the major principles on which Western civilization rests.

HUYGHE: Doubtless civilization is currently undergoing an extremely serious crisis. The knowledge that this is true has practically become common knowledge shared by a wide audience. In 1968, the West—and France in particular— witnessed a move by young people to interpret the crisis in an almost animal and instinctive fashion as they, in a spasm of agony, rebelled against prospects for the future.

Nothing could be more contrary to the spirit that dominated the nineteenth century, when humanity entertained the heretofore unprecedented idea that the world was in a state of continual progress. The idea of Progress (with a capital P) was fundamental and was celebrated by such poets as Victor Hugo who, posing as a clairvoyant, predicted that humanity would march toward happiness and ever-expanding light.

In the twentieth century, the situation has been completely reversed. Eventual history, as it is called today—history seeking causes in events, which are actually, however, manifest reactions to very profound and concealed mutations—tries to explain everything on the basis of the two global wars of the first half of the century: on the basis of the millions of dead, the devastation, and the resultant economic exhaustion. These wars fueled the collapse of the Western world—especially Europe—and its hegemony over peoples of Asia and Africa.

At the same time, as successor, the United States—a European offshoot on another continent—has taken in hand the destiny of the scientific and technological civilization evolved by the West and has continued the triumphal march. But the United States suffers from the same defect that brought on the decline of Europe. Its progress, as inevitable as it seems, will encounter the same obstacles, on perhaps an even greater scale, in direct proportion to its material success.

Behind the jolts, certain forces are at work that have exerted constantly increasing pressure and led the West and its civilization to the present crisis, in which may be seen both destiny and, perhaps, ruin—in spite of the appearance of inevitable progress.

In the elements that have assured its most triumphal successes, the nineteenth century carried the seeds of the evils that poisoned the future. To what did it owe its most intoxicating successes? The nineteenth century brought to perfection a new mode of civilization, roughed out in the seventeenth and established in the eighteenth century and based on scientific knowledge. The physical sciences, the first to be propounded and developed, brought many technical achievements. Although they made life practical and more agreeable, they were limited to that role, because progress, the pinnacle of the sciences, concerns only the material world. The physical sciences which have only one object, namely, matter in space, have undeniably succeeded in enabling humanity quickly and easily to gain the upper hand in arranging natural data for the better satisfaction of concrete human desires.

People thought only of demanding more. And the constant growth of technology and its powers led them to believe that their requirements could not but continue to be satisfied. It was believed that science would take care of everything.

In the past few years, however, we have been forced to change our tune. The petroleum and energy crisis was a rude awakening. We have begun to learn to live with it, but solutions escape us. The knife the oil-producing nations hold to our throats will not let us wait for the substitute energy sources science has promised—at a later date.

Once we demanded a lot. Now we are reduced to wanting to hold our own. But that is not all. People have begun making *other* demands. Who, yesterday, would have suspected that a pressing need would emerge to satisfy different aspirations that are inherent in our nature and that have wakened all the more vigorously because they have been so outrageously neglected? Intoxicated with material progress, we have forgotten that we possess an internal life, a spirit, a soul (I deliberately string together these words which, for a number of us, have been tossed aside almost long enough to have lost meaning). We have allowed these needs to starve. Now they object. Tomorrow they will imperiously demand to be taken into account afresh. The French Jesuit philosopher Pierre Teilhard de Chardin has commented, "No matter what one says, our century is religious, probably more religious than all others. It is only that it has not yet found the God it can adore." This provocative statement is less paradoxical than it seems.

IKEDA: As you point out, people are now beginning to have second thoughts about the idea of progress, the symbol of scientific civilization. I agree with your comments on progress. But it is difficult for us to criticize it fairly, as long as we remain dependent on the conveniences made possible by scientific technology. It is easy to criticize the idea of scientific progress from the outside but much harder to master the situation from the inside.

The petroleum crisis brought home to many shocked people the seriousness of depleting natural resources by pointing out the immense demands imposed on those resources by the system needed to support modern scientific technology. When the first oil shock struck, most Japanese first sought to ensure their own supplies and only then adopted conservation policies. At about the same time, rumor had it that, as a consequence of the petroleum shortage, supplies of toilet tissue were running out. Market prices for this commodity shot up, and housewives immediately lined up at stores to buy, then hoard, as much as possible. I suspect that reactions of this kind are not peculiar to the Japanese people and that they illustrate the energy with which human beings think and act in reaction to matters that concern them directly. The same holds true of pollution. People tend to move into action with great speed and rancor when their own immediate surroundings become polluted. They are much less likely to demonstrate concern for such instances of environmental pollution as the high lead content discovered in Arctic ice or nylon stockings recovered in the stomach of an Antarctic whale.

In pointing these things out, instead of criticizing the ugly aspects of human nature, I am merely suggesting that such an attitude is deeply rooted in the human instinct for self-preservation. A human being who sits by idly waiting for death in the face of danger is a human being in name only.

Immediate danger sometimes inspires human beings to act radically, as in the case of the French students in 1968. The more profound the danger, the more violent, even panicky, the reaction against it.

Current second thoughts about our ideas of progress offer an excellent opportunity to give sincere thought to ways of averting the crisis we now face. Instead of being limited to specialists or politicians, however, our efforts must be cooperative and universal.

For many years I have been insisting that progress deals solely with the external material world. It is now time for us to turn our eyes to humanity's inner aspects. We must reaffirm our own independence by controlling and guiding the artificial environment we have created instead of allowing ourselves to be controlled by it. In order to have the kind of wisdom needed to accomplish this, the human spirit must be filled with the pulsing force of universal life that permeates humanity, nature, and all things.

HUYGHE: The crisis involving humanity is complex and is attacking us on many planes, including that of our material appetites, to which a mental aberration over two centuries old has led us to devote ourselves entirely. Tomorrow, it will strike on the plane of our spiritual appetites, which we have put aside all too readily.

I propose that you and I approach these planes successively. In order to examine each in its turn, I suggest we distinguish material crises, which strike at our physical integrity; psychological crises, which occur in conjunction with physical crises and which threaten our mental integrity; and, finally, the ultimate, moral crises, which suffocate our spiritual life.

1

The Material Crisis

HUYGHE: Once the mechanism of scientific and technological progress seemed faultless. Human beings had only to examine their needs, one by one, and then methodically undertake to satisfy them. It was the duty of science to make this possible.

The Encore Effect

HUYGHE: The important question, however, is how satisfaction is achieved. First a goal for attainment is assigned. Then, when this goal has been defined, it becomes necessary to discover the proper lever with which to accomplish it. Once this appeared simple, but the approach overlooks a weakness in the human mental mechanism. When engaged in reasoning—especially in the technical domain—human beings fail to envisage the infinite complexity of reality and are satisfied to have isolated cause A as resulting in effect B. Failing to understand that the world is a complex tangle of causes and effects, they overlook unforeseen reactions—which I once called encore effects. These sometimes very important effects are unforeseen since, though the benefits are usually limited to expectations, the damage a course of action may produce can be limitless.

This kind of thing has been observed in the prodigious progress of medicine. We frequently seek specific medicines—cortisone for example—to cure specific sicknesses. Later, however, when abstract discovery confronts living reality, it becomes necessary to admit that, in addition to the attainment of the anticipated results, things unforeseen by science have happened. For instance, the very medicine that was intended to be a cure engenders in the organism—in other organs or in the entire body—problems as difficult to overcome as the original complaint. I might mention the kidney ailment that struck workers in an aspirin factory and, thus, brought to light harmful side effects of a medicine reputed to be highly inoffensive. In other words, technology produces uncontrollable consequences.

The kind of thing observable in a field like medicine occurs in all domains in which administrative and rational methods are applied. This is why, in spite of logic and development in such new disciplines as economic science, human beings remain unable to master events.

A formidable phenomenon like inflation can spread inexorably throughout the whole world without our innumerable economists being able, so far, to find a remedy. Indeed, the measures that have been conceived have only aggravated the problem.

Industrial developments once seemed marvelous. They created all the machines one could desire and used them to turn out an infinite number of products, including such previously unknown substances as plastics. But one day it became necessary to change our tune and admit that, to keep industry supplied with primary materials and energy, it was necessary to irreversibly exhaust natural resources that were already being destroyed. It was essential to realize that the pollution we were creating was attacking our physical health and that, in the process, our moral health was being affected. New lifestyles, intensified by technology and speed, involve stresses that upset the psychic equilibrium by creating ruptures in normal biological rhythms.

We shall return to these points later in our discussion. At this juncture, we will content ourselves with giving an impressive enumeration of them. The twentieth century must settle the account. Going beyond the satisfaction of attained objectives, it must make a statement of unforeseen consequences that have proved to be harmful reactions. Little by little, the idea of progress has faded; and now, having arrived at the end of the twentieth century, people find themselves unhappy.

IKEDA: I should hope we would be able to do more than enumerate the sufferings unfortunately now being cited on all sides as indication of the profundity of the modern malady. I agree that humanity today is going through a grave period of crisis but should like to hear you speak in more detail about the nature of that crisis, the areas in which it is manifesting itself, and the disorder from which it arises.

Observers of the contemporary period see in it unprecedented changes fundamentally related to civilizational progress. Which problems faced by contemporary society pose the most basic threats to the future?

HUYGHE: Their great number and complexity demand their methodically ordered enumeration. Attacked from all sides, we are like a traveler lost in the night, watching as the circle of wolves about to attack closes in gradually. In sketching our account, then, let us start with the most positive factors, those that seem most important to our contemporaries and that, in the eyes of some, are the sole valid ones.

The Consumer Society

HUYGHE: Our civilization has justly been defined as one devoted to consumption; that is, one that consumes, absorbs, and takes from the surrounding world resources to satisfy our bodies' needs as well as appetites and desires. Our contemporaries seem to confine themselves to a program aimed at first supplying food; then ensuring comfort; reducing the need for effort; and, finally, providing sensual satisfaction or distractions furnishing scope for sexuality. The more needs are satisfied, however, the more exacting human beings become. This indicates dangerous deviation and degradation. But, at the present stage, let us confine ourselves to positive evidence.

The most striking, in my view, is the ceaseless growth of the world's population and, therefore, of consumers. Everything is geared to increasing an individual's capacity and will to consume. But the planet's stock of primary minerals cannot be augmented. In short, everything that we take from the Earth is an irreversible deduction from a total that must someday be exhausted.

The same is true of vegetable and other food products. The forests of the world are receding and, according to some calculations, once destroyed may never be restored. Modern technology can stimulate the recovery of agrarian lands, though only by means of chemical fertilizers. Such increase cannot continue limitlessly, even if the admittedly immense expanses of still uncultivated land are fertilized. Enormous quantities of water would be needed for increased agriculture—and this at a time when diminution of the world's water supply is cause for concern. In addition, the action of chemicals may exhaust the soil and may harm crops. These effects, only now being considered, occur at great expense to human health. For example, who can say whether the continual spread of cancer today is not brought on, in part, by the ingestion of chemical substances and the abuse of medicines?

Our bodies are made to absorb biologically produced substances—vegetable or animal substances. It is frightening that the brutal intrusion of artificially obtained substances might have disturbing effects on us. We measure these effects poorly because our simplistic and complacent mentality wishes to see nothing but immediate results and is nonplused by unforeseen rebounds.

The 34 percent increase in agrarian yield that occurred between 1951 and 1966 was achieved only at the price of a 36 percent increase in the use of nitrogen fertilizers and a 300 percent increase in the use of chemical pesticides. As is well known, these pesticides have harmful effects on species of animals against which they are not intended and which are indispensable to the biological equilibrium of the globe. Ironically, the insects against whom the pesticides are used adapt and, finally, become immune. Owing to the vast numbers of generations they produce during one human generation, an estimated 250 species of insect pests have managed to develop resistance against pesticides.

IKEDA: Like the land, the seas too are being damaged. When I was a child, my family made a living from edible seaweed taken from the waters of Tokyo Bay. Although not true agriculture, our work was, nonetheless, a primary industry. It was possible for my family to make a living this way at that time, but such is no longer the case.

Indeed in Japan the primary industries are clearly failing. Since Japan is small, it is considered more efficient and profitable to use what little land is available for secondary industry and to purchase foodstuffs abroad. If this attitude reflects a feeling that secondary industries should be given preference over primary industries, it can pose a grave threat to the future.

The population of the world is growing in geometric progression, no longer gradually but explosively. But, in spite of improvements in farming techniques, agricultural production is growing very slowly. The situation is clearly catastrophic.

From the ecological viewpoint, the growth of a single species to a much greater extent than any of its fellow creatures poses extraordinary dangers. When a species continues to increase after its environment becomes incapable of supporting it, disaster is inevitable. The many instances in which herbivores have multiplied, eaten all available pasture down to the roots, and then perished are not without relevance to our own situation. It is impossible to reject the forecast that a global famine may strike and bring us all to miserable destruction. Indeed, world famine threatens even now.

Taken globally, human dietary conditions are already wretched. Only some of the industrialized nations enjoy surpluses of foodstuffs. Most of the developing countries take a very pessimistic view of the likelihood that agricultural technology will catch up with population increases. The general tragedy is aggravated by a prevailing imbalance in which people in the industrialized nations overeat to the extent that diet-related cardiac illness, diabetes, and other disorders are major causes of death, while peoples in many other parts of the world are on the verge of starvation.

In what amounts to an immoral act, industrialized nations—of which Japan is an excellent example—willingly abandon the idea of agricultural self-sufficiency and, concentrating on industry, content themselves with purchasing all the food they need from poor nations, where supplies are likely to be far from ample. The result is that popular welfare in the poor nations is sacrificed for the sake of sales.

Japan, which relies on other nations for a great deal of its food, produces more rice than it needs, a fact that has inspired the government to adopt the strange policy of limiting the amount of land under rice cultivation. While wheat may be grown on land on which rice cultivation is officially forbidden. This is not done, however, since wheat crops are not subject to the same economic protection afforded rice crops. Clearly, politically caused imbalances of this kind must be corrected.

In connection with the artificial agriculture supplements that you mention, we would all, no doubt, be shocked if we knew precisely what some of the things we eat actually contain. To make most efficient use of limited agricultural land, it is necessary to use artificial fertilizers and pesticides. Often, owing to food-supply and labor conditions, these substances are applied before possible effects on the human body have been properly determined. The same kind of thing occurs in connection with animal husbandry and the fisheries industry.

A case in point is pig farming. To fatten them in minimum time, pigs are immobilized, artificially fed, and given digestive drugs and hormone supplements to enable their bodies to ingest the maximum amount of nourishment. But meat from such pigs is excessively fatty and repleat with toxic substances.

Marine products are similarly polluted as a result of the continuing pollution of the oceans, and fish and shellfish that have been insufficiently inspected for pollutants often reach the market. In addition, excessively large catches threaten some species of sea creatures with extinction. Now that pollutants and harmful preservatives and additives in foods have been shown to make the dietary environment perilous, the time has surely come to admit the folly of continuing to believe the myth that the enormous size of the planet and its great expanses of sea ensure us an inexhaustible food supply and an environment overflowing with energy sources. We are not being pessimistic, but merely realistic, when we recognize that, by the end of the century, the problems of agriculture and food supply will have become the most pressing issues facing humanity.

The question of food must be approached from two standpoints: supply and consumption. Among the many problems related to supply is the amount of land put to agrarian use. On a global level, while area expansion is still possible—as is crop production without resort to chemicals and industrial methods—it is bound by limitations. Therefore, although it may not provide a fundamental solution to the problem, I suggest that an examination of our dietary habits can provide some relief.

To begin with, relying heavily on meat entails the wasteful use of fodder in bringing animals to marketable maturity. It is said that ten times the amount of vegetable feed is required to enable human beings to obtain from meat the same amount of energy that could be obtained directly from vegetables. A simple calculation shows that, if we were to shift from an omnivorous to a vegetarian diet, the current amount of arable land would feed ten times as many people as it does now. Of course, it would be impossible to effect such a shift suddenly. Furthermore, even if the change were successfully made, the problem of supplementing the diet with the necessary animal proteins would remain. Nonetheless, ideas of this kind must be given serious consideration.

Changing to a vegetarian diet could bring a double benefit, since excess consumption of meat leads to many of the serious illnesses plaguing adults in modern society. For while the prohibition against eating meat that is maintained by some

Buddhist sects arises from a spirit of compassion for all life, it is also conducive to a longer life for those who abide by it.

The core of the consumer side of the issue is control of the world's population, without which no amount of improvement in agricultural production can bring about a fundamental solution. In my view, the problems of supply and consumption hinge on the issue of population control. We can only hope to solve the crises facing our civilization if, instead of taking piecemeal measures, we tackle this essential question.

In the past, war has been regarded as the most expedient way of thinning populations, though other methods have also been applied. For instance, the poor people of Japan once found infanticide—called *mabiki,* or thinning—necessary to survival. In our time, however, when such methods are totally unconscionable, contraception is considered the ideal method of population control. Lacking the mating seasons and estrus common to other animals, human beings must apply their wisdom to controlling themselves in this connection. Far from considering it immoral, I look upon contraception as highly humane.

As I said earlier, a single species that increases excessively runs the risk of annihilation. To avoid this, humanity must control itself. For centuries we have idealized the multiplication of the species and material well-being achieved through progress based on the conquest of nature. The time has come for us to realize that such progress can go too far and to see that true morality is not represented by development based on conquest, but by peace and harmony with all things. Civilization should be characterized not by production and consumption, but by diffusion.

Although they have known past periods of material glory, with their Eastern tradition of philosophy, including that of Buddhism, the peoples of the Orient currently lag behind those of the West in terms of science and technology. No doubt, from the standpoint of the industrialized nations, peoples who make little or no effort to absorb the scientific and technological aspects of civilization seem to lead poor, wretched lives. But it should be realized that these Eastern peoples may simply prefer to live within the limits of the blessings of nature. Though meager and poor, they consider theirs to be the right way for human beings to live.

Certainly poverty and life on the verge of starvation are not good. But, to live harmoniously and successfully with the world of nature, human beings must control their desires. Overemphasis on ease and comfort has in part caused the population explosion that jeopardizes the continued existence of humanity.

In summary then, avoiding the use of industrial and chemical methods and relying on nature and human effort, agriculture should attempt to increase production as much as possible. In addition, every effort must be made to limit world population. These are the two major elements of a solution to the material crisis facing the world. To effect this solution, it is essential that humanity now enter a period of peace and stability.

Exhaustion of Natural Resources

HUYGHE: As was recommended in a report, entitled *The Limits of Growth,* made at the request of the Club of Rome by the Massachusetts Institute of Technology in 1972, everything should incite human beings to limit growth. Human beings must stop growing for the sake of growing, producing for the sake of producing, and consuming for the sake of consuming. But ideas can have great sway. The report was subjected to violent discussions, and certain political parties did not hesitate to reject its conclusions a priori in the interests of their own electoral propaganda.

Nonetheless, the facts remain. The global population, estimated at 4.5 billion people, grows by from 2 percent to 3 percent a year and will have doubled shortly after the year 2000. Furthermore, since the increase is no longer linear but exponential, if things continue as they are, the population of the world should have reached something like 15 billion in a century. (As an illustrative example, assume that the amount of a pond surface covered by water lilies doubles daily and that the lilies cover the entire pond in 30 days. Half of the total coverage will be effected between the twenty-ninth and thirtieth days. The speed of the increase accelerates, becoming wilder and wilder. The same will be true in the case of world population.)

While rich nations now tend to decelerate them, birth rates are increasing in poor nations, making apparent the menace to the future. In 150 years, Caucasians, who now account for a fifth of the world's population, will constitute only 13 percent of it; in less than 15 years, their fecundity has dropped by half.

According to statisticians, at the present rate of consumption—even if increases in demand are prevented—known reserves of lead, mercury, gold, tin, silver, and zinc will be exhausted in 20 years; those of copper and tungsten in 30 years; those of aluminum and nickel in 70 years; and those of iron in a century.

Even supposing that they are pessimistic and fail to take into consideration still unknown resources, these figures underscore certain peril. The situation will be catastrophic in a hundred years—and irreversible in thirty.

In a general fashion, MIT advanced analogous figures for substances more indispensable to human life. One day, even our water resources will be insufficient. On an average, an inhabitant of Paris uses 50 liters of water a day. Simply multiply that figure by the world's population. . . .

Those who think that our supply of air is unlimited are forgetting the extent to which machines increase oxygen combustion. For instance, in traveling 1,000 kilometers, one automobile uses up the same amount of oxygen that one human being breathes in a whole year. Furthermore, sources of supply renewal are limited. The decreasing number of trees in the world is only a minor ill. The greatest of all oxygen producers, marine plankton, account for an estimated 75 to 80 percent of the oxygen generated in the world. But increasing pollution of the oceans is destroying these creatures. It has been calculated that human waste products, especially hydrocarbons spilled by oil freighters, will soon have destroyed plankton in at least 4 million square kilometers of a total sea surface area of some 280 million square kilometers.

Moreover, our civilization has created new needs and depends almost entirely on the consumption of energy, the principal sources of which are limited. The energy needs of the industrialized nations alone double every decade. Coal supplies are rapidly decreasing. We search feverishly for unexploited sources of petroleum, the supply of which can, as we know only too well, pose problems capable of upsetting the economy of the whole world. Nor is the supply of uranium limitless.

The World Energy Conference recently estimated current terrestrial reserves at 11,200 billion tons of combustible minerals (primarily coal), 740 billion tons of combustible liquids (essentially petroleum), and 630 billion tons of natural gas. These figures might seem enormous—even reassuring. But it must be added that only about a third of the resources are in a condition permitting extraction. In addition, it is supposed that 10 percent of the stocks will have been used up before the end of the century; that is, in barely two generations' time. In fact, owing to the increasing growth of the population and of individual consumption, no more than 22 percent of the world's resources will remain by 2050. Moreover, it has been forecast that, in only forty years, consumption of electricity alone will have doubled. Statistics of this kind should be made available far and wide to open the eyes of die-hard optimists whose offspring may still be alive then.

It is certainly reasonable to imagine that, as a countermeasure, science will have discovered new means of utilizing the permanent sources of energy offered by the wind, the sun, the ocean, and geothermal sources. Scientific research has picked up speed in this field in the hope of countering intensifying penury in energy sources. But only about a century remains to accomplish the necessary unprecedented revolution. It will be a very close game.

Recourse to atomic energy is, of course, eminently conceivable. But B.M. Berkovsky, the Russian specialist in thermophysics, has noted that delays in the application of nuclear energy insufficiently manifest our impatience. During the 35 years that have passed since the problem of its utilization was first broached, atomic energy has come to account for no more than 1 percent of the energy produced in the world. It has always taken about sixty years for a new energy source to replace an old energy source with a new one—as was the case when petroleum replaced coal and natural gas, in turn, replaced petroleum. In a century at most, it will be impossible to expect anything from traditional sources.

IKEDA: In addition to the issue of the exhaustion of energy sources, you have touched on the pollution of the sea and air caused by the application of certain kinds of energy. One of the likely replacements for petroleum as an energy source is nuclear energy. France is especially interested in this field, but it must be remembered that pollution from nuclear energy is far more grave than that from petroleum.

Is it wise to assume that, in the future, humanity should continue making ever greater demands for energy sources? As long as a relentless pursuit of the satisfaction of material desires is considered correct, increased energy demands will be seen as unavoidable. But, if the correctness of the pursuit is reexamined, steps to reduce energy consumption should be possible.

When consumption reduction is the goal, we should be able to attack the problem of developing inexhaustible, nonpolluting energy sources. What is your opinion of this idea?

HUYGHE: Energy resources, much like other resources, have been exploited by contemporary civilization at a frantic rate, in defiance of the spirit of collaboration with nature that human beings have demonstrated in the past. Certainly, if we wish nature to satisfy our needs, we must take reciprocity into consideration. In other words, we must keep an eye out for our own welfare. One of the great benefits of interplanetary rocket travel has been that we have been able to view our own planet from a distance. Seen from space, Earth looks like a sphere with a definite content. Much like a child with a bag of marbles, as he plays with them, the child must remember how many marbles remain in the bag. One day it will be empty, and that day will come all the sooner the more recklessly he squanders its contents. Since the Earth is no more inexhaustible than the child's bag of marbles, sooner or later, humanity will find itself out of resources. To see how things will one day be, we need only take into account the constant population increase and the growing rate of individual consumption. Although devoted to quantities, our epoch is strangely reticent when it comes to making this necessary calculation.

Humanity today faces dangers that, expressed graphically in curves, can be seen to be growing in geometrical progression. The day will come when this increase will border on absurdity. In the face of these facts, our epoch, as devoted to the rational as it is to quantities, is able to do no more than present sophisticated arguments.

Numerous people are blindly confident in scientific technology, which they believe is perfectly capable of pulling us out of our scrape since it was capable of putting us in it. Such reasoning is a little naive.

How can we restrain and discipline the mad greed of a humanity more liberated by present civilization than at any other time? Attaining this goal presupposes a preliminary and profound mental reformation. In this domain, fear may prove more effective than reason.

The usage to which, in the immediate interests of their own propaganda, political parties have put this problem is not reassuring. In this connection too, direct interest and cupidity for votes, not conscience, have spoken most loudly. Concern for the needs of humanity has carried little weight. What few injunctions against consumption have been issued have been regarded by some as reflecting the wish to restrict the growing comforts of the common people. It is blind frivolity to allow the struggle among classes to take precedence over the struggle for human survival. When a captain attempts to keep his ship from sinking, knowledge of the relative numbers of first- and third-class passengers his action will benefit is a matter of secondary importance. The important thing is to want to save the entire ship. Is it so difficult to conceive of a global solidarity of humanity united in a common front? Is it necessary to go on trying to find polemics to deaden an awareness that grows more indispensable every day?

Throughout history, humanity has rarely demonstrated the sagacity required of it. Today, besotted with scientific progress, technological power, and the material advantages the two have brought, human beings are all the less disposed to manifest the wisdom needed. In these circumstances, since things show little sign of immediate change, we face a brutal crisis. No doubt the very brutality of the crisis will constrain man to reverse truths that he refuses to modify. And in this way only will it be possible to escape from what, for the moment, looks like a vicious circle of blindness.

As you justly point out, even assuming that atomic energy can ensure the indispensable relief, its use will only aggravate the danger of pollution, which we must now examine closely and from all angles.

Pollution

HUYGHE: Let us conduct a point-by-point examination of the subject. At its initial appearance, the living cell ensures its existence by means of two functions: absorption for the sake of nourishment and excretion for the sake of ridding itself of unassimilable or dangerous wastes. This functional duality remains fundamental in the most highly developed organisms. Without it, life could not go on. The duality remains valid for human societies which, to grow, augment their capacity to absorb, or their consumption. Then it becomes necessary for them to rid themselves of wastes, which increase in direct proportion to consumption growth. In other words, the elimination of wastes can take place only in an environment in which an organism nourishes itself. Thus this vexatious combination creates a cycle in which precisely those substances that ought to be eliminated are blended with those substances that we absorb. Nonetheless, until the present, human beings have been scattered about so sparsely in nature that the danger has been negligible.

The situation has been made dangerous by certain factors: increases in population; enormous urban concentrations; and, above all, the use of machinery, since world industry grows at a rate of nearly 7 percent a year has steadily become the main consumer of energy resources.

For thousands of years, the power of human beings, animals, and later of water and wind have sufficed in many instances. In more recent times, however, energy obtained by means of transmutation has progressively been substituted for primitive power. From the day when fire was first used to generate steam, large-scale industry became possible. Wastes from industrial combustion were dumped into the air and water. And, concomitant with scientific progress, the residues of chemical operations have increased to a frightening degree. At present, to avoid hindering the economy, consumption of energy must account for 4 percent of the gross national product. But at what cost! The atmosphere is filled with sulfur dioxide, carbon monoxide, and unconsumed hydrocarbons. Experiments on mice have shown that such pollutants in the atmosphere as anthracene, pyrene, and benzopyrene are carcinogens. All too often, factories poison bodies of water, which carry and diffuse chemical residues just as they do detergents, the use of which is steadily growing. The disappearance of various kinds of fish bears ample witness to the destructive power of these polluting substances.

The burning of a ton of coal launches twenty kilograms of anhydrous sulfur into the atmosphere. Three and a half million tons of this are emitted into the air over France annually. The factories of Saint-Denis and Boulogne alone annually emit 30,000 tons. And the situation is aggravated by the use, for domestic heating, of fuel oils in quantities rivaling those employed by industry. When anhydrous sulfur comes into contact with water suspended in the atmosphere, it undergoes a series of transformations that eventually produce sulfuric acid.

The end result of this pollution is, of course, harmful to the tissues of the human body, especially the lungs. But it is equally damaging to monumental works of architecture and sculpture. The Parthenon, the cathedrals of France, the sculpture at Versailles, and the buildings of Venice are all testaments to this. The work of destruction is so rapid that, left in the open as they are, statues become unrecognizable in fifty years.

According to one estimate, the skies over a city like Milan receive 100,000 tons of vaporized sulfuric acid annually, an amount that would require 3,000 tank trucks to transport. Paris, it has been calculated, annually must deal with 90,000 tons of cinders and 15,000 tons of dust, among other pollutants. And in New York City, forty tons of toxic waste are estimated to be suspended over every square kilometer of the city. In 1944, before corrective measures were taken, the city of Pittsburgh held the record, with 400 tons of such waste for every square kilometer. In addition to its direct chemical actions, this screen of suspended waste blocks sunlight which is indispensable to photosynthesis and therefore to life. Twenty years ago, the solar illumination of Paris had dropped to one-quarter of what it had been in 1900.

Certainly remedies are possible. Factories could—indeed ought to—be outfitted with filters. Polluted water could be evaporated in boilers at temperatures high enough to destroy some of the pollutants. But all of this is expensive. Furthermore, it would be essential to reach an international accord in this connection; and which nation would agree to accept, and legalize, such a cost handicap without the assurance that parallel measures were being taken by foreign rivals? Rarely do economies—the dominant, almost obsessive preoccupation of governments—willingly make sacrifices of this kind.

What then about the new sources of energy derived from either atomic fusion or fission? Allowing that part of public opinion passionately exaggerates the risks, the specialists' reassuring arguments seem a little complaisant. From time to time, the facts belie the engineers' belief in the infallibility of their precautions. For instance, in 1978, radiation leaks at an English factory affected the health of the majority of the employees, although for weeks nothing was suspected of having gone wrong.

As Leprince-Ringuet, professor of physics at the Collège de France, remarked on television in 1973, in the natural course of things, our senses have become accustomed to detecting danger from unfamiliar sights, sounds, odors, or tastes. In the case of nuclear danger, however, our organism reacts only to damage after the fact, when it is already too late. Only artificial detectors, hazardous to employ, can put us on our guard. People speak of events that are purely accidental. But, owing to the magnitude they can assume, it is precisely accidents 'that we dread.

The Hiroshima bomb—a mere toy by comparison with contemporary bombs and considerably surpassed by the widely criticized bomb that General De Gaulle sponsored—is a memorable warning. But our dilemma is great. In France alone, 200 atomic-energy plants are foreseen by the year 2000. And they will, apparently, be indispensable to the normal functioning of our society.

As long as we lack the assurance that we can prevent technical accidents, which can be catastrophic, how can we counter the awesome and long-lasting effects of nuclear wastes? There are, of course, proposals that envisage the projection of such wastes into pockets vitrified in the bosom of the Earth by an atomic explosion, or, this proving impossible, their projection to the sun or into interstellar space. But who knows when such things will become possible? At present, thousands of tons of extremely toxic wastes are annually buried a sea in special concrete casings. How long will these containers resist the action of the tides and what will happen when they rupture?

An example of what might happen comes to mind. In 1970, it became necessary for the United States to dispose of dangerous nerve gas; 12,500 shells of the substance were sunk to a depth of 5,000 meters off the Florida coast. The shells rapidly corroded and disintegrated. Although cement would last longer, it is not eternal.

These are some of the major risks to which human beings

submit themselves in the name of progress, the utilitarian developments of which seem to offer an easy downhill ride. But that ride might become a fall from which there is no getting up.

Parrying

IKEDA: Of course, you are correct. But parrying the problem by halting progress is difficult. For instance, how is it possible to limit consumption of energy or natural resources in a society founded on the principles of a free economy? In a free society, the majority of the people derive material benefits from development. Competing as they consume natural resources, businesses produce and market large quantities of products. Abundance and consequent competition among businesses bring down product prices, to the delight of the consumer.

Introduction of a totalitarian system instead of free competition would put the brakes on the wasteful consumption of resources. But it would also increase the interference of the authorities in the actions of individuals. As a person who has experienced life under a totalitarian regime, I have no wish that such a thing occur.

Consequently, I believe that the only way is to deepen each individual's awareness of the limited nature of our resources and thus to stimulate self-imposed limitations on both material consumption and production competition.

In the case of nuclear energy, the issue surpasses considerations of finite resources, since, even though the required resources are still available, the wastes produced as a result of their use jeopardize human life. It is true that petroleum wastes too are harmful, but the danger involved in the case of nuclear energy is many times greater.

We must totally alter our attitude toward the consumption of all our natural resources, but we must also realize that the question of nuclear energy is unlike anything humanity has ever experienced before. Until they exceed certain quantitative limits, wastes from nonnuclear energy sources, however harmful, are not fatal. The smallest amount of nuclear waste, on the other hand, is potentially fatal. This is why the development and application of nuclear energy, even for peaceful purposes, must be submitted to the closest scrutiny. Should absolutely foolproof methods of dealing with dangerous wastes be developed, the resumption of the use of nuclear power could be considered. Until such time, however, I feel it would be better to halt its use and stimulate modern science to pool its efforts in the development of energy sources that produce no harmful wastes and that can be recycled, so that there is no danger of their being exhausted.

Since I am not a specialist, I have no concrete proposals to make. I do suspect that you are correct, however, when you say we must work in cooperation with nature. Surely we can find hope-inducing hints in solar energy, the motion of the Earth's oceans and atmosphere, and in the tremendous power of gravity. I feel certain that applying the best of human wisdom will enable us to go beyond the simple watermill and windmill to develop highly efficient and widely applicable sources of energy from natural forces.

In addition, it is essential that forecasts, based on facts and figures, take both dogmas and theories into consideration. Unexpected results can be forthcoming if this is not done and if too much faith is put in scientific optimism. On the other hand, excessive pessimism can be as counterproductive as the excessive optimism against which it is a reaction.

The dangers you have pointed out must not be underestimated, and we must be prepared for the unanticipated. You and I agree that we must take steps to deal with important dangers that, sooner or later, will demand urgent attention.

HUYGHE: Some voices have been raised in favor of confidence. For example, Alfred Sauvy, a professor of demography at the Collège de France, has observed that the laws of nature tend to work in the name of equilibrium and to compensate for excess by means of a thrust in the opposite direction. Joseph Basile, a professor at the Université de Louvain, in Belgium, has said that, in a similar fashion, ecological variables operate inversely to ensure relative consistency in the sum total. In more general terms, the effect is that of cybernetic feedback, which can serve as a corrective autoreaction.

It is necessary to observe, however, that this new notion, which finds verification most of all in the biological and psychological aspects of life, is intended to serve as a corrective to those singlemindedly materialistic and rationalistic views that paralyze our times and lead us blindly to perdition. The simplistic and most dogmatic conviction that an experimentally verified, determined cause mathematically produces a no less determined effect fails to take into consideration the element that might be called the elasticity of reality, which seems endowed with an ability to compensate for excesses committed against it. Instead of going on and on without interruption and thus leading to absurdity, an excess breaking the norms of reality curiously encounters a retort tending to neutralize it. This has been experimentally demonstrated with rats. When a given threshold is exceeded, per-area population increases among rats evoke destructive actions (such as aggressiveness among their own kind) that tend to normalize population density. The idea that human demographic excesses may have provoked epidemics and wars for the sake of neutralization is scarcely reassuring.

Scientific consideration involves the kind of change of mind that we require and that can save us from the mental mechanism that I call materialist rationalism. We must stop blindly believing in a determinism strictly based on a consistent relationship between cause and effect. We must admit the existence in nature of a kind of corrective force operating at the pace of what religions call providence. Perhaps doing this would be the first step toward the spiritual revolution that is our sole hope of salvation but that we can reasonably consider only after having examined the psychological aspects of the crisis.

2

The Psychological Crisis

IKEDA: It is now time to advance our discussion from strictly material facts to the realm of psychology. As we have already seen, humanity has reached limits in connection with many aspects of material life. In the psychological field, too, crisis is exerting various debilitating influences, perhaps even more clearly and profoundly than elsewhere. But in these cases, scientific methods are insufficient and useless to analyze the situation.

Nuisances

HUYGHE: In remaining faithful to our guiding lines, let us pass from the material to the psychological realm using, as transition, the nervous system that is related to both. The noxious effects of modern civilization can here be seen to manifest themselves not as pollution, but as what may be called public nuisances.

Clearly, noise occupies the first rank among the factors that attack the nervous system. As you know, experiments have shown that by raising the decibel level of sounds to which they are submitted, it is possible to cause animals to lose their memory and, then, to drive them wild or even to kill them. How are human beings to cope with the increasing noise in

28

their environment? Technical solutions exist: soundproof walls; double windows; and a turnabout in the concept of the house resulting in placing the front not facing the street, which has become dangerous, but facing a planted, enclosed, and protected interior space.

But noise is not the only problem. Our sensory integrity is constantly the victim of other, more subtle attacks, for instance, from the excessively glaring lights of cities and from highly developed information media.

Radio and television result in the attrition of active attention as a consequence of the fascination they arouse in the general public. Numerous educators have demonstrated this on their pupils. As can be verified, the many young people who assiduously follow television programs become used to receiving information passively and, little by little, grow incapable of responding. I wonder if you knew that, according to a recent estimate, an American born today is destined to spend eighteen years of his life in front of a television set.

Perhaps young people are persistently confrontational because they instinctively sense that human beings are being reduced to a level where they passively accept constant sensory intrusion. A desire to preserve their interior autonomy incites them to a state of insurrection, which may include some intuitive wisdom, no matter how unreasonable its manifestations.

In the many years that I have been preoccupied with the power of images*, I have found that mental passivity leads, little by little, to virtual slavery.

It must now be admitted that publicity does more than merely invade our homes: it becomes dictatorial. Statistics show that insistent, overbearing presentations ultimately constrain housekeepers to buy the products advertised. This is the start of docility and mental servitude. Such a state of affairs strikes me as dangerous and loaded with forbidding consequences.

As specialists in psychophysiology realize, when faced with

* In 1965, Flammarion published Monsieur Huyghe's book *Puissances de l'image*.

constant solicitation, in the form of publicity, and aggression, in the form of lights, neon signs, noise—particularly of automobiles—and traffic, the nervous system is exposed to physiological risks and to tension that is bad for the cardiac, circulatory, and mental systems.

Once again, certain remedies are possible. New kinds of urban traffic and street organization are being considered. Certain projects envisage channeling automobiles in underground galleries from which exhaust fumes can be eliminated. Others envisage stage gradations of traffic.

Le Corbusier repeatedly commented on his astonishment at being able to discover in Venice an idea from the past eminently suitable for the future. It seems that the city of the Doges suggested to him a model for an ideal system of what might be called progressively diminishing traffic. Such a system would require first a principal artery, corresponding to the Grand Canal, accommodating the fastest and noisiest means of transportation—the ones responsible for the greatest amounts of exhaust fumes. Such a main artery could be conceived of as a loop highway—or belt as the Americans call it— encircling the city. It would be accompanied by a system for more moderate traffic, similar to the network of *rii* in Venice and, finally, by rigorously protected streets for pedestrian traffic. In Venice pedestrian passages enjoy the advantage of being almost always perpendicular to canals, which must be crossed by means of bridges.

The nervous system and the aggression to which it is subject lead us now to something more complex—what I call moral aggression involving not merely our physical or even psychophysiological being, but our very existence.

Here, again, we must stick to the facts and avoid principles and theories. We know that in modern urban centers, which have been hastily and excessively materialistically conceived, the number of cases of mental illness surpasses the total number of cardiac ailments and cancer.

In old people it leads to disgust with life and even suicide, whereas in the young it produces inverse reactions of aggressiveness. The phenomenon is the same, except that the old person succumbs whereas the stronger young one fights back. This is one of the major causes of the juvenile delinquency and criminal behavior prevalent in low-income housing complexes.

As you know, certain mental maladies have been named for big new cities. In France, after the construction of Sarcelles, about eleven kilometers north of Paris, psychiatrists began speaking of a psychological condition called *sarcellite.*

A very unusual phenomenon accompanied the building of Brasilia, the capital of Brazil. During the construction work, a disorderly, temporary encampment—a kind of bivouac—was created to house laborers. When the city was completed, the inhabitants decided not to abandon their bivouacs, which they preferred to the new housing that, though theoretically perfect, was to their way of thinking too schematic and less alive and varied. Something called the Brasilia sickness resulted. And experts traveled from Brazil all the way to Europe to see what was happening in our modern cities, to compare causes, and to determine remedies.

The modern human nervous system and psychic functioning are profoundly disturbed, especially in the urban environment, where the scale and nature of the noxious elements to which we are exposed increase and become aggravated. Like scientific vocabulary, current vocabulary in this field has been compelled to adopt terms to describe the unprecedented and increasingly important state of affairs. The first of these terms is *aggressions*, which is used to signify disturbing actions directed against us ceaselessly by our surroundings. The second term is *stress*, that refers to the brusque, defensive starts our organisms are forced to make.

In 1936, the Canadian physiologist Hans Selye (1907–1982) first employed the term stress to mean the "alarm reaction" to which our body and, most of all, our nervous system are unceasingly subjected. This same reaction disturbs our neurochemical system, which responds by accelerating the pulse, increasing the temperature and blood pressure, and by causing chemical imbalances that affect both blood, urine, and alkaline reserves and protein and glucose levels. In the long run, these incessant starts or alerts, and the control efforts with which we respond to them, can engender such functional troubles as organic lesions and can result in changes of disposition and psychological state.

The Escape Reflex

HUYGHE: Human beings have not delayed in responding to this situation. If I were to name a psychological phenomenon symptomatic of our times, I would call it the escape reflex. Contemporary human beings dream of nothing but getting away. This is first noticeable in completely ordinary manifestations that are in no way disturbing in themselves.

One of these is the increasing number of people who own second homes, which actually represent an abnormal need. In the past, outside the especially privileged sectors, the custom of resorting to such a residential dichotomy did not exist. Today, on the other hand, the simplest people economize or borrow—repayment sometimes wipes them out financially—to procure a weekend house outside the city. In France, the number of such houses more than quintupled from 300,000 in 1939 to 1,600,000 in 1975. They attract more than a million families to Nature Rediscovered.

Those who cannot afford this luxury—albeit vulgarized luxury—resign themselves to long and tiring daily commuting in order to live in the country, or at least in the suburbs, far from the city to which they are bound by work.

Still another escape phenomenon is the annual vacation, which takes the form of a veritable migration and has been made possible by the development of tourism. The direction taken by humanity on holiday is noteworthy. Vacationers usually travel to the least technically developed countries. This accounts for the tourist successes of first Spain and now of Turkey and the Caribbean. As a consequence, however, these regions are able to grow economically in a way that, little by little, results in the disappointment of the tourists.

Sometimes people flee from the present into relics of the past. In France, young people voluntarily serving on archaeological teams offer new evidence of the extraordinary attraction of centuries long gone. People fly to nature, to those things that are not industrial.

The nonparticipation of the hippie movement, too, was an escape phenomenon. It systematically rejected actual life in the consumption society, in which each increase in income seems to stimulate an increase in expenditure. The hippies wanted no part of such a system and set themselves apart from it by a manner of dress inspired often by the costumes of primitive peoples. The hippies' aggressive break with urban customs accentuated their separation and retreat, which provocatively underscored their rejection of norms and rules.

But the hippie phenomenon had an intellectual significance that must not be overlooked. When it did not degenerate into mere mummery, the movement was concerned with the philosophies of India, the philosophies of renunciation and nonbeing. The hippie challenge to Occidental thought and the pursuit of Oriental thought, the origins of which are remote in both time and space and which negates practical activities and interests—to the point of envisioning existence as an absence of being—were an escape phenomenon.

But the ultimate, radical escape is achieved through artificial dreams and drugs, the increasing ravages of which signify a panicky reaction of abandon and oblivion.

3

The Moral Crisis

IKEDA: After having clarified the natures of its material, physical, and spiritual sides, we must now turn to the moral aspect of the crisis facing humanity today. This is the very core of the problem.

HUYGHE: I agree. A need to create new terms corresponds to the development of new and pressing realities. We have just seen how our contemporaries complain of the aggressions to which they are submitted by their environments. In addition to *aggression,* the word *frustration* is widely used. The importance attached to the notion of frustration by Herbert Marcuse, one of the cult figures of young people during the 1960s, is well known. The idea takes us directly to the heart of the moral ill suffered by modern man, who feels himself frustrated; that is, arbitrarily deprived of his due. This, in turn, is to say that we expect the fulfillment of our being to be naturally ensured and that we revolt, as if it were our right, when such fulfillment is blocked or obstructed.

Since they would be interminable and fruitless, let us avoid discussions of what is called Nature and of the natural. Let us say simply that, when cast into this world, the human being finds himself in the presence of certain fundamental data according to the functions of which it is necessary to organize life. The first such datum is certainly exterior reality, with which the human being comes into contact by means of body and senses and which presents itself to us in two dimensions, apart from which we are incapable of conceiving anything: one of them appears as space and the other, which combines with the first, as time.

Nonetheless, we perceive ourselves as distinct from this exterior reality. We experience ourselves as an interior reality, directly perceived within and, in a way, constituting ourselves. It is in this interior reality that the "I," or the personality, is nourished and in which thoughts, feelings, desires, and will-power exist. The three fields of space, time, and interior life—which corresponds more precisely with what Henri Bergson called the *durée*—are the only places in which we can realize ourselves. The three are offered to us, and within each of them we hope to enjoy the conditions of normal existence. When we complain of frustration it is because we are being deprived of one of these conditions.

IKEDA: I should now like to approach each of these fields—time, space, and the interior life—to discover wherein, according to your analysis, they have ceased to correspond to the requirements of our deeper nature.

Disarray in Space

HUYGHE: First, what do we encounter in relation to space? The connections human beings have maintained with space since time immemorial have been profoundly disturbed in our day. The virtually exclusive development of urban civilization, with ceaseless accentuation of its characteristics in combination with dizzying population growth, stifles us and deprives us of a field of normal expansion. We are stricken with a new sickness in the form of the loss of a sense of scale.

Growing numbers of births and urbanization of the population deprive the individual of a normal proportional relation with the group to which he belongs. The new idea of the mass takes the place of this relation. But the crowding together of people in masses can have tragic consequences.

As can be observed even in prehistoric times, life has always suppressed things that exceed proper scale. It seems likely that dinosaurs disappeared from the planet because their physical size was too great in proportion to the speed of their nerve impulses.

As has been demonstrated in experiments with rats, over-crowding leads to aggression. Human history may well offer cases analogous to those of rats and other animals. For instance, at some time Easter Island, isolated far in the Pacific, became overpopulated. Owing to a lack of historical documentation, we do not know what happened; but the island population was suddenly reduced to a tiny group by some catastrophe that sparked life's corrective autoreaction, which is endowed with devastating force that surpasses ideas and reason.

To prevent the mass from overwhelming the individual, it is essential to establish transitional stages between the two. It is all too easy to be willing, without the required reflection, to destroy all ideas inherited from the past. But the individual human being requires intermediaries between his own person and the collective global reality. Such past institutions as the family and, in a second circle beyond the family, other groups leading to cities and then to nations provided these intermediaries.

Biological gradations should find urban equivalents—like the neighborhood. A survey conducted in certain low-income urban housing complexes shows that it is possible to eliminate conspicuous rates of neuroses and suicide by establishing, through private initiative, meetings with interested and stimulating intermediary groups. This kind of thing shows clearly both the limitations and the responsibility of disproportionately large population masses.

Merely limiting size, however, is not enough to make a group aware of its proportion and unity; it is equally important to locate a center. Old cities were built around very evident centers.

We human beings require symbols. In those countries where it survives, the monarchy has its deepest reason for existing as a symbol of national unity. Similarly, in certain cities, the cathedral belfry is a landmark reminding people, perhaps only obscurely, that they belong to an organized group gravitating toward a point with only symbolic meaning. In towers visible from all around, the ringing bells are a real presence rhythmically marking the hours of the day.

At the same time, the human being needs to obey the laws of the living cell of which, after all, he is but an elaboration. As we all know, the living cell is an isolated portion of space with a nucleus and a cell wall, which must be permeable in two senses. It must facilitate effusion toward the exterior, the excretion of wastes outside the confines of the cell, and communication with the environment. At the same time, it must permit provisioning from the surroundings. The law of the cell is our law, too. This is why people talk today of the "human bubble."

We need to establish an aura, or a personal zone. Animal psychology confirms the existence of this need. Dogs and cats set up their own territories and mark out their boundaries by natural means to make them apparent to the olfactory senses of other animals. Warned by this scent, other animals must not, if they abide by natural agreement, cross the boundary. Beyond the primary territory is a secondary, mixed one, into which other animals are admitted as long as they respect certain rules of courtesy. Beyond this is the unknown world of adventure.

The kind of division of space into zones of progressively greater access found among many animals has its equivalent in human life. In our homes, we claim full personal autonomy, which extends to the family. We forbid intrusions from the exterior world, even those of an aural nature. Beyond this we expect to take advantage of a zone of mixed association. This is the neighborhood, where people associate, get to know each other, and form groups. It corresponds to the second of the animals' two zones. Beyond it begin society and its collective mass. While advancing into an increasing anonymity, human beings need to be able to protect their own reserve as they communicate with other human beings.

But the principle of communication concerns more than human beings and must be safeguarded with nature as well, since we must both participate in a society outside our own personal retreats and consciously take part in the whole. The Romantics perceived and developed the awareness of participation in the whole to an extreme degree.

Although the most individualistic of all creative artists, by a trick of natural compensation, the Romantics dreamed of fusing with—of being swallowed up by—nature. Their attitude is fresh proof of the dialectic of isolation and communication without which human beings cannot realize themselves normally.

Similarly, in our mental lives we experience an equally strong need to use our intellectual means to give the world an accessible and assimilable representation and, at the same time, to employ our resources of sensitivity to establish in it a communion permitting our lives to rediscover a sense of participating in the universal. These are the two poles between which we must remain balanced if we are to find equilibrium.

Contact with other beings, contact with nature and things, contact with sources of communion and the universal through art and the religious spirit are the indispensable steps leading each individual to the necessary flow between the self, jealous of its independence, and the whole, the supreme fulfillment.

Disarray in Time

HUYGHE: The exigencies we experience in connection with space have equivalents in the field of time. We can no more abstract ourselves from the temporal than from the spatial continuum. Time situates us in a present that, balanced between the past and the future, slides along its course like a cursor on its track. It demands both forward looks to the future, as is proper to the vital force, and solidarity with the past and the continued efforts humanity has expended in connection with it. We need to feel that we belong to time just as vividly as we feel the need to belong to nature. This contact may be ensured through the past and culture—poorly understood today because it has been caricatured and transformed into pedantry. It is the source of the importance of the monuments that are its witnesses and the historical centers—themselves works of art—it has left us.

Being exclusively absorbed in the present, an attitude we proudly describe as modernistic, is the surest sign of stagnation. In ideas for the sake of which many young people (and adults too) willingly destroy the past, the historian detects sclerotic, established commonplaces, and often repeated and paraphrased catechisms closely resembling the very things that are condemned as obsolete. We should be on our guard against the blind convictions of the present, since they can be more paralyzing than traditions from the past. All they need do to achieve this aim is to succeed their predecessors and become dogmatic and authoritarian.

But there is always the future, which, by its nature, does not oppose itself to the past. A continuum of man exists in both time and space. What is behind us is as important as what lies ahead. And we must live in time as in space with our full dimensions. Arbitrary amputation of the past is stupidly pushed to the point where history courses are constantly being cut from educational systems.

We must not abuse the future in our prejudgments. While I approve of forecasts in principle, I mistrust excesses in making them because they all too often attempt to make the future conform with the present in a dictatorial fashion. Human beings must be free. And the greatest human freedom is the future. Of course we must attempt to foresee dangers, in order to avert them, and tasks, in order to fulfill them; but we must respect the liberty of the future since, in doing so, we will be respecting the liberty of humanity.

The future does not exist to continue either us or the ideas we have of ourselves. Its purpose is to complete and sometimes to correct us. Consequently, we should not attempt to impose on it our more or less simplistic and arbitrary doctrines. We should pay more attention to what it can teach us than to what we pretend to inculcate in it through planning.

Internal Disarray

IKEDA: What you have been saying pertains to the space and time dimensions of external reality. We must now show how modern life is a source of perturbation in our interior reality, the importance of which you have already underscored.

HUYGHE: Here again, modern life deprives us of the total fulfillment toward which our nature aspires. Now we are speaking of our interior dimension, where, again, we are incomplete. Contemporary civilization leads us to restrain and cut away our interior dimension through a process of progressive intellectualization.

What does this mean and why is it dangerous? In this age, dominated by economy and technology, our contacts are increasingly limited to the concrete world, the world of matter. We are driven to give priority to the excessive, even exclusive, development of faculties for practically representing positive reality—the role of our intellectual faculties.

But the intellectual function is insufficient for our total interior life, which it asphyxiates if its abusive application trammels complimentary functions, that of sensitivity in particular. Intellect and sensitivity are made to associate and balance each other like the two phases of breathing. Sensitivity enables us to respond and participate. Between us and reality our intellectual functions interpose practicable representations in the form of a transparent but impassable screen. And, although it facilitates using reality, this screen is false to it in nature because, to be usable, it must transcribe everything that changes, moves, and diversifies itself into fixed, permanent, simple, and defined models—the *"idées claires et distinctes"* of which Descartes speaks. Life is complex and rejects fixedness and permanence. It is ceaselessly self-questioning and, therefore, rejects definition.

The intellect reduces everything to an image of spatial forms. It abstracts continuity, which is understood only by our sensitivity. This is why, as important or even indispensable as it is, the intellectual representation of reality must constantly be irrigated, amplified, and corrected through affective communications. To our misfortune, we find ourselves under obligation to adapt ourselves more and more to machines—even to the extent of modeling ourselves on them. Since machines work only on the geometrizing of fixed and determined elements, this obligation atrophies and devaluates our sensitive participation in reality. The cult of the geometric—especially of the rectilinear—in our ideas and images is an index of this.

Arbitrary simplification is imposed to the maximum extent in urban design and architecture, which constitute a fixed framework of our lives. From the Bauhaus to Le Corbusier (who did not pass over into the opposite camp until late, with the church called Notre-Dame du Haut, at Ronchamp) the straight and the orthogonal became a kind of moral obligation, a gauge of modernism—to be elevated to a cult in the art of Mondrian.

Square urban layouts, based on the American block, reigned supreme. The resulting so-called purism created a state of mental asepsis excluding activities of the living being and contributing to the urban psychoses that we spoke warningly of earlier. Life demands the curve, which is a sign of flexibility and motion and affirms the need to use both bending to balance the straight and liberty to balance rectitude.

It would seem that the facts have imposed similar obligations on the engineer. The ideal straight road to which he once aspired was forced to curve as soon as increasing rapidity in the automobile demanded the abandonment of abstractions and consideration, not only of space, but also of the realities of time imposed by speed. Highway interchanges that, perforce, replaced intersections of straight roads are admirable examples of a new flexibility.

Similarly, when problems of forces in protracted action, pressure, and traction forced it to abandon the arbitrarily imposed orthogonal, modern architecture itself was led inexorably to curves, which became the basis of a new style popularized by Oscar Niemeyer, Pier Luigi Nervi, Eero Saarinen, Guillaume Gillet, and others. Once again, the force of things triumphed over conceptual conventions.

Later, the revolutionary architecture of Jacques Couëlle and his former collaborator Grataloup attempted, through reaction and liberation, to abandon themselves unrestrainedly to soft, unforeseen, semispontaneous undulations. Laozi observed that the straight is united with death whereas the curve is bound to life.

But the simplified geometrizing, which we impose on life and which deforms life as a result of our wish to make it conform with our mentality, can take command of our ways of thinking and divorce them from reality to the point of desiccation. By refusing to take into account the variable peculiarities of human existence, the technocracy that invades national administrations treats human life as if it were inert, neutral matter subject to preconceived and levelling schematics. Such standardizing simplification stifles the life of the individual and adds arbitrary urban schemes to other constraints. Everywhere mental patterns, so-called mind fixes, submit the free play of life to their own structures.

Possibly the symmetrical mental pattern is the most formidable of all, since it demands that we constantly make absurd choices between for and against, good and bad, black and white, or right and left. It not only ignores evident nuances, but also attempts to obscure the logic of the contradictory that has impressed the most perceptive spirits from Heraclitus to the contemporary philosopher Stephane Lupasco.

We must preserve the fecund motion that, according to the Hegelian scheme, leads to a synthesis from the opposition of thesis and antithesis. Only the inert is totally whole. It is blind to the need and fertility of all things living between two adverse poles. But the inert is dead.

Another mental model evolving from symmetry is what Christopher Alexander calls arboreal thinking, which could be described as thought in brackets. It originates with the formula "one of two things" and, continuously subdividing by making obligatory choices, reduces problems to artificial ramifications that fail to take into consideration the exchanges and interexchanges by means of which life operates. Alexander has demonstrated the ravages produced by this rational method in the field of urban design. This method neatly appropriates separate zones for commerce, work, leisure, residence, and so on. But, in doing so, it ignores—or tries to ignore—the continual interferences occurring in human activity, in which relaxation should, or must, be possible nearby if not at the actual place of work. Playgrounds at schools are a lesson born of experience.

Furthermore, Alexander has shown how a mode of thinking in patterns of latticelike intersections has already restored some of the communications formerly cut off by a system greedy for artificial clarity. In the field of philosophy, Roger Caillois has reacted similarly with his insistence on "diagonal thinking."

In order to dissipate the false prestige of such methods, it may be necessary to open up to psychology a complete field of studies that would take the place of efficiency and certainty of mental function, which seduce by means of apparent ease of reasoning. It seems likely that mental stereotyping results from a system of education for masses of people, who, lacking the time to develop them fully, prefer to mechanize their individual selves. Furthermore, this system itself ultimately evolves from a fundamental materialism inculcated by the nineteenth-century triumph of the physical sciences, which are limited to inert matter and uniform laws and incapable of understanding, or admitting, that the salient characteristic of the living being—and most of all of the psychic being—is respect and development of the particular.

The profound illness can go so far as to result in crisis and generate new terminology born of new pressures. To the word *frustration,* which we have already mentioned, it is necessary to add *alienation,* a term currently on all lips. The use of such words is justifiable because they reflect authentic anguish. Contemporary human beings call themselves alienated because they realize they are being diverted from their true natures, just as they call themselves frustrated because they realize that certain of their possibilities and essential needs can neither be exercised nor satisfied.

But their reaction is as blind as that of an ill person who aggravates his malady by running wild and writhing about. Struggle—another key word—often takes place with the support of simplistic ideas that, while appearing revolutionary, are actually no more than residues of stifling dogmas. Acquiring a true awareness of the false situations in which our epoch has enchained itself will require a slow, patient, and objective work of elucidation.

For those who are not afraid of being engulfed in them, to counter categorical and elementary dogmas—the likeliest to find support—it is essential to rediscover direct experience of psychological realities. We must attempt to discover the forces behind all ideas, whether inherited from the past or imposed by present modes because, before congealing into theories, living realities are forces—first unperceived, then perceived and affective. And herein lies the truth.

I should like to return to the means available to us for redressing ourselves in this situation. At present, we may point to two: education for the young and art for peoples of all ages.

A child should be formed—and I realize that attempts are being made to do this—by means of a revised educational method teaching him to share direct experience. Such education should be sensory and should give the child a sense of things and objects and of the reality of contact. On the basis of instruction of this kind, it is possible to advance to general notions when they are acquired during actually lived experience. We must never begin with abstract ideas, as many intellectuals advocate and practice.

Obviously, later, abstract notions may serve to consolidate and order experiences. Or they may be useful as aids to memorization. But this stage of education, which it would be a grave error to neglect, cannot be attained without a sure basis rich in effectively experienced experimentation.

This is why we must preserve the culture of artisans, the culture of the hands. In addition, we must develop the sense of art and increase the role of museums. The success art enjoys today arises from the instinctive human desire to extract from the communication and effusion of works of art things that technology cannot give. Technology permits us to operate on the world, not to live in symbiosis with it.

In order to avoid making conjectures and thus running the risk of imprisoning them within our own limitations, we must prepare for the people of the year 2000 an enlarged awareness of their tasks and reinstruct them in asserting and assuming their complete human nature. No matter how devaluated the word has become—and I wonder why such devaluation has occurred—I hope for the institution of a new, unrestricted humanism. There must be no humanity without humanism.

It is to be hoped that, though harried by the difficult problems confronting him and exalted by overflowing awareness, the man of the year 2000 will be a Reformation and a Renaissance man. Otherwise, misled by the illusion of false progress, the dangerous countereffects of which he is beginning to perceive, he has nothing less to fear than his own perdition.

4

The Crisis Manifest in Art

IKEDA: As you clearly indicate, the crisis that is deeply ingrained in material facts exerts a considerable influence on human morality. Many intellectuals have pointed out the crisis situation into which contemporary civilization has fallen. But, with their acute intuition, artists must have perceived it and the deep effect it has on our sensitivity earlier than others and no doubt expressed the insecurity and suffering associated with it. A specialist in art, like you, is in an excellent position to analyze this situation.

HUYGHE: It is extremely interesting to question art on this subject. If nothing else, art is eminently a mode of both intentional and unconscious expression. It is a way of listening to the human soul.

Artistic expression can be read in two ways. Personal expression is manifested on the individual level, and all the more strongly when the individual is especially gifted. Into his work, the artist projects the reflections and images of his own character—of his psyche. But, together with this capacity for individual expression, art is endowed with another capacity for collective expression. In inverse proportion to the importance he places on his particular problems, each individual expresses the general mentality in which he participates, thus reflecting its aspirations, anxieties, and sufferings.

It is important to study contemporary art in order to point out common traits that, owing to their very repetition, are seen as repercussions of a general state of affairs confronting all individuals, no matter how diverse. I have attempted to point out these characteristics on several occasions.

From Happiness to Suffering

HUYGHE: Without doubt, anxiety is one of the most striking traits of our time. Critics have often pointed it out, not only among writers, with whom it amounts to a veritable leitmotif, but among other creative artists as well.

As you have suggested, art provided forewarnings of what was to come even when the euphoria of the nineteenth century was at its apogee. With the Impressionists, the euphoria persisted until the end of that century and even beyond—Monet, for instance, was painting until his death in 1926. True to the optimism of the century of science, the Impressionists took as the basis of their approach scientific positivism, to which, in the field of art, realism and observation of the physical world correspond. They felt that their task was confined to perfecting the representation of appearances according to newly discovered laws of optics and prided themselves on great scientific accuracy.

But the school of Impressionism had something else to convey: a defense of the joy of living. In their time, the world of nature was still very close to cities. Living in Paris, they were still able to encounter at the very gates of the capital the countryside, where they could go boating and rediscover rural pleasures in charming country settings, like that of Grenouillère, which they celebrated. Renoir, Monet, Sisley, and others sang the beauty of this way of life as it glimmered in the light. To this, Renoir added the pleasures of the flesh and, on occasion, those of a picnic or of the table, in the form of a still life. Into the middle of the twentieth century, such painters as Bonnard and Dufy remained faithful to the idea of painting as a defense of the joy of living.

Other painters, however, kept themselves apart from this current, indicating, from the time of Romanticism, premonitory anxiety about an exclusively material and physical civilization. More and more boldly, they announced themselves to be antirealists. Initiated by the Romanticists, this reaction, together with the ideas of the symbolists, developed during the very heyday of Impressionism.

Antirealist painters turned toward the interior life and its mysteries and avoided the physical joys afforded by the visible world that Impressionism celebrated. Gustave Moreau and Odilon Redon claimed that the important thing is not the visible but the invisible.

In this way, such artists recoiled from the blind optimism of the nineteenth century and paved the way for an art of suffering and unhappiness. Since our own time has given up expressing aspiration toward happiness, Impressionism can be called the last manifestation of the dream of euphoria.

From the time of the Impressionists, everything seems to have been turned round. With the advent of Expressionism, in the 1880s, especially in northern Europe, irrepressible interior torment became the major expressive element. At that time, Sweden and Norway were avant-garde countries in both literature—Ibsen and Bjornson—and art—Edvard Munch (1863–1944). People of this kind helped germinate—especially in Germany—the agonizing Expressionist movement.

The natal thrust, the progression, whereby this movement developed can be traced in a series of canvases painted by Munch between 1882 and 1884. The first shows a street in Oslo on Sunday. People are strolling, and a military band is present, all brightly lighted in a way suggesting Impressionism. Munch repeatedly treated the same theme, altering its meaning each time he did so: the street becomes dimly lighted; while wearing the same bourgeois clothes and then fashionable tall hats, the strollers become haggard and a little mad in appearance. A secret panic seems to be germinating among the crowd. The culmination of the series is the painting called "The Scream." In it, at the seaside, on a kind of jetty, the lines of which rush unexpectedly toward the spectator, stands a creature stripped of all individual character. Its eyes are dilated in terror; its mouth wide open in a shriek. It covers both ears as if not to hear some unimaginable threat. In the background, nature has been stripped of all security. The unstable seashore undulates. The sky is crossed by great blood-red streaks. Everything gives the impression of a universe that has lost its foundations and has been transformed into an agitated, fluid mass. The world of peace has been abandoned for a world of oppression.

The same premonitory quality is strikingly present in the paintings and engravings of a Belgian contemporary of Munch, James Sydney Ensor (1860–1949), who was haunted by the idea of the mask and the ambiguity of the human being (what is behind appearances) and by the idea of death, which is made present in his pictures by skeletons mingled with living people.

At the opening of the twentieth century, Fauvism and Expressionism emerged as connective links with these premonitory developments. Soon Cubism abandoned nature: in Cubist works, forms lose regular security to be crushed like debris and then reconstructed according to a logic alien to that of reality. After World War I, first the Dada movement brutally and sarcastically rejected tradition, morality, and rationality; then Surrealism came to full flower.

As the evolution of psychology and medical science led to psychoanalysis, so Surrealism proscribed reason and exterior reality, which scientific thought had allowed to reign supreme, and sought sources and truth in the subconscious, in things not yet put in order by the mind, that are impulsive and related by means of fantasy.

Uncovered by occidental art, these tendencies reached nations like Japan, where intensive modernization opened the way for European influences while stimulating the renunciation of local traditional art.

Thus, more or less subconsciously, artists perceived and manifested the changing times. Unable to explain why, by an almost animal instinct, they realized that art is no longer capable of offering an image of happiness. They realized that art can now announce only the arrival of troubled, sick times plunged into insecurity and the unknown. As is usual, art preceded lucid awareness.

Divorce from Reality

HUYGHE: A closer analysis reveals still other traits. Beginning with the twentieth century, art more and more stopped reproducing, or even reflecting reality, demonstrating instead a certain distance from or even hostility toward it. This is an indication of a rupture, a divorce, between humanity and nature. The coordination that had prevailed between them in earlier agrarian societies was broken.

The modern artist, however, takes refuge in an entirely subjective or intellectual world that is violently arbitrary. The triumph in a few decades of abstract art—especially in its geometrical aspect—demonstrates this. No two things could be more diametrically opposed than the rationally conceived structures of abstract pictures and the complex, multifarious, and changing spectacle of the reality surrounding us. Abstract paintings underscore our excessive and increasingly exclusive recourse to rational faculties. The attitude of this art is characterized by Mondrian and his innumerable followers.

Still another aspect of incompatibility with reality might seem to contradict this one. The paintings of Mark Tobey, Jackson Pollock, and Jean Dubuffet lack compositions and develop by means of a kind of rupture or a dispersion of elements—signs of which are to be found in Cubism. Of course, the Cubists did not flatly refuse rapport with reality but, for the first time, proposed images not in conformity with actual physical organization, which Cubist painters fragmented and then arbitrarily reassembled. In these cases, the viewer seems to be witnessing the crumbling of form or the dispersion of outline, as if a projection or explosion had just occurred. Arman (or Armand Fernandez) proceeds by a simple accumulation of preexisting, moreover useless, objects.

To these might be added such other characteristics as an obsession with the empty, or the obstacle, or the barrier that is encountered in representational as well as abstract works. All of these traits spring from what in psychopathological terms could be called a schizophrenic mentality. But it is not merely the painter's problem.

This is an extremely important point. The images of art are, in a way, projections of our mental life. If we can find syndromes of this kind widespread in the art of our time, we must admit that contemporary society is a carrier of the blemish of latent schizophrenia. Through the obsessions of its art, our society confesses to an incapacity to adhere to reality or to conquer it globally by means of the spirit, if not by means of the partial operations undertaken by technology and science. Arbitrary constructions, which are human mental elaborations, are founded in all domains on a kind of flight from reality.

At the beginning of this century, the German philosopher Wilhelm Worringer, who contributed considerably to the emergence of abstract art, if only in the influence he exerted on the thought of Wassily Kandinsky (1866–1944), had already advanced the significance of art's rejection of reality. He believed that representation and nonrepresentation in art are periodic phenomena. According to him, representational art corresponds to happy civilizations or to classicism, that is, to adhesion to the surrounding world. Abstract art, on the other hand, he saw as a rejection of a painful or even insupportable reality.

The same kind of thing can be observed in such more recent manifestations as insistence on the gratuitousness of art, which strives to flee into itself, abandoning all social functions even to the extent of refusing to communicate—although art is, first and foremost, a means of expression. Many artists in our times profess to disdain oneness with the spectator and are ambitious for nothing but self-expression. Their shutting themselves up in their own creative work is a different kind of flight.

Another of these trends might be called antiutility and is represented by Jean Tinguely, who created and displayed in New York an utterly useless machine and a self-destructive machine to protest against the useful and the technology devoted to it.

Certain regression phenomena, too, might be cited. For

instance, there is regression toward the coarse, as in Dubuffet, or regression toward the formless and to soft matter as in César Baldaccini (1921–   ). To these I might add regression toward the unorganized and the germinating. Is this the capitulation and abnegation of art? Pop Art is evidence that art is not to be differentiated from despised modern reality. Flight can go so far as to suppress the durability of a work of art. What else can be the meaning of the so-called happening? In an inversion of what has always occurred in preceding civilizations, in which concurrence with reality, under various forms, has been the rule, modern art ceaselessly bears witness to a rupture with contemporary reality in all its forms.

Frequently occurring art images enable us to make a kind of auscultation from which evolves a more precise diagnosis of the illness of our time.

IKEDA: You have been analyzing the elite arts—art proper. But the new technology of modern civilization has given birth to previously unknown art forms. One of these forms, the motion picture has a much wider and more catholic audience than other arts. The little screen of the television has by now entered virtually every private home. The development of these mass media, which have become the favorite recreation of a large segment of the population, is a characteristic of contemporary technological society.

To be popular, the mass media must reflect the tastes of contemporary people much more directly than such traditional art forms as painting. This is why their frequent themes are distrust, eroticism, violence, and the appeal of money. Certainly, in our savage modern world, trust is often betrayed. Society is run by the cold mechanism of power and the greed and tyranny of people in power. Adults who believe that material wealth and positions of authority are the most reliable things in the world are unlikely to be attracted to art offering idealism and sweet ethical doctrines. Such people will be much more keenly in tune with works that acutely represent the ugliness of reality.

The presentation of such works by the mass-media, however,

presents a problem. In Japan, television, which occupies a place of prominence among the media, broadcasts considerable numbers of dramas and other programs including fairly erotic and violent scenes. It is possible to prevent minors from attending motion-picture houses where such material is shown, but television reveals it to the eyes of all, including young people who lack the experience enabling them to judge properly the merit of what they watch.

In numerous instances, acts of juvenile delinquency may be traced to stimulus from television dramas. But a still greater cause of concern is the gradually accumulating influence undesirable television programs have on the minds of young people who must be tomorrow's leaders.

I believe that education should be centered on efforts to teach young people that, even when they are removed from the actualities of society, lofty ideals of trust and the courage to respect justice are goals all human beings should aspire to attain. Of course, education that leaves children blind to the ugliness of society produces adults who are too fragile to respond successfully to the actualities of real life. This is why I oppose attempts to eliminate violence and sensuality from such mass media as television and even more strongly reject restrictions on creative art in the wider sense, including motion pictures and drama. Nonetheless, scruples should be exercised in cases of broadcasts of media that can be seen by everyone.

Restrictions must not be imposed on artistic creativity; freedom of expression must be respected. But directors and television bureau heads, who determine program content, are not artists. They should be aware that they occupy positions of great social responsibility. If they reflect this responsibility in determining programming, they will give idealistic artists opportunities to work and exert a wholesome and stimulating influence on viewers.

I consider the artist to be more than a person who passively reflects the ugliness of actual society and believe that many outstanding artists are capable of acutely observing society without losing their trust in humanity or their lofty idealistic propensities. But often, in our liberal society, commercialism threatens to smother such artists. Nevertheless, by providing outstanding artists with opportunities to act, it is possible to correct the influence art has on future generations without repressing freedom of expression.

Compensatory Aspirations

IKEDA: Art is, however, more than a mere reflection of its time. The things it expresses have a profound influence on people and create the climate of the epoch. Certainly it is possible to view contemporary art as an expression, not of happiness and joy, but of insecurity, discord, and despair. But, for the sake of future generations, should we condone this approach? What are your thoughts on the matter?

HUYGHE: True, motion pictures and television, not only in Japan, but in other countries as well, are too preoccupied with success and profit to concern themselves with doing more than humoring the lowest appetites of the public and make no effort to awaken a new spirit capable of dealing with the fatal tendencies of our times. But then neither do the traditional arts, which call individual creativity into play. As we have already seen, painting and sculpture reflect the agonies of our civilization without remaining content with its blemishes. Their content is much richer than that.

Art always reflects not only the situations imposed on its epoch and the dangers it experiences, but also, inevitably, its compensatory aspirations, its desire to rediscover a state free of constraints.

It is possible therefore to learn from a diagnosis of art not only a record, or report, of what actually is, but also the more or less well formulated desire for a lost state, a secret aspiration for something else. It may even be possible to detect seeds of future developments as well.

Art, the sources of which are for the most part intuitive, can help us in this way. Unlike literature, philosophy, and science, which require a process of reflection and intellectualization, the graphic and plastic arts flow forth spontaneously in inspirations. They are, therefore, more open to presentiments, which they represent more easily than modes of expression subject to disciplines of thought and logic. Indeed, it was precisely art that testified to the reaction, latent in our times, against the growing and stifling empire of the rational which, drawing its nets ever tighter, threatens to compromise the life of sensitivity and even the existence of the individual.

The subconscious quickly became a constituent element of Surrealism, which appeared in about 1919–20, shortly after the end of World War I. This very profound movement, which cut through our epoch, demonstrated a visceral fear of the rational, an uncompromising return to the most innate, subconscious sources, operating within us before being worked out by logical thought. Precursors of this development were already apparent in the nineteenth century in the role of the imaginary in Romanticism, which attempted to arrange a refuge from then current positivistic, scientific bourgeois thought. Part of this attempt entailed fleeing far from contemporary society to the past—the medieval period most of all—or to the Orient.

In the twentieth century, signs of similar rejections became all the more violent; and Surrealism bound itself to reaction as it plunged resolutely into the subconscious. Thus rationalism was not only counterbalanced by Romantic reverie, but also thereafter excluded when recourse was made to things that escape it.

To this first sign of compensatory reaction must be added another—also introduced by Romanticism—in the form of an increasingly provocative affirmation of the individual temperament. In this connection, subjectivity was exalted at the expense of the objectivity required with increasing vigor by scientific, materialistic, and technical directives tending to reinforce collective rules. Artists intuitively perceived the menace posed by the collectivization implied by rational laws; the objective methods of science; and the kind of political evolution that, as a parallel, tended to subject the individual to the demands of the masses.

In the face of this threatening oppression, art tried to

strengthen the affirmation of the individual. Whereas in the past they had contented themselves with modulating it, in the nineteenth century and all the more strongly in the twentieth century, they became aggressive in relation to the collective vision and were unafraid to contradict it violently through free interpretations, deformations, and willful impulses that Expressionism, for instance, had not attempted.

It is impossible to pay too much attention to these new traits, which confirm the diagnosis we have already made of our time.

IKEDA: Although it confirms our fears, is it not possible that art gives grounds for some hope and, by indicating things that need changing, points the way to a solution of the crisis? You yourself have often said that artists sometimes vaguely sense things that become generally clear only much later.

HUYGHE: The true artist can be a clairvoyant. The profound sources of his intuition and sensitivity enable him to register signs that are still obscure to thought, which can elucidate them only later, when the evidence is available and when leisure has been provided to interpret it. Since the artist commands the faculty of, if not prescience, at least of presentiment, we ought to ask whether he can perceive in depths still veiled to our times, germs of a saving reaction that can correct the difficult conditions threatening us at present. They should be correctable, even though perhaps only sporadically.

With some artists, it is possible to sense a desire to escape from contemporary materialistic levelling and stifling. In this instance too, precursors are to be found in nineteenth-century Romanticism. For instance, an examination of the work of Delacroix—even an examination limited to large decorative masterpieces like *Triomphe d'Appollon sur le Serpent Python,* in the Louvre, or *Combat de Jacob et de L'Ange,* at Saint-Sulpice—shows that the artist had a presentiment of the need for battle (indeed his motto was *Dimicandum,* meaning one must fight). In the case of the former picture, Apollo, god of light and the spirit, battles against the material instincts, represented by a monster, or dragon. The second is a call to a confrontation between the spirit and the divinity, represented by the angel.

At the end of the nineteenth century, the Symbolists stated this aspiration toward the spiritual. An example is the revindicating elevation that Verlaine expresses in his sonnet dedicated to Ludwig II of Bavaria, at the time of his death in 1886. The poet praises the king fervently for having wished to die avenging his reason.

> *Des choses de la politique et du délire*
> *De cette Science intruse dans la maison,*
> *De cette Science assassin de l'Oraison*
> *Et du Chant et de l'Art et de toute la Lyre.*

The same aspiration is perceptible in twentieth-century art. For the rest of his life after 1913, the great sculptor Constantin Brancusi (1876–1957) was occupied with the theme of flight, abolition of weight, extraction from the Earth and ascension toward free space. This is the meaning of his *Oiseau,* which he once called *Maiastra.* A parallel theme, seen in his *Colonne sans fin,* is a different response to the same deep aspiration: to leave the zero level, which represents matter, and to attain knowledge as a result of limitless elevation, to escape the threat of standardization. A more recent painting by Chapelin-Midy showing petrified hands in the desert desperately reaching toward a flight of birds crossing the sky confirms the urgency of this need.

It is possible to find other significant manifestations of the same kind, for example in the art of the American sculptor Richard Lippold (1915–), which appears on the surface to be a tributary of the technological civilization in that his exclusive use of metals appears at first to signify obedience to the mechanical world. Actually, however, his radiating constructions of wires stretching out from a balanced center signify expansion to the heart of the light that causes the strands to scintillate.

Brancusi once demonstrated a similar interest in light. In his studio, he himself photographed his *Oiseau* at the time of day when the sun struck the top of the sculpture and seemed to substitute a burst of light, a dazzling brilliance, for the actual form. All of this is profoundly meaningful. And Brancusi's having wanted to keep a photograph showing his work transformed in this way indicates the importance he attached to the idea.

In conclusion, an attempt to decipher them indicates that images projected by art as bearers of meaning, partly subconscious, striving to become consistent, visible, and evident reflect two positions in connection with contemporary society. First, they indicate an increasingly profound awareness of a pathological condition evinced by our civilization's failings, excesses and threats. This awareness can stimulate the second position, namely, a desire to flee. With some people, however, the images assume the form of a positive not negative need, obscuring the drive to rise so as to escape the weight of matter, and rush upward toward the Spirit.

PART TWO

Historical Significance

HUYGHE: In spite of the scale of the crisis rocking modern civilization and of its material, moral, and spiritual consequences, many people give in to the temptation to minimize its bearing on the future and find reassurance in citing previous examples. Since the time of Paul Valery, people have repeatedly said that civilizations are mortal. One after another, all have fallen victim to senescence and survive only in human memory and in monuments indicating their bent toward philosophy, literature, or art. Is it not possible, then, that we now find ourselves at the end of a civilizational phase? Is what we are experiencing now not a sign of a new departure, a new drive, marking another stage in the perpetual regeneration of humanity?

After all, people often object, the blow shaking our world cannot be worse than the one that toppled the Roman Empire and brought an end to Antiquity. The twilight of that time mingled at its very beginning with the dawn of the Christian Middle Ages, a period which had its own brilliance and which greatly enriched the history and heritage of humanity. This line of thought questions the significance of these phases of transition which, though seriously disturbing at the time they occur, ultimately do no more than mark the eternal rhythm leading humanity to periodic regeneration. But the analogy is superficial. If we are to understand both its true dimensions and its true origins, we must place the nature of the present crisis in an overall historical perspective.

1

Human Evolution: Three Ages

IKEDA: Although, as you say, some thinkers judge it to be no more than a periodic phase of suffering, a precursor to a new departure, others—including some modern scientific researchers—perceive that the present crisis affects the very basis of civilization to the extent of jeopardizing the continued existence of humanity. I agree that a judgment on this issue can be made only if we relate the crisis to history in general, and should like to hear your opinions on the topic.

HUYGHE: You are quite correct. In my view, the crisis we are undergoing is unprecedented in terms of the scope of its effects.

Certainly the Middle Ages knew tragic periods, such as pro-tracted warfare, epidemics, and the Black Death of the fifteenth century that profoundly upset the existing equilibrium. To go back still further in history, by permitting the development of the causes of the exhaustion that plagued it, the Roman Empire assisted in bringing about the downfall not only of a civiliza-tion, but of all Antiquity as well.

It is necessary to remember, however, that all these ruined, even annihilated, civilizations belonged to the same cycle: the agricultural mode of life that began to form and develop in the third millennium before Jesus Christ. Consequently, the crises we refer to in the history of the past five thousand years are no more than internal disturbances in an unfolding continuity.

Today, the entire continuity is being radically torn asunder. A disruption on this scale is unprecedented and is comparable to the transition from prehistoric to agrarian civilization. It cannot be compared with the phases of a greater cycle and, therefore assumes a gravity unlike that of anything except the fundamental mutations that separated what may be called the Ages of Humanity. In the past, in a collective work entitled *L'Art et l'Homme,* I attempted to describe as strongly as possible the nature of these mutations, which, as is to be expected, art recorded with the greatest fidelity. They profoundly changed the relations between humanity and its surroundings and modified the way human beings perceived the world, worked to draw from it the things they wanted, and imposed on it organizational forms. But the number of mutations is considerably smaller than might be expected, and they establish only three principle phases.

Prehistory

HUYGHE: In this period, human beings were practically completely unarmed. They lacked the means to understand the world, to impose their laws on it, and to defend themselves against it. They were limited to extending, by means of the great invention of the tool (weapon), the natural means of action and defense in which they were no better qualified than other animals.

Art is the sole surviving evidence of the concept that human beings of this age had of their world. But this art is difficult to interpret, owing to the absence of oral and written traditions and the consequent need to rely on hypotheses to elucidate its true significance. Nonetheless, thanks to the brilliant pioneering work of the Abbé Breuill (professor of prehistory at the College de France) and the later work of Leroy-Gourhan, it is safe to say that prehistoric human beings employed symbols and symbolic images believed to possess magical powers to appease or invoke the forces that made nature mysterious to them.

It is difficult to determine, however, whether the magic involved is simply a hunting magic—as discovered by the German ethnologist Frobenius among primitive African peoples—or a fertility symbolism emphasizing sexuality as supported by Leroy-Gourhan. While Abbé Breuill supports the former interpretation, these variants define an attitude prevalent among primitive humanity until the end of the prehistoric period, when civilization turned to agriculture.

Agrarian Society

HUYGHE: Agrarian humanity established a new civilization in about the third millennium before Jesus Christ. Although an agricultural way of life had appeared at the end of the prehistoric period—the end of the Neolithic period—it did not assume a distinctive form until the time of the great agrarian empires of Egypt; Mesopotamia farther east; India, where archaeological traces of an analogous civilization are to be found; and, finally, China, where the agricultural way of life became so firmly established that it continues to dominate today.

For the sake of definition, it is possible to say that, with the appearance of agrarian civilization, humanity formed an alliance with the forces of the world—or, as they came to be called, the forces of nature—instead of defending itself against them. Agricultural human beings understood that they should accept the good things nature brings but that acceptance should be accompanied by both attempts to adapt and the intelligence to take part in the process. They saw that this intelligence makes several things possible: surpassing blind, passive natural existence; divining latent possibilities in nature; and helping to realize these potentialities. This, indeed, is the principle on which agriculture rests.

Man sees the plant that nourishes him growing naturally from the sustaining earth. He then attempts to discover how he can employ seeds and cultivation to increase output and thus derive new possibilities from the plants. Then he goes further to employ fertilization to enrich soil and plant together.

From this point, he explores further possibilities. He senses latent capacities in animals and plants. From a single wild plant, like the eglantine, he develops the visual beauty and the fragrance of the cultivated rose; both of these attractive qualities existed originally as only potentialities. In addition, he attempts to collect qualities existing but dispersed in the world of nature. For instance, the speed of one dog is added to the scenting capability or strength of another to produce a more effective hunting instrument. The basis of the agrarian system, then, was perfecting things.

This explains why, from the early Egyptian period until the nineteenth century, agriculture, true to the life-style it represented, concerned itself first of all with the reproduction of nature. Nurtured by the cult of "what is," it strove to transcribe visual appearances in recognizable ways. In other words, it was realistic.

It must be noted, however, that, while realistic, this civilization was constantly preoccupied—as has already been noted in connection with agricultural techniques—with perfecting existing things and taming them to its own convenience. The logical end of this tendency is the concept of ideal beauty, a doctrine that dominated Europe again in the early nineteenth century with the advent of neoclassicism.

Up to the threshold of the twentieth century, academic art felt obligated to respect nature and to conform to natural appearances, which were to be cultivated with suitable human means in the fashion of the gardener and the farmer. In other words, without thwarting or violating it according to their own ideas of beauty, human beings attempted to improve nature in the raw, which they respected and from which they themselves originated.

This then is the second great phase of human history. In the West, it developed without interruption and established a philosophy of humanity that impregnated religions and founded a civilization that, today, is threatened with annihilation.

That civilization has been rocked and virtually ruined by tendencies, the seeds of which it contained within itself, that have suddenly developed in brutal and exclusive ways. Stimulated by the advantages he enjoyed from collaboration with it, the farmer inevitably came to exercise increasing sway over nature, which he began modifying and bending to his own designs by, for example, pushing back and destroying forests for the sake of more arable land. Wars began when greed for land stimulated human rivalries. The earliest skeletons bearing fragments of weapons date from the Neolithic period, the era of early attempts at agrarian culture.

Nonetheless, early aggressiveness and acts of degradation and destruction remained dominated by a general principle of harmony, which was not repudiated until the advent of the new scientific and industrial civilization. It is the West that produced this civilization, in the creation of which the East, initially at least, played no part. Nonetheless, the East has been tainted with the perverting and degrading contagion, as no doubt Africa soon will be. The spreading of the contagion will have the same lamentable consequences in the Orient that it has had in the Occident—a topic to which we shall return.

The Industrial Age

HUYGHE: Since the beginning of this age, human beings have wished to push still farther and to acquire power to assault and violate nature. The alliance between the two has been broken and replaced by human aggression.

Human beings are no longer content with taking the best of what nature promises and with assisting her in keeping her word. Instead they want to attack and tame nature and enforce her exploitation. Within a century after their discovery, reserves of coal found within the Earth were already facing depletion. Though perhaps not yet fully apparent, open-cut mining gashes the scenery, shaves away hills, and destroys landscapes.

No longer satisfied with exploiting such natural energy as can be obtained through wheels and mills from water and wind, humankind went to the very heart of energy, which became a new divinity. In the middle of the nineteenth century, the old established idea of matter was replaced with the notion of energy and the idea that matter is no more than a variant—an incarnation, if I may use the word in this sense— of energy. Man began to extract from energy, enclosed in the appearances imparted to it by matter, new possibilities, the most important of all being electricity. Then, one day, he sought energy at its source, its origin, by approaching the atom, the very name of which indicates the indivisibility it was once thought to possess. In splitting it, man liberated a power that should have remained concealed. It is impossible to force nature any farther than constraining her to surrender her most secret resources. The risks entailed in this gigantic shock are themselves gigantic.

I recall that, while pursuing her research before World War II, the famous French physicist Irene Joliot-Curie was greatly preoccupied with ways to prevent the catastrophe of a chain reaction. Once the energy of an atom has been liberated, how is it possible to prevent the explosion from propagating itself from atom to atom? An unbridled chain reaction could, conceivably, lead to the step-by-step destruction of all matter on the globe and of the planet itself. The great problem, which persisted in the following years and was at the heart of research on the atom bomb, was devising a method of restraint to block the chain reaction that man started and that threatened to turn on him. (This was the heavy-water problem, which played an important role in the first years of the war; but that is another story.)

Thanks to the violence—which as we shall see will probably produce reactions—and injuries he continuously inflicts on nature, man is overreaching the natural condition. It is hardly necessary to recall the consequences of industrial development and its renewing demands for sources of energy. In the past, the forces of nature—the wind in the case of windmills, flowing liquids in the case of the water wheel and the turbine—sufficed. Later industry demanded constant expansion to new energy sources that, ultimately, began to give out, as has been true in the cases of coal and petroleum.

But this is only one aspect of the problem. At the cost of

exhausting energy resources, products turned out by factories must find incessantly growing outlets. The price paid for this is the degradation of humanity.

To augment consumption it is essential to resort to advertising to pervert man's natural tastes and to create artificial needs by applying to him the system of conditioned reflex that the Russian physiologist Ivan P. Pavlov proved eminently effective with animals. In this way is created a kind of human hyperaesthesia in which, under the irritating and exciting effects of publicity, artificial needs drive us to consume to a pernicious excess. Such has been the case with alcohol and tobacco, two means of self-destruction, and their vertiginous extension, narcotics.

But even this is not the whole story. Factory production requires energy transformation, which, however, has two aspects. Its voluntary, positive aspect permits production. Its involuntary but inevitable aspect generates wastes, which, as we have said, blindly dumped into the natural environment, have noxious, polluting effects with terrible consequences that have already become apparent in our time.

2

The Industrial Age and Its Failings

IKEDA: In dealing with this issue, we must take into consideration the basic nature of industry. Hunting and gathering depend totally on the natural order. Although it involves tampering with nature, in general agriculture, too, depends on the same order. Modern industry, however, far from relying on it, actually operates in ways that are destructive of the natural order and that rebound by causing rapid environmental changes that threaten human life.

Do you agree that, in order to restore and maintain harmony between humanity and nature, we must conduct a fundamental examination of what industry is like and what it ought, ideally, to be?

Nature under Attack

HUYGHE: Actually industry rests on an artificial principle that fails to take the normal order into account. Nature strives constantly for equilibrium. As we have already seen, it acts in a rhythmic, compensatory, and dialectic way, always correcting itself in order to avoid extremes and excesses. This indeed may be living nature's profoundest law. Man disrupts this spontaneous compensation because, owing to his intellectual constitution, his undertakings always begin with abstract principles and proceed, unilaterally and implacably, by deduction and logical continuity. Once an idea has determined a direction, it proceeds straight ahead and is capable of envisioning corrections only when confronted with evidence of defeat or catastrophe, the sole conceivable contradictions. Actually, it would probably often be wiser to turn aside to avoid obstacles in the way.

Man can outstretch his hand only toward envisaged goals that have been determined as concepts. But he sometimes stumbles as a result of doing so. To adapt himself better to the battle in which he is engaged, man has developed exclusively his positive, practical, and rational faculties. And, in doing so, he has devalued all those faculties that put him into contact with the profound and mysterious nature of things. He has thus unbalanced himself. In this connection we are witnessing the opening of a new era, the consequences of which are, as yet, unforeseen.

IKEDA: The Industrial Revolution detonated a complete change in relations between humanity and nature. In the distant past, man feared and respected nature and conformed to it. After he tamed fire and learned the techniques of working iron and bronze, his intellectual abilities became a menace to other animals, which had formerly lived in complete freedom. Now, his boundless tyranny over nature runs to the extent of leveling mountains, filling in seas, and slicing away continents.

Biologically speaking, if our own epoch is taken as a terminus, humanity is only a sudden and very late intruder in the long history of life on Earth. This newcomer must not be permitted to assume powers of life and death over all other creatures, rewrite biological history, and destroy the natural environment in ways that influence the entire planet. Man must realize that, instead of being an absolute despot, he is no more than one component element on the Earth, which nurtures life, and, although others may be discovered in the future, at present seems to be the only planet in the universe capable of supporting life. Clearly, if human beings destroy the Earth on which they depend entirely, they destroy themselves as well.

In thinking of modern humanity's pride, I am reminded of an

incident in the famous and popular Chinese novel *The Way West (Xiyuji)*, in which the magical monkey Sun Wukong, who is capable of all kinds of tricks including leaping to the edge of the universe, is unable, despite his apparently miraculous abilities, to find his way off the Buddha Shakyamuni's hand. Similarly, although they can subdue and subject all kinds of individual things within in it, human beings cannot escape from the operations of the total natural universe.

Buddhism teaches that human beings and the world of nature depend on, and ought to assist each other. It seems likely that the climatically favorable ecological environment of Asia was important in the formation of this idea. In a harsh climate, human beings fight against and learn to fear nature. When fertile soil, temperate climate, and abundant rains make possible rich harvests and a more comfortable way of life, however, human beings come to interpret nature as protective. Naturally, under such conditions, man and nature meld and coalesce.

But even amidst the blessings of nature, human beings exercise a powerful influence on their environment for the sake of mere existence. And, when under the command of his own egoism, man takes advantage of that silent nature to which he ought, instead, to be grateful for the many benefits he receives.

Turning to agriculture after hunting and gathering and then animal husbandry, human beings began to undertake such projects as altering the courses of rivers. Now attempts at remaking nature have gone beyond the mere necessities of life to extend to egoistical violation of natural laws for the sake of such minor considerations as a desire for transportation convenience or for such luxury articles as rare furs. Human conceit has inspired the slaughtering of animals for sport and pleasure. It is unthinkable that humanity, with its mere two million years of existence, should be allowed to rewrite the more than three billion years of the history of life on Earth.

Encroachments on nature will no doubt continue as long as human beings and the evil of human egoism persist. Buddhism regards this as the most doleful of all human karma. Had human beings never come into existence, the other animals would probably have existed in peace. Of course, animals devour each other for food, but this is in keeping with the inevitable need to survive. Until the emergence of conscious human efforts to that end, nature was never altered by something outside herself.

At the bottom of the Buddhist teaching that delusion is evil and that we should regard the world around us with boundless love is the belief that pride and egoism are the basis of the various evils humanity perpetrates against the harmony of nature and the universe.

Human beings have used their brains to develop fearsome weapons that make killing easy. Realizing that, without some restraints, human evil can expand limitlessly, Buddhism makes the taking of life the paramount sin. A profound sense of the evil human beings are capable of led some thinkers in the Hinayana Buddhist tradition to consider the destruction of one's own existence as the most laudable of all acts. Inheriting elements from the Brahman tradition, such people submitted themselves to ascetic practices difficult for us today to comprehend. Buddhist stories tell of a number of ascetics who attempted to save hungry beasts by offering them their own bodies as food. During the war in Vietnam, some Vietnamese Buddhist monks immolated themselves to protest against the government. These acts of direct, violent protest trace their origins to elements in this ascetic Buddhist discipline.

The ultimate value of such an approach is, however, open to question. Certainly we human beings should realize that we are a part of the totality of nature and that in many respects other animals are superior to us. But, an awareness of sin and the belief that the appearance of humanity on the planet was a mistake cannot solve the problem.

First realizing the basic anthropocentricity of most human actions and then examining ways of altering this attitude constitute a much more promising approach.

Undeniably capable of killing, the human being is also capable of profoundly appreciating the value of life. Mahayana Buddhism teaches that the delusion causing human beings to suffer and supreme wisdom are, ultimately, the same thing.

This means that, instead of regarding delusion and enlightenment as two separate entities, we should always be aware of the delusion-inspired karma behind our actions and strive to alter that karma for the better. This is the way to face our relations with the natural environment.

In the past, human beings have acted—especially in the case of science and technology—for the sake of attaining their own goals without giving much consideration to whether the goals are good or bad. In the future, such consideration will be imperative, not solely from the standpoint of humanity, but from that of the natural environment and the whole planet, too. Afraid of being bested in competition, people often swing into practical action on a given issue without taking all of the pros and cons of the situation into consideration. Under existing circumstances, the human intellect is incapable of considering everything. Nonetheless, if we are to live in harmony with the world of nature, the most complete consideration possible is essential.

For instance, industrial products should not be marketed until ways of disposing of them after use have been mapped out. Japan has been so intoxicated with the convenience of plastic articles that disposing of them has become a major worry. We must not leap thoughtlessly into the production of such things. There is plenty of time to produce after sound recycling methods have been evolved.

In creating a road or altering the course of a river, we must remember that such steps affect the natural as well as the human environment. Making the decision to take such a step only on the basis of economic considerations can result in unforeseen natural disaster at a later date.

The Folly of Rationalism

HUYGHE: Decisions of the kind you mention are often made because they are considered logical. In such a context, however, logic is a dangerous deformation that, I fear, may become a characteristic of our era. My fear stems from the sus-

picion that this kind of logic is an exacerbated Western rationalism that is insufficient for dealing with nature, which
requires infinite experience.

IKEDA: I have the instinctive feeling that the Western interpretation of cause and effect is analytical and individualizing,
whereas the Eastern interpretation is synthetical and generaliz-
ing. In the analytical Western method, everything is divided
into constituent elements, and causal relations are sought
within these simplified elements. Each element is understood
as a closed cause-and-effect system. In contrast, the synthesiz-
ing Eastern method emphasizes mutual relations among things.
Since it discovers causality in mutual interrelations, it interprets
individual phenomena in an open system, to all parts of which
cause-and-effect relations extend. The Western method manifests its strength in interpreting parts. The Eastern one, while
taking a wider, general view, attempts to interpret mutual relations among individual parts correctly.

You have said that Westerners seek causes for the effects
they desire to produce without taking into consideration the
complexities involved in those effects. Perhaps this is because
they view causes as closed systems. In terms of space,
Buddhism regards total mutual relations as a kind of circular
cause-and-effect continuum. In terms of time, it is seen as an
infinitely repetitive cause-and-effect cycle. The former is basically described as the twelve-link chain of causal relations, and
the latter as transmigration or metempsychosis. In early
Buddhist scriptures, the former is set forth concisely in the following set of statements: "If this exists, that exists. If this comes
into being, that comes into being. If this is not, that is not. If
this goes out of being, that goes out of being." The ideas represented by these statements were later given more perfect form
in the doctrines of the inseparability of the individual and its
environment (called *Eshō-Funi* in Japanese) and the Three
Thousand Realms in the Single Thought (*Ichinen Sanzen*). The
doctrine of transmigration was later elaborated into the teachings of the Four Forces Generating Phenomena (production,

duration, change, and annihilation) and the Four Periods (formation, continuance, decline, and disintegration). In simple terms, both of these doctrines set forth the principle that all things are subject to cycles of generation, growth, stability, decline, and annihilation. In my view, this interpretation has never been more significant than it is today.

Of course, I do not imply the total absence in the West of an interpretation of cause-and-effect systems on the basis of the idea of mutual interrelations. But, since ecology was tardy in emerging, it can be said that such an interpretation did not appear in the West until fairly late. And, even after it did emerge, Westerners remained either completely uninterested or, at best, only slightly interested in the influence their treatment of the natural environment could exert on human society.

The traditional Western interpretation of the nonhuman natural world involves the Old Testament formula according to which creatures are divided into God; human beings who are on God's side; and nonhuman beings, all of which are subject to the dominion of man. This arrangement is clearly set forth in the first chapter of the Book of Genesis: "And God said unto them . . . have dominion over the fish of the sea, and over the fowl of the air, and over every living thing that moveth upon the earth." (Genesis 1:28)

But this interpretation differs from the Eastern one. The Japanese word *shizen,* now employed in the same sense as the English word *nature,* came into usage in that significance comparatively late. To express what is currently meant by *shizen,* the Japanese of the more distant past used compound listings of actual natural phenomena like *sansensōmoku* (mountain, river, grass, tree) or *kachōfugetsu* (flower, bird, wind, moon). The absence of a word meaning nature in general suggests that the Japanese thought, not in terms of the objective totality, but in terms of those concrete phenomena with which daily association generated a sense of union. No doubt, other peoples interpret nature in a similar way.

The word *shizen* is a Chinese term (*ziran*) meaning something that exists of itself in conformity with the most fundamental principles. It indicates a kind of ideal, true to itself and free of the petty calculations and falsities with which human beings are often concerned.

Peoples who regard nature as something existing of itself can feel closer to plants and other animals. Furthermore, if they embrace the concept of reincarnation, they have no problem regarding human beings and animals as equals. This probably explains the complete equanimity with which a group of Japanese students were able to accept a lecture by a surprised European scholar on the Darwinian theory of evolution at a time when it was causing considerable stir in the West.

Traditional belief in the oneness of humanity and nonhuman nature prevented the development in the Orient of modern objectifying, analytical science. Nonetheless, it seems to me that the Oriental view of this oneness is urgently needed by humanity today. While endowed by scientific technology with the power to control nature to a certain extent, human beings are no more than one element in the natural world and are, therefore, bound to exist under the same law of life as all other elements. Having experienced severe retaliation from the natural world, human beings are just beginning to be aware of this truth.

Behind progress in the natural sciences and developments in technology I sense a confluence of the distinctively Western view of nature, dominated by the will of God, and the drive to satisfy human desires. Efforts to dominate nature in accordance with the will of God can be thought to have overlapped with activities for the gratification of desires. In my view, the energy of the West may be traced to a consequent absolute confidence in self-affirmation and justification of desire gratification.

Freed from divine bondage by science, humanity ultimately banished the idea of God, whose place was taken by reason, the source of science. Nonetheless, desires still lurked behind reason. Founding itself on the reason that had brought liberation from God's bondage, science was free of all restraints and could proceed along any course it chose.

I find grossly deluded the generally accepted image of reasoning as an infallible power of judgment, with a refined spirit of its own, and as something in which we are justified in putting absolute trust. Although reason may be the guiding force, human judgment is often founded on something the operation of which precedes that of reason. In many instances, that something is desire of one kind or another; and rational powers of judgment are called into action in order to justify and effectively realize the satisfaction of desire. In short, modern scientific-technological civilization has made human desire its driving power.

God's bonds may have been broken, but the Old Testament notion that nature is something exterior to be used for man's benefit lingers. Indeed, now that the brakes represented by God have been abandoned, plundering of the natural environment grows worse. The most important problem facing human civilization is controlling human desire—if, indeed, control is still possible.

You mention the problem of energy. People today demand inexhaustible energy sources for the sake of still greater comfort than they enjoy at present. Even supposing that utilization of solar energy or of nuclear fusion provides limitless supplies of energy, raw materials on which to apply the energy are finite. In other words, the problem we must address is not energy itself but the human desire for limitless energy.

Inability to develop sources of limitless energy until we are able to control our desires would actually be for the good of humanity. No doubt human beings would compete to exhaust raw materials available on the planet were they to acquire an inexhaustible source of cheap energy soon. And, as you say, such a development would generate more toxic industrial wastes to aggravate environmental pollution to a point beyond the possibility of correction.

On the basis of a vast chain of causes and effects, the natural world maintains splendid equilibrium through a huge system of circulation. Industry should be restructured to produce a similar cycle. Since, under such an industrial structure, human beings cannot expect greater luxury than what they enjoy at the present, the control of desire will become an unavoidable task.

Everyone understands rationally that, without a system of

controls, we have no future. But we must not trust entirely to reason, which is incapable of detecting the legal fictions of a justice based on desire. This is why I believe we must effect a conversion in the very foundation of reason itself. And this is what, in its ultimate essence, Buddhism teaches.

Modern human beings approve of the endless pursuit of satisfaction of their instinctive desires where they expect to find supreme happiness. But, no more than pleasing sensual stimulation, instinctive satisfaction grows stale as it becomes familiar, generating a craving for stronger stimulation. Because satisfaction is noncumulative, it is immediately succeeded by a sense of emptiness. Contemporary society vividly illustrates the effect of this vicious circle. Under such circumstances, the degradation of human tastes that you mention is scarcely surprising.

Buddhism teaches that, because they are instinctive, the seductions of sensual pleasure are strong and difficult to combat. But it has perceived the source of unhappiness in submission to desires, and has devised a way to liberation.

Through profound observation of human nature and acute examination of all phenomena, Buddhism has uncovered a Law permeating everything and shows how, by assimilating that Law, the individual life can find perfect liberation; that is, freedom from everything that enslaves human nature. The basis of this Law is cause and effect, a manifestation of the phenomenon of life itself. I am certain that this approach can be very useful in dealing with the problems facing contemporary society. Nonetheless, since no true solutions can be achieved through rational understanding alone, I insist that, in addition to philosophy, religion is of the utmost importance.

HUYGHE: The flaw in modern man is not only unwillingness to heed anything but his own ego and willingness to exploit the world indiscriminately, but also the blindness of his egoism in abandoning himself thoughtlessly to his own avidity. He sees only the coveted prey and the way of obtaining it and fails to take into account the dangerous, even irreparable, consequences a superficially successful action can have for him. What has been referred to here as the encore effect entails imagining an aim, selecting the shortest way to achieve it, and relying often on blind logic. But nature is complex and frequently defeats our unilateral and simplistic views. When she does, what we take for a success ends up by launching disasters—those unforeseen disasters you mention.

A single example will illustrate the imbalance you quite rightly point out in the natural environment. That example is the gigantic dam that, in his singular preoccupation with assuring Egypt of a source of energy capable of supplying the industry of which he dreamed, Gamel Abdel Nasser built on the River Nile at Aswan.

The engineers carried out the task imposed on them. But, after a few years, a perturbed nature struck back in ways totally unforeseen by the scientific sages. The transformation the dam caused in the water system damaged agriculture, modified the climate, and ruined the ecological system from which Egypt has been formed. In addition, populations were displaced and monuments were moved. Even some forecasts ended up in defeat. Everyone praised the technical triumph involved in lifting the temple of Abu Simbel from its endangered location at the base of a cliff to the top of the plateau. (This feat was made possible by global cooperation sponsored by UNESCO.) People now begin to see, however, that in its new location, the temple is subject to desert winds that will, little by little, wear away stones preserved for thousands of years in the original location.

Our over-rationalized way of thinking can discover the cause that produces a desired effect but can perceive neither the infinite complexity of reality nor the unanticipated disturbances our acts can generate. Standing in a room with a gun, we can hit a bull's eye on a target but fail to realize that repercussions from the shock may shatter the glass in the windows.

The Third World

IKEDA: Western by origin, the present crisis may spell the downfall of the West. History shows that ordinarily, when one civilization falls, another is waiting to flourish in its place. Do you believe we can expect what is now called the Third World to play such a role in the age to come?

HUYGHE: Apparently, we cannot hope for the kind of counterweight or regulating possibility that has always existed before. Beside the great civilizations of the past were always human masses who never or rarely came into contact with their civilized neighbors and who constituted an intact factor ready to emerge upon the scene as soon as renewal became necessary.

For instance, next to the Roman civilization waited the so-called Barbarians—the Romans considered Barbarians those people who lacked the benefits of the technical, urban, and social developments in which the great peoples of Antiquity had already made considerable progress. Furthermore, when a civilization began to be self-destructive or to sink in senility, there were always fresh virgin zones in reserve in the world. It was often from these regions that healthy vitality arose to attack worn-out and, in a sense, rotten civilizations. After overturning them by force, peoples from unspoiled regions infused older civilizations with new blood and, each time, through this violent injection, made possible fresh starts toward new destinies. In this way, the great barbarian invasions that flooded Europe at the end of the Roman Empire led, after four or five centuries, to the genesis of the Middle Ages, which were to have a brilliance of their own.

Today, however, no such phenomenon exists, because the new technological civilization has invaded the entire globe. The Third World, which in a sense corresponds to the ancient barbarians, will not attack the so-called civilized world because, first of all, it lacks the technological means and would be crushed by our superiority in this field. In adopting bronze and applying it on a wider scale, the ancient barbarian Gauls acquired a technological advantage that permitted them to advance and conquer all the way to Rome and Asia Minor. To their own healthy, fresh energy they added the resources of a novel means of combat. The nations of the Third World today are unable to duplicate this achievement since all means of

combat are monopolized by the scientific technological civilization. But, if they someday gain access to the atomic bomb, as it
seems they may. . . .

Moreover, the nations of the Third World are dazzled, virtually spellbound, by the phase called progress. Granted they preserve autonomy and the capability to resist, they will have but
one idea: to develop rapidly without considering the failings
and dangers entailed.

During my voyages to North Africa, I have often been
impressed by the impossibility of explaining to audiences there
(I was about to say an audience of students, but at any rate an
intellectual audience) the risks inherent in Western civilization.
The immediate reply to such an assertion is usually, "Oh no!
You are ahead of us. And that is unfair. First we must correct
that situation. We will have plenty of time to consider restrictions on the uses of technology and energy when we have
reached the point where you are now." People who assume
this viewpoint fail to see that the whole world faces the same
predicament and that there are no longer any pristine regions
to be sources of assistance.

Japan, the first to have been fascinated by and to have assim-
ilated Western mechanical development, has now become not
merely a competitor, but also a formidable competitor for occidental economies. Thanks to its people's powers of imitation,
intelligence, and skill, Japan has entered into competitive relations with the greatest Western nations, the very creators of
science and its practical applications. It should be remembered
that China, too, which was much less advanced than Japan
(and which may be one of those reserves making renewal possible) has already produced a number of leading physicists
who have won Nobel Prizes.

Thus, from all viewpoints, the current situation is without
historical antecedents that might serve as reference. Things will
not be in the future as they have been in past situations we
consider comparable to our own. It is impossible to be too disturbed by this state of affairs.

IKEDA: The agrarian civilization, literally rooted in the land for the past five millennia, centered on the relationships between the Earth and human beings, and between human beings and nature. Although these relationships have varied widely to include bitter struggle, appeasement, and cooperation, they have always been intimate.

In no more than three decades, however, scientific technological civilization has far outstripped the achievements agrarian civilization made in five thousand years and has converted close humanity-nature relations into relations among human beings, machines, and nature.

As long as they lived in awareness of their relations with it, human beings frequently remembered the inferiority of their own powers to those of nature and tended to control their own pride. But technological science has given human beings the power to subdue nature. And we, the possessors of this powerful science, delude ourselves into believing in our own omnipotence and, therefore, behave in an arrogant fashion.

Misuse of science has brought about all kinds of disasters and has generated a situation totally unforeseen by believers in the omnipotence of scientific methods. Some people interpret these disasters as nature's vengeance. But, without ascribing such arbitrariness to nature, it is probably more correct to say that encounters with the complexities of reality have thrown into confusion the prejudiced and peremptory human view of science as omnipotent.

As part of the natural world, human beings should attempt to cooperate with, and not to conquer, nature. The most important thing in dealing with the crisis we face now is to put a curb on aggressive violence of reason and to build within ourselves a device to control our conceit.

You have pointed out the unlikelihood of the kind of infusion of fresh blood that barbarian invasions in the past provided when established civilizations fell. In my opinion, the source of new life for us today must come, not from a material or spatial exterior element, but from the development of our own inner life.

I was especially interested to hear you say you were unable to convince audiences in North Africa of the dangers inherent in scientific civilization but were told there will be time enough for instruction in such matters when backward nations have reached the level of development at which we stand today. What a peculiar way of thinking! When they have reached that level, there will be no need to instruct them in anything; and no doubt they will already have suffered such irreparable losses that further instruction will be meaningless. I suspect that they answered you in this way because, less interested in dangers they can only envisage as possibilities in the distant future, they are concerned with such present suffering as poverty and plague. In other words, they are not so much enthralled with the idea of scientific technological civilization as they are worried about overcoming current hardships.

Nonetheless, since the crisis affects all humanity to some extent, it is not enough for the peoples of the industrialized nations to be cognizant of the danger. The peoples of Third World nations, too, must be made aware. Discovering the right method of informing them, however, is difficult.

These peoples are deeply dissatisfied with the excessively wide gap separating them from the industrialized nations, at whose hands they have endured deeply resented tyranny and selfishness. Far from being confined to North Africa, emotions of this kind are general and very widespread. Resentment greatly aggravates the difficulty of convincing the peoples of the Third World of the dangers they face if they fail to avoid the errors and mistakes already made by the industrialized West. No amount of preaching about harmony and cooperation with nature can be effective in the face of mistrust and existing differences in living standards. We must first strive to eliminate distrust by rectifying discrepancies between the Third World nations and the industrialized ones. Then, we must act sincerely to offer words of caution about the crisis.

3

Society

IKEDA: Because the originally Western industrial-technological civilization now influences the entire globe, it is especially important to clarify the conditions of its origin and growth.

The Rise of the Bourgeoisie

HUYGHE: To understand its origins and growth better, we must recall that preparations for modern civilization were laid by the irresistible rise, from the twelfth and thirteenth century, of the bourgeoisie, a new class of merchants and administrators.

As great a difference separates the farmer and the merchant as sets the farmer apart from the nomad. The merchant cultivates no land and comes into no direct contact with nature. He acquires products made by other people—for example, cloth. The shepherd raises the flocks and shears the sheep to obtain the wool, which his wife spins. At this point in the process, the merchant purchases the yarn, which he passes on to the weavers. At first, weaving was the work of artisans, later it was industrialized.

The merchant then acquires already-made products, which he evaluates and the sale of which he organizes so as to generate profit. He is interested in materials and economics. It was the merchants who built around castles and palaces the cities that gave birth to the bourgeois class.

Gradually, a considerable mutation took place in this class. Prehistoric and agrarian human beings were essentially religious. The bourgeois class inherited from their ancestors and was, therefore, at first penetrated by religious dogmas and cults. But a new spirit progressively dulled these dogmas and, after initial contact, ultimately destroyed religion. This new spirit was realism, but not the realism of love for—or brotherhood with—nature.

The bourgeois created towns, in which he closed himself up. He attenuated and then cut his ties with the rural world, from which he required no more than products. Because he had to estimate exact, profitable purchase prices of the things offered to him, the realism he needed for his profession was that of material goods. He could no longer afford to confuse wool, cotton, or linen. He had to use his sight and other senses to estimate from actual experience the value of the merchandise—or as people came to say later, the value of things.

Next he began commissioning the production and manufacture of goods (the laborer, who was destined to take the place of the artisan, worked under him in increasing numbers). He began concerning himself with the display of merchandise, supply as a stimulus of demand, the encouragement of commerce, and the barter of goods for coin or monetary values.

Certainly this kind of activity had existed for a long time, but the people who engaged in it earlier had no knowledge of the methods—especially banking methods—to which the bourgeoisie dedicated itself.

IKEDA: What were the consequences brought on by this new spirit?

HUYGHE: The germs were present from the time when the first merchants in Egypt, Mesopotamia, and China introduced this spirit, the triumph of which is associated with the predominance of the bourgeoisie.

The bourgeois individual became the practical man believing

in nothing but concrete, positive facts capable of immediate translation into commercial values, hard cash, and figures. With this development we have entered the realm of the material and of quantities, which forms a firm alliance with the realm of the abstract. Actually, the bourgeoisie was simultaneously rational and concrete, a pair of traits evoking and complementing each other.

In contrast, everything arising from profound creative sensibility was eliminated as disturbing order and reason. All trace of dream, imagination, myth, and flight toward spirituality became suspect as a divergence from "reality." The subjective was repudiated for the sake of the objective, which, dedicated to knowledge of the exterior world, reduced all things to facts that were productive, negotiable, and immediately translatable into monetary figures. Such is the spirit that, as it developed and systematized itself according to a rigorous method, generated science and the technology arising from it.

In the West, the bourgeoisie came into being in the twelfth and thirteenth centuries, the era in which lived Saint Francis of Assisi (1181–1226), whose life deserves some study in this connection. The son of a cloth merchant, Francis had a profound faith, amounting to mysticism, that preserved and exalted in him all the sources of sensitivity. In a recent book, Francois Chenique has shown that, owing to the convergence between his way of thinking and that of oriental mystics, Saint Francis, or Poverello, as he was called because of the life of poverty he advocated, rediscovered fundamental spiritual ways amounting virtually to an evocation of a kind of spiritual Yoga.

His way of life stirred up so much scandal that he was rejected by his own father, by society and, most important, by the Church of his time. Gaining acceptance for the sensitive, religious, and mystical values within him cost Saint Francis an admirable and exhausting struggle.

Nonetheless, he actually contributed to the evolution of science. He adored God through His physical creation, through all nature from "Brother Sun" to "My brothers the birds and animals." The Franciscan order, born of his efforts, was most deeply attached to the realities of the things of the visible world.

The term *experimental science* was originated not in the Renaissance, but in the thirteenth century, at the height of the Middle Ages, by a Franciscan monk named Roger Bacon (1214–94). This Bacon is not, of course, to be confused with Francis Bacon (1561–1626), who put the scientific method on sure footing at the end of the sixteenth century. But the appearance of the term *experimental* three centuries before his time clearly indicates that a new concept was already evolving.

A similar transition may be observed in the evolution of theology. Until the thirteenth century—the century of the bourgeoisie—Plato was the accepted master of thought. From that time on, however, the prestige of Aristotle grew until he finally came to dominate the field. The problem was reexamined during the Renaissance; but, until then, effective authentication took precedence over absolute ideas.

The Scientific Era

HUYGHE: From the time of Copernicus and Galileo, the scientific concept, an original phenomenon, began to take form in conflict with traditional religion. Although not clearly established until the eighteenth century, this concept was gradually to transform the world. During the eighteenth century, The Age of Enlightenment, techniques aimed at conquering the physical universe and industrial production began to grow rapidly under impetus supplied by the Encyclopaedists, thus preparing the way for the consumer civilization.

Parallel with the formulation of science, the eighteenth century lost religious faith and substituted positivistic and rationalistic ideas for the mystical spirit. Science and technology sanctified this idea, in which were associated experimental knowledge and the means of action generated by it. The mechanical sciences opened an immense field, producing big industry and all its social consequences, the most important of which were to be the creation and exploitation of the proletariat.

With this development began a new era that was to expand further in the nineteenth century, the great turning point. The physical sciences grew vigorously, directing human attention exclusively to matter in space. For its part, society became increasingly materialistic. Chemistry added to mineral and vegetable products numerous artificial things that either did not exist naturally or could not even be extracted from natural materials by means harmonious with nature. This state of affairs totally reverses the relation between nature and agrarian peoples and results in a completely different view of the world.

This view has been reduced to exclusive positivism. The physical sciences, the first to develop, concern themselves solely with matter in space and evolve laws controlling it. But modern science has shown that nothing exists except energy. And matter, the most elementary stage of reality, corresponds to an inscription of energy in space, where, in a sense, it assumes being and stabilizes in a definite form.

But people who desired to know only matter could believe in no law but the one governing it, that is, determinism—the same cause always produces the same effect. At the elementary stage, this is the basis of scientific laws. Matter does not evolve. A billion years ago or today, a quartz crystal grows inexorably according to the same geometry.

Human beings persuaded themselves that they could become masters of fate by mastering the physical causes engendering the effects they desired. The astronomer Pierre Simon, Marquis de Laplace (1749–1827), claimed that total knowledge of all facts made it possible to deduce inevitable consequences and thus to know the future. The sole change that has taken place since then is "progress;" that is, development of scientific and technological methods enabling human beings to take greater possession, on a boundless scale, of the world's resources.

This system of thought, which in philosophy is the positivism of Auguste Comte, was completely formulated at about the middle of the nineteenth century. As the name positivism indicates, consideration in it is given only to real, or positive, things, from which laws can be derived. But, contrary to the general opinion, the thought of Karl Marx, coeval with that of Auguste Comte, is profoundly penetrated by bourgeois philosophy. Marx's bitter struggle against the bourgeoisie and its power excesses was conceived within the educational and cultural mold implanted by bourgeois philosophy, with which he himself was pervaded. Nor did he question materialism, which is, indeed, the very foundation of his teaching.

Materialism triumphed with the new governing class, which was intensely reviled by Marx. One day in an open session of parliament, Guizot, a minister under Louis-Philippe, proclaimed his own doctrine by saying, "Gentlemen, get rich!" The only people trying to escape from the triumphal materialistic flood were literary and artistic rebels struggling desperately to maintain the rights of subjectivity. But they were rejected by a scandalized public opinion that described them as "the damned."

IKEDA: The situation today is very different. Now, scientists themselves are clearly aware of and react sensitively to the crisis of modern civilization. Patently scientific progress has not fulfilled its promise of benefiting and advancing the human spirit.

Even fully realizing that the fruits of their work can be or even sometimes are intended to be employed for horrendous purposes, some scientists pretend that scientific research is neutral and that its users are culpable when it is applied for evil ends. Neutrality may be a more correct stance than former deliberate contributions to progress in the blind belief that it is necessarily good. Nonetheless, I regard it as a cowardly stance. Those who advocate it are hiding behind grand words like, "Scientific research is for neither good nor evil," while actually often cooperating with evil.

This is why I believe scientists must reflect profoundly on the sentiment you have expressed to the effect that scientific discoveries in the name of the satisfaction of individual human desires can end up destroying all humanity. In addition, they must conscientiously control their own research on the basis of a firm understanding of the supreme dignity of life itself.

In the past, it has sometimes been believed that exaltation of national dignity was the supreme justice and that service in its name constituted good conscience. No doubt this is a higher ideal than mere personal profit or glory. Nonetheless, if it costs millions of human lives, service to the exaltation of national dignity must be seen as a horrible evil. It is impossible to give tacit approval to the self-contradictory maxim "He who kills one person is a criminal; he who kills millions is a hero."

The true basis of a good conscience must be the realization that nothing in the world is as precious and irreplaceable as life. Scientists whose research can entail immense forces capable of destroying millions and tens of millions of human lives must make this realization the unshakable foundation of their consciences.

They must be aware of the ways in which the fruits of their studies will be put to use within the complex political and social structure and its dynamic principles. I do not imply that all scientists must become specialists in political and social sciences. They must, however, be broadly cultivated and aware of what is happening in contemporary society. Moreover they must have the courage to abandon research if they learn that, within the mechanism of contemporary society, its results pose a danger to large numbers of human beings.

HUYGHE: Unfortunately, together with the "objective-research" mentality, the utilitarian and practical mentality common in our time has stifled scruples among many responsible persons, although certain very eminent scientists have been agonized by scruples of their own. We must remember that even the great Julius Oppenheimer was tried in court for refusing to participate in work the results of which he considered dangerous to humanity.

The Psychological Mutation

HUYGHE: This is true because, under the pressure of materi-

alism, developed in the nineteenth century, a profound mutation has taken place in the human spirit. In the first stages, the
newly developing civilization remained enveloped by the older
Christian civilization. In the name of gentility, the bourgeois
preferred to see themselves as belonging to a continuation of
the aristocratic classes, which they had overturned and
replaced. They copied aristocratic manners, tastes, and culture
and, in France and Italy, affirmed themselves profoundly
Roman Catholic, as in Germany and England they affirmed
themselves firmly Protestant.

But developing together with scientific and technological
progress and under the influence of economic impetus, materialism made a breach in the ramparts of faith. Society remained
faithful to the rites and ceremonies of the Church but more out
of habit and respect for custom than out of deep conviction.

The twentieth century has been a time of reckoning.
Remolded and absorbed by urban and industrial society, agrarian society found itself progressively farther and farther
removed from the profound and universal ways of nature. It
had not consecrated itself to the intensive exploitation of
resources that simultaneously generated capitalism and the
consumer society and reordered social classes. The aristocracy
had become nothing but an honorific and worldly survivor,
regilding its heraldry through alliances with the bourgeoisie.
The bourgeoisie controlled industry and exploited the worker
by striving to pay the lowest possible wage for his work.
Having come into existence, with the aid of socialism, which
envisioned a new society where workers' rights were proportional to their fundamental role, the proletariat became aware
of both its misery and its weight.

At this point began an enormous crisis of mutation in which,
progressively eaten away, agrarian society lost its very reason
for existence as it found itself increasingly mechanized. The
agrarian world gave way to an urban, industrial civilization.
Statistics show an inexorable diminution in numbers of farmers
occurring as urban populations became enormous. Man's new
milieu is the city, where life is isolated from reality and increas-

ingly abstract, technical, and mechanical. Escape from this environment is now possible only in weekend escapades and vacations.

Simultaneous with the social change occurred a transformation in the individual's psychological constitution. Like all other conscious beings man has, from his origins, distinguished between himself on the one hand and nature and reality on the other, in order to confront them for the sake of external knowledge. As an animal, he observes with his senses and possesses in his psyche an ensemble of instinctive reactions, that are both hereditary and acquired through experience, that dictate an effective, if routine, form of conduct. But, thanks to his mental development, he has been able to add to such directly acquired information and the reflexes responding to it, a capacity that is distinctive of his intelligence, to construct a system of representation that can, among other things, evolve the general from the particular, establish causal relations and envision goals. This undeniably enormous advance has separated—abstracted, in the meaningful sense of pulling away—him from the exterior world, which has become an object of observation and action. He has substituted for real nature his artificially made image and idea of it. This image is like a mirror that, while exact, is glassy and impenetrable to life.

The intellectual faculties cannot be developed with impunity in the exclusive fashion adopted by modern society. Technocracy and its desiccating forces must be counterbalanced by a reinforcement of everything in our psyche that links us directly and intermingles us with reality. Similarly, a tree cannot rise unless its roots are intimately mingled with the soil, from which derives the sap without which it shrivels and dies. The faculties of observation must be counterbalanced by the gifts of participation, that enable us not to conceive, but to experience. Such faculties arise from the indeterminant and shifting realm of sensitivity, which extends from the most unconscious pulsations to supernatural revelations. Through them we bathe in and enter into or remain in direct, profound communication with being. These faculties manifest themselves in us through intuition and perceptions arising from great depths and evading rational explanation. Understanding this well, Buddhism perceives the level of the "self" behind the individual "I." At this substratum is the great center where all things come together. It is like an ocean from which waves separate themselves temporarily, only to fall back again into the common mass.

Like a wave, the human being is an isolated particle centering on his "I," the existence of which he struggles to preserve. His autonomy is, however, as precarious and illusory as that of a wave. Though isolated from it for a time, the human being is a fragment of the universe. He is of the same substance as all those things surrounding him and subsists only through the constant physical and spiritual exchanges he maintains with them.

The primitive cell exists only as a result of the ceaseless coming and going of nutrients and wastes passing through the cell wall that gives it existence. The cell remains alive only because of an equilibrium between that which distinguishes it from all else and that which continues to rebind it to all other things. As we have already said, the same is true of human beings.

Modern civilization threatens this subtle balance by ceaselessly accentuating the things that distance and cut man off from the world, which has become for him nothing but an exterior object, a spectacle, a prey, and even an adversary (in the strict meaning of the Latin *ad-versus*, or turned against). This civilization stifles the inner voice calling man to rejoin the world harmoniously with all other things. The voice is, in other words, the cry of the subconscious from which arise intuitions that, while irrational, can reveal secrets, or aspirations of spirituality, which strive eventually to rejoin being or God. Modern civilization takes up a place of ambush behind portholes and shuts itself up in the mechanism of intellect as if before an equipment panel.

Suppressing all forces except consumer or predatory greed, this civilization confines itself to the logical proliferation of abstract principles and mental formulas, imprinted in the head by means of the mass media. Such is the civilization being founded in our day.

Modern Humanity

IKEDA: And how would you describe the predicament of humanity in modern civilization?

HUYGHE: During the agrarian age, humankind flourished in all ways that, while permitting participation in nature, at the same time add innately human resources of perfection, quality, and elevation. Now, however, humankind finds itself challenged, atrophied, and excluded.

On the one hand, the new civilization certainly makes possible a heretofore undreamed-of mastery of the exterior world. On the other hand, however, humanity has had to pay for this advantage, which concerns nothing but human needs and desires, with an interior imbalance, even an amputation. This is because, in the exchange, he has been constrained to atrophy and stifle the most profound and elevated functions of life.

Independent of sensations and rational thought, when permitted by sensitivity to pass to a more conscious level, our intuitions concerning the universe ascend to spiritual aspirations. Such intuitions present to us, behind the appearances of the material world in space, a reality of which appearances are only the cladding, a kind of skin or mask forming a legible and convenient screen but separating us from another, completely immaterial reality that is perhaps the soul of the world.

To those who object that such a conception is incompatible with science, I have only to refer to the illustrious originator of the quantum theory and Nobel Prize winner Max Planck, who at a conference in 1929, said, "The edifice of physics rests on measurements, which like all measurements are bound to sensory perception. The notions of physics are borrowed from the world of the senses."*

Planck goes on to say that we must admit " . . . behind the

world of the senses, the existence of a second, real, world possessing its own autonomous existence, independent of man. We can understand only through the interpretations of our perceptions made possible by means of the signs it communicates to us. We can never understand it directly."

Here, open wide, is the door that scientists, shivering with cold, hold shut and that conceals a world inaccessible to and denied by them. This is the door at which we must knock.

Another perhaps even better-known physicist, Albert Einstein, goes still further. In his book *Out of My Later Years,* written at the close of his life, he professes, "I affirm that the cosmic religious experience is the greatest and most noble directing energy behind scientific research."

I do not believe I am very far from these men's convictions when I insist on the immaterial reality beyond that of sense and measurement, with which, at the foundation of our being, we can effect a rejoining through our own instinctive, intuitive depths. By means of these depths we perceive the nature of the world which, at that level, is our own. But, it is equally our own at the other extreme; that is, at the summit sometimes glimpsed because of our very aspiration to scale it. This aspiration constitutes the spirituality compelling us to transcend our selves.

Having become a pragmatic, utilitarian, and dogmatic theoretician, modern man has lost the intuitive resources of depth and transcendence. He closes himself up in and confines himself to the median zone of the practical. But how can he amputate with impunity all his other faculties and resources? These faculties too, like all things occurring in an organic ensemble, must be exercised, or the whole will be compromised. It is well known that atrophy of the legs, causing suffering to the whole organism, results when creatures do not walk. Similarly, even if the liver and intestines are preserved intact, removing the stomach damages the whole organism. What is true physiologically is true psychologically as well.

* Planck, Max: *L'image du mond dans la physique moderne,* Gonthier ed.

The civilization fashioned by our times has become a prison. A person who shuts himself up in a room two meters wide, two meters deep, and two meters high will surely be asphyxiated. Just as surely, a person who limits himself to the application of rational capacities to concrete problems will suffocate. A supply of oxygen provided beforehand will permit another moment of life but, one day—and perhaps ours is that day—asphyxiation will begin. The asphyxiation faced by our civilization is one of morality, sensitivity, and the spirit.

This is the third phase, upon entering which humanity has, little by little, severed all bonds and ties with the past, agrarian world, which produced all the great religions of civilization. A complete separation is made for the sake of passing into a new era where excessive obsession with material conquests must be purchased at the price of a human restraint entailing an anguish and insecurity evident in all those means of literary and artistic expression that persist as a zone of compensation. Literature, poetry, and art are preserves resembling in a way the reservations the Americans set aside for their Indian predecessors. But all of them convey the torture tormenting a humanity that has lost its axis or is, as people are fond of saying today, frustrated.

It is normal and healthy for man to refuse to remain fixed in the norms of past epochs. It is normal and healthy for him to initiate a new era and expect new civilizations to come into being in keeping with new needs. Our tragedy lies in our inability to create such a new civilization on a human scale. Responding to the situation by developing the most efficacious faculties is insufficient if, in the process, the rest of the total human being suffers fatally. This is the origin of the present crisis.

In what can we put our hope? Can we count on life itself? Certainly, with its infallible instinct, life can ensure the reactions necessary to the times. Life moves with alternate steps guaranteeing equilibrium.

But we must not be lazy and leave everything to life. We must not trust blindly in the counterbalance effect that we have said evokes "feedback," to use modern scientific jargon. Going too far in one direction evokes reaction in the opposite direction. We know that when a boat tips to the right, it tends to balance itself by tipping back to the left. But two possibilities exist in such cases: balance may be restored, or the boat may continue tipping in one direction till it capsizes. This is catastrophe.

We must realize that such is the alternative involved in our present destiny. Either we react in an effort to restore balance—and such a reaction may be painful since it will run counter to tendencies enslaving us—or we obstinately continue tipping in the same direction until the boat capsizes, swamping us. It is we who shall drown. The wooden boat will rise and float while we are dragged under.

The boat is life. Life will always persist but perhaps without us. The problem, then, is to ensure that we survive with life. To this end, we must assist life by giving of ourselves.

Man has made great strides in conquering the world but at the price of loss of self-possession. Absorbed by sordid material cupidity, he forgets his own mission—his reason for being. We must relearn how to master ourselves and rediscover the meaning of true flourishing.

4

Japan, France, and the New Civilization

IKEDA: Now that you have plotted the general course of our discussion, I should like to return to some of the individual points you have raised. In particular, I should like to consider the effects modern civilization is likely to have on Japan, situated as she is on the opposite side of the world from Europe. Japan was the first non-European nation to import modern Western technology and, in so doing, suddenly changed her ancient agricultural life style.

The Fate of Agriculture

IKEDA: Since it provides humanity with essential nourishment, agriculture will never lose its importance. The so-called shift from an agrarian to an industrial civilization has actually affected only the industrialized nations and only their urban regions. The peoples of the industrialized world still rely on farmers—and from the international viewpoint on developing nations—for the food they must have. People who regard breaking with the agrarian tradition as a sign of development and progress denigrate the effort on which their own sustenance depends and in this way jeopardize their own continued existence. To my great concern, Japan is one of the nations making this mistake. But other nations make it too. And peoples everywhere must revise their attitudes. What is your impression of the significance of agriculture in the future?

HUYGHE: As you point out, the suppression of agriculture is a prominent feature of the new civilization characteristic of our era. By means of it, human beings have learned to confront the environment by bending it to their own needs. Nonetheless, in the past, even though cultivation over the millenia always implied some kind of transforming action such as the pushing back of forests to make way for arable land, the process took place in a spirit of balance and collaboration between humanity and nature. But, with technical progress, the development of science, and the emergence of what might be called the engineer mentality, industry began to expand. When this happened, the old rapport between them gave way to an exploitation of nature by humanity in a way implying ceaseless violation. When the proletariat came into being, the will to exploit was directed against weak human beings as well. At one time, the lower classes had occasionally been able to discover their own vital kind of equilibrium. Under the rod of the industrial bourgeoisie, however, they came to know an oppression more implacable than any they had previously experienced.

Incontestably, this mutation, which originated in the Occident, contributed to the West's military superiority, which was in its turn a factor making colonialism possible. The first to feel the blow, nonoccidental peoples were initially subjugated. Then, in accordance with the alternating and compensatory rhythm that is a law of life, they began striking back. Suddenly, the tutelage of the Western world was shaken off and formerly subjected peoples recovered their independence.

They could do this, however, only by assimilating the means of domination that once had oppressed them. Blazing the way for other countries, while freeing itself politically, the Orient yielded intellectually and even acquired the Occident's faults. With the dynamism predisposing it to assimilate the Western spirit rapidly, Japan was the first to undergo this conversion.

Open to commerce with European nations since the middle

of the nineteenth century, Japan quickly learned the industrial lesson and adopted the military methods of occidental nations. Japan had, as we say, modernized. Japan had left agrarian civilization in order to convert itself into an industrial civilization. But if this civilization has been a Western triumph, it also threatens to push the West toward ruin as a consequence of interior degradation and spiritual impoverishment.

The danger has become obvious. By Westernizing, the rest of the world, where religions have often preserved a sense of spiritual vocation—as in the case of Buddhism, for example—is threatened with the same process of abandoning the resources of the interior life for the sake of the exclusive triumph of practical and utilitarian capacities. Little by little, the trinity of science-technology-industry has appeared in all countries that have considered themselves liberated and is preparing a new kind of slavery for them. As you say, this danger is especially serious in Japan.

At the same time, special attention must always be devoted to the kind of revolutionary events that shook Iran. French political parties leapt at the chance to fit these events into their own rigid, preconceived schemes and even demonstrated solidarity with the so-called popular Iranian masses aligned against the monarchy. The error of this approach is complete and proves how some minds—too many minds—are incapable of conceiving or foreseeing anything beyond ready-made formulas.

Actually the Iranian masses have risen up against modern Western civilization in order to preserve the religious spirit and customs of a bygone age—customs which seem backward to us. They seek refuge against a transformation that they wholly and instinctively reject. Their actions are, in the strictest sense of the word, a reactionary attempt to reintegrate the past, where they hope to find protection. Their approach is a blunder because it runs counter to the meaning of history. It is an instinctive recoil. Nonetheless, no matter how clumsy it is, we must pay attention to it as a warning of a rejection of the direction in which we wish to bind other peoples. Perhaps we must seek and propose other revised directions better adapted to the future.

We must remember, however, that all these peoples face contagion with what I have called the Western malaise, which, as you clearly describe it, is the replacement of human aspirations with human appetites localized in the desire to gratify immediate, present interests.

Although lasting existence is possible only with the assistance of a sense of duration making possible responses to the most profound needs of our nature, destination, and perhaps role in the universe, modern humanity is capable of seeing and thinking of nothing but the present. The malaise is grave and menaces the entire world.

Certainly agriculture is still practiced and becomes increasingly necessary in guaranteeing food for the growing masses of the population. But to satisfy these diverse needs, it is being transformed at the cost of its atavistic character. By employing artificial and industrial methods it works a deep transformation in rural psychology.

The fruitful coexistence once established by agriculture between humanity and nature permitted the simultaneous nourishment of the former and the improvement of the latter. But it has now been replaced by a novel conception inspired by industrial methods. Instead of caring attentively and experimentally in ways that restore to nature a maximum of her possibilities, people now exploit her "to death." Instead of worrying about exhausting natural resources, they employ chemical means in the pursuit of immediate profit. Concerned solely with quick turnover, the egoism of the modern world, even when it does not deliberately sacrifice them, worries very little about the needs of future humanity. Indeed, egoism of the instant, satisfaction of momentary deeds, could be called the very basis of our civilization, as problems of pollution and environmental destruction demonstrate everywhere.

Another danger exists in the moral dimension. The farmer once realized splendidly the ultimate profound equilibrium of the human being in nature, with which he lived in contact, their close association serving as a source of harmony. As a consequence of the disappearance of small family cultivation—increasingly becoming no more than a memory—tomorrow's farmer, perforce both a mechanic and a chemist, will be an employee at the service of too vast and, therefore, abstract systems. And even political parties eager to fly to the farmer's aid will be unable to do anything but aggravate the malady.

Take for instance the transformation of socialism, which, while pretending to answer present needs, allows itself to be overtaken by a mentality of abstract, schematic thinking and relies on administrative solutions instead of solutions that were once found in living, individual contact. In this instance too, a tremendous mutation has taken place. In comparison with nineteenth-century socialism, imbued with generosity and spontaneous love, that of today is dogmatic, throttling, and state-oriented. How can we expect a remedy from socialism when it has fallen victim to the very disease against which we are supposed to do battle?

It has given in to the temptation to excessive control of a kind that substitutes an abstract administration, steeped in principles and rules, for the concrete experience characteristic of the individual or family contacts farmers once had with reality.

Such systems of control are conceived in offices by men who, even if they open a window, probably fail to see a tree or the Earth itself and, therefore, merely multiply their own errors. We have seen examples of this kind of thing in France. For instance, a statistic arriving in the offices of the administrative services indicates a surplus—let us say, in rice which these same services had decided to plant in the valley of the Rhône. The same thing would be true in the case of orchard or vineyard products. Immediately a rule—an ukase—is issued. Replace the crop unbalancing the statistics. Then, a few years later, the same abstract system of controls, confronted with new statistics, takes the reverse steps by ordering the replanting of the formerly discontinued crop. All of this is done without realizing that nature takes time and demands attentive care and patient delays incompatible with the volte-face of human thought.

I fear that Japan is hurtling along a dangerous path. Returning there after an absence of a dozen years or so, I was greatly stricken by the radical transformation that has taken place in the country. In the past, I had admired a Japanese conservatism that, through family and religious traditions, preserved continuity with and the quality of the past while applying practical intelligence to assimilating technical discoveries. On the occasion of my first contact with Japan, I hoped to have found a civilization balanced between intact atavistic forces and borrowings from the modern West. On my last trip, however, I saw that, in the space of a few years, the balance had been upset and that Western-style urban industrial civilization had spread like an epidemic threatening to kill, almost methodically, the spiritual resources the Japanese had seemed dedicated to safeguarding. As in the West, increasing materialism is all that can be expected from so radical a conversion.

This is why I greatly admire your efforts to make the Japanese people aware of the spiritual needs that Buddhism has staunchly advocated and disseminated. Your task is vital and embodies the hope that the growth of the illness can be retarded and counterbalanced.

We must remember, however, that the Orient sometimes demonstrates a certain lucid fear of the dangers of Westernization. Mao Zedong's China was a case in point. I cannot say what path China will follow tomorrow, but certainly Mao sensed the risks of too sudden an assimilation of Western civilization. On the other hand, he was hesitant to adhere too blindly to Soviet communism, with its devotion to industrial materialism.

Whether in the hands of the state or those of private capital, materialism is a factor in the destruction of the world today. Mao seems to have understood that the vastness of China permits balance between urban development on the one hand and the maintenance of agricultural resources on the other. Though perhaps simplistic and brutal, constraining intellectuals to go into the country to do agricultural work—as has been abundantly underscored by the press—may indicate uneasiness at the possibility of an over-intellectualized, excessively abstract society. With the development of the mass media, the intellectual has often played a harmful role in urban society. He has believed too strongly and at an increasing rate of frequency that thought consists in manipulating abstractions and playing with gratuitous ideas and that his own role is to disseminate intellectual-style theories and words that, owing to their superficiality and schematic and partial nature, disturb the human balance. Since the eighteenth century, the intellectual class has advocated the indiscriminate triumph of rationalism and, in this connection, has attached itself to dogmatic Marxism and its materialism.

But let us return to Mao Zedong. It is impossible to overstress his efforts at avoiding great industrial concentrations and to replace them with a dispersed industry scaled to rural life. Never having been in China, I know neither on what these tendencies rest nor the scope of their realization. But I seem to sense in that country the beginnings of an awareness of the dangers inherent as much in the Western capitalist as in the Soviet Marxist civilization.

Everything indicates that it is now time to find a way out of these impasses which, though no doubt contradictory, are blighted with the same disease. Our civilization is in peril and, since there is little hope of finding a political solution to the problem, must address itself to the reformation of its own spirit.

Loss of Autonomy

IKEDA: In the modern era, Japan has striven to build itself through industry and commerce to the extent that agriculture, once the backbone of the national economy, has been strictly suppressed. The outcome has been sharp loss of self-sufficiency in food provision. Indeed, with the exception of rice, Japan is so reliant on imports for practically all foodstuffs that severance of overseas supplies would certainly cause a crisis. Although some parties realize the need to reexamine official policies with an eye to providing the rural agricultural population with greater security and enabling them to maintain their own distinctive lifestyle, in general, industrialization still takes first place while pressure on agriculture continues unabated.

Although a certain degree of division of labor is essential for the sake of total global economic development and the advancement of international cooperation, the current situation is unbalanced and unwholesome. I should be happy to hear your views on the approach Japan and the other industrialized nations ought to take toward their future attitudes, especially in relation to agriculture.

HUYGHE: You have indicated one of the risks inherent in membership in the new civilization. In almost fanatically industrializing, Japan is losing its balance and becoming dependent on other nations.

A nation is a large-scale organism, all the parts of which must complement each other in reciprocal action, as is the case in the human body. Nothing can exist without the capacity of biological functions associated among themselves for the sake of united self-sufficiency. As it is with our bodies, so it is with the family and larger groups, especially the nation.

In international politics, dependence on another state that possesses an indispensable natural resource must be avoided at all costs. A striking example of the reason for this is the exorbitant power possessed by Arab nations producing a large percentage of the world's petroleum. Nations deprived of such resources must either submit to the demands of producer nations or resort to force. The frantic quest for new energy sources such nations are compelled to make indicates the price of shortsighted imprudence. Deprived of its agriculture, Japan will lose its autonomy.

On the scale of present needs, the organic constitution must be extended to groupings larger than single stages. Current effort to establish a united and coherent Europe reveals how pressing this need is. United, Europe is equal in power and resources to either of the super powers—the United States or the Soviet Union. Divided and partitioned, Europe runs the danger of falling under the protection of one or the other.

The modern world changes scale with developments in transport, speed, and information and, as this happens, traditional balances are destroyed. The crisis lies in the agonized search for new balances, as may be verified from the social viewpoint. In the past, a wise division of labor among the various social categories prevailed in the bosom of each nation. But later, organized and disseminated class hatred replaced and found support in international solidarities that broke through the walls of the national cell, the existence of which it compromised. In the past the existence of each state depended on the balanced harmony of different individual functions. As long as the eyes remain unclouded by nineteenth-century systematic deformations of the political spirit, we can see that, even though it was less comfortable because of a more difficult struggle for natural resources, life in the past was at least more harmonious than it is now.

An example of the way in which political deformations affect historical interpretations may be seen in the false ideas prevailing about the Middle Ages. The limited social cell of those times corresponded in size to the extent of a given feudal lord's lands and included the fecund fields tilled by the peasant. Nearer to the lord, the town, where the bourgeoisie came into being, was organized at the base of the castle walls. In the town, industry, still at the artisan stage, furnished the peasant with, for instance, cloth in exchange for the produce of his land. The town became the center of commerce and of relations first with neighboring cells and then with cells increasingly farther away.

At the pinnacle of the organization was the lord who, except in the case of an unbalanced person, was not the tyrant that certain people have imagined. It is to be noted that in the twentieth century, literature and even history as taught in schools are not always as objective as they are thought to be.

The lord was the person in charge; he had functions to fulfill, one of which was hunting. His aim in hunting was not solely, as at a later time, his own pleasure and was far from being the careless destruction of crops (as legends based on exceptional cases claim), since this would have worked counter to his own interests. In hunting, he was performing the indispensable task of periodically thinning out harmful beasts, a cause of damage to the peasant, his domestic animals, and his crops, in order to keep their numbers within reasonable limits. From time immemorial, the hunt has had profound significance.

Another equally protective function of the lord was war to check foreign invasions and depredations. In principle, the medieval system was perfectly constructed although, like all systems, in practice it could be distorted and abused. Thus, each individual in these small, very limited societies was a specialist who, like an organ in a living organism, through division of labor contributed to the life of the whole.

Comment is often heard concerning the weight of taxes and duties in the Middle Ages. But I seriously doubt that taxes imposed by modern national states today are any lighter.

In the nineteenth century, imitating the excesses of the aristocracy of preceding centuries, the bourgeoisie upset the social balance. A voracious extension of industry and mistress of an economy in a society living solely for its good, the bourgeoisie developed ways to exploit both nature and the laborer simultaneously. The class struggle came into being as a fatal repercussion of this development.

But when the various organs within an organism can no longer coexist peacefully, the whole is threatened with death—at least as long as no more inclusive substitute wholes are available. This explains why the twentieth century has demonstrated a tendency to internationalism, paralleling tendencies imposed on the economy and capitalism. But transitions of this kind are always perilous undertakings. Once again, the law that disruption of harmony spells the threat of death for the whole living organization finds verification.

IKEDA: I agree that, as in the case of self-sufficiency in food supply, it is essential to maintain the harmonious and correct operation of both instinctive resources and rational capacities within the organism. In a sense, the modernization process has consisted of reducing or obliterating the autonomy of the small social unit, which was then reassembled as only part of a social structure of much larger units.

As you point out, in the Middle Ages, societies that grew up in small, local regions produced everything they needed for daily life. Things they could not produce were regarded as rare luxury items to be imported from distant places.

Such self-sufficient societies were enclosed and stagnant. But their walls were to be broken down, probably because of an increasing desire for rare luxury items and the consequent development of means of travel and transport. A growing ambition for power stimulated the establishment of larger social units, as increasingly sophisticated means of transport facilitated circulation of materials in large quantities. Aided by the division of labor, this development expanded the field of goods transportation beyond the luxury items that had once been the main item of traffic to include such indispensables as food and clothing.

Certainly, from the standpoint of satisfying large material demands, there is a good reason behind the shift from a small-unit to a large-unit society. First, it is more efficient to produce one article on a large scale than for each individual to produce many different articles on a small scale in limited quantities. Furthermore, specialization and exchange satisfy needs more effectively. But the individual human being has paid for increased efficiency with the loss of autonomy in the society he himself built.

This development can be regarded as an expansion of a society based on autonomy. But, when such a society grows beyond human powers of comprehension, the individual feels dwarfed and consequently loses affection and a sense of responsibility for the control of society.

In connection with balance and harmony between the human being and society, Aristotle observed that, ideally, a city should be no larger than the limits to which the voice of a shouting person standing in the central plaza is audible. Today voices carried on radio waves are heard by countless people over vast distances. But the exchange is one-way. The voice of the person wishing to reply or object to what is being said cannot be heard. Under such circumstances, communication runs the danger of becoming a unilateral imposition of opinion.

Human beings feel true affection for, membership in, and responsibility for, the operation of a society within the limits of their own awareness and understanding, the voices of all other members of which are audible to them. This attitude is deeply related to what you call instinctive resources.

In exchange for the material riches and convenience obtained as a consequence of the shift from a micro-society to a macro-society, in which the smaller unit has lost autonomy and become no more than a part of the larger unit, human beings have deprived themselves of the spiritual fulfillment and stability derivable from a profound sense of oneness with society. And, as a consequence, having become passive benefi-ciaries, we have lost the ability to act deliberately and sponta-neously in the management of society.

Of course, a mere return to the ways of the past can solve nothing. The walls of the large social unit called the state have already been broken down. Economic transactions and cultural exchanges on a global scale take place daily. Every day fruit, fish, meat, and other comestibles imported from distant lands appear on our tables. The very paper on which I am now writing may have been made from logs imported from Canada.

First of all, we must come to regard the whole world affec-tionately and with a sense of responsibility as the foundation of our very lives. In addition, we must become acutely aware of what we have lost—and continue to lose—in the moderniza-tion process, as a result of extreme division of labor in the name of increased convenience and efficiency, and must make an independent effort to recoup our losses.

The commune movement among the youth of the industrial-ized nations may be regarded as a manifestation of the desire to do precisely this. These youths are, however, too escapist. Reflecting then actualizing ideas in society is what is needed.

HUYGHE: The kinds of young people you mention manifest-ed a necessary reaction, but it remained at a very elementary stage. In the present phase of generalized crises, the scale on which it is essential to plant the notion of harmonious balance, as required by the various parts of an organism, is much larger. And this cannot be achieved without a mental reformation of man himself. This, in turn, demands the reestablishment of the balance already compromised within the human organism and psyche. We must make our instinctive resources and our rational capacities cooperate once again. Instinctive resources are derived from the profound intuitions of our sensitivities and from their organization as effected by tradition and gradually transmitted into secular experience. By establishing reasoned rules, rational capacities clarify old experiences and make possible rapid functional action. It is impossible to establish a social life solely on either blind tradition or administrative rationalism. Either extreme can lead only to the death of the organism.

Unfortunately, I am afraid that our civilization is so engrossed in the partial, biased solution represented by administrative rationalism that reestablishing equilibrium will be difficult and we will be unable not only to return to the past, but also to take compensatory measures. It is to be feared that, in a case as advanced as our own, the experience is irreversible and must continue to the end—perhaps to catastrophe. Indeed maybe catastrophe is necessary to awaken endangered humanity to the nature of the needs and to stimulate a fresh start with a new civilization capable of correcting the excesses of its predecessor. The fear that this is true is inescapable since, far from changing itself, our kind of civilization is spreading inexorably throughout the whole world. Perhaps the only egress will be an instinctive, violent crisis in which much suffering must be endured before the way is finally rediscovered.

Natural Conditions

IKEDA: No doubt fortunate climatic and geographic conditions have played an important part in making France more successful and noteworthy in terms of agriculture than other

Western European nations. But is it not true that the French people have a special respect for agriculture?

HUYGHE: Certainly the influence of climatic and geographic conditions has helped give France the characteristic you mention. A balanced abundance of resources in France brought about an exceptional natural flowering of the agrarian way of life and the mental attitudes suited to peasants. Attentive and practical work and the ready development of natural instincts in combination with sensibility, good sense, and rationalism have contributed to the evolution of traditional solidity. Favored by the land, this way of life has made the inhabitants prize qualities proper to farming people.

This is why the advent of the modern world, characterized by elements alien to traditional French ways, disoriented France more than any other nation. France found herself fundamentally altered by the triumph of urban industrial civilization. The malaise was grave, as is confirmed by the initial decline of French preeminence in Europe and the world from the time when that new civilization began evolving. It should be noted that it was only under the pressure of competition from England, later reinforced by competition from Germany, that France adopted this civilization. The growth of these two great industrial powers compelled France to develop methods that disrupted harmony at home.

This French sickness, of which much was said after the appearance of a remarkable book by Peyrefitte, resulted from the substitution of a systematic rationalism, a rootless incarnation of administrative technology, for the peasant wisdom that had been perfected through a kind of reason found compatible to the French.

IKEDA: On each of the numerous occasions on which I have visited France, I have always been astounded by the beauty of the countryside and the rich variety of the flavors of agricultural products.

In Japan, France is known best for art and fine food. The painting entitled *L'Angelus*, by Jean Francois Millet, was my first encounter with French art. I was deeply impressed by the naturalistic beauty of the man and woman, who make their living on the land, standing at the end of the work day in humble prayer as the sound of the Angelus bells floats toward them from a distant church.

Since my first encounter with this picture, I dreamed of someday standing in a field in France and experiencing the mood Millet depicted. By the time I was able to visit your country, however, most of the villages Millet had known a century earlier had already disappeared. Furthermore, my own schedule usually kept me busy. Nonetheless, I did manage to visit a village where I was deeply moved to be able to savor something of the mood of *L'Angelus*.

Although farming methods have been modernized and mechanized and the daily life of the rural population has changed, whenever I am in France I feel that the people truly value agriculture. Furthermore, the French attitude that union and harmony with the Earth and nature are the foundation of life is deeply reflected in all aspects of the life of the people.

Agriculture—or the farmer's way of thinking—is the basis of both French art and French gastronomy. By this I mean the way in which the French take nature as it is and, without attempting to destroy, will try to enhance and deepen her beauty and richness.

As we have already said, such an attitude is one important aspect of civilization as it ought to be. Although, as you say, in the turbulence of modernization France may have lost, and may still be losing, traditional and fundamental attitudes, I hope she will be able to preserve as many of them as possible. We Japanese, too, must open our eyes to the importance of conserving typically and distinctively Japanese traits.

HUYGHE: Like the agricultural nations, the fishing nations are losing many of their traditional ways. Has not modern civilization upset this essential way of life in Japan?

IKEDA: Fishing, which supplies a vital source of animal proteins, is highly important to Japan. But, with the declaration of the 200-nautical-mile limits by nations like the United States and the Soviet Union, Japanese deep-sea fishing fell on hard times. Of course, in the background are certain Japanese legal malpractices related to overfishing certain species to the brink of extinction. But, on the wider scale, the time has come to switch from a primitive hunting (fishing) phase to a phase of sea-life cultivation. Such a transition would correspond to the change from a hunting to an agricultural economy on dry land. In other words, instead of merely catching all we want of the fish existing naturally in the seas, we must breed the fish we catch.

The Japanese are already successfully operating breeding farms on a large, industrial scale for certain species, including trout and eel, in various parts of the country. But in almost all cases, the fish raised in this way inhabit fresh water (ponds or lakes) and their role in the Japanese diet is still relatively small. For most of the fish consumed in Japan, we must rely on the seas: the Sea of Okhotsk, the South Pacific, and the Indian Ocean. The only truly marine creatures successfully cultivated for human consumption at present are such shellfish as the scallop.

Surrounded by seas, at a point where a cold current from the direction of the Arctic Ocean meets a warm current from the south, Japan once enjoyed an abundance of fish and shellfish. During modernization, however, a more efficient fishing industry began recording excessive catches that helped severely reduce sea life in Japanese coastal waters. It is saddening to hear that famous local delicacies, once prepared with fish and shrimps from nearby waters, now must be made with seafood imported from such distant places as the African coasts. All that remains of their former truly local character are their names.

Each year back-and-forth jostling takes place between the Soviet Union and Japan over fishing rights in the Sea of Okhotsk. The Soviets are so concerned about stock depletion that they apply strict limits to control the Japanese, who are eager to ensure the largest catches possible. Although I do not necessarily agree one hundred percent with the Soviets, they are attempting to care for their own country. The Japanese should devote some thought to the dangers of over-fishing natural stocks.

Since the imposition of the 200-nautical-mile limitation, the Japanese situation has become even more difficult. The dilemma is very real for many harbor towns that can no longer send fishing fleets to the northern waters. This problem could arise, and has indeed arisen, in many other parts of the world.

The situation affects the daily lives of the Japanese people. In the past, fish was an indispensable, inexpensive source of protein in the daily diet. Today it has become too costly to appear on the menu as often as once was the case. (The complicated Japanese system of cargo distribution contributes to the high prices of seafood products.)

Fish is a wholesome source of protein in the diet. According to some specialists, the increase in such so-called adult diseases as hypertension among the Japanese may be ascribed to a reduction in the consumption of fish and a reliance on meats like beef and pork, which have a much higher cholesterol content. Widespread realization of the superior quality of the protein in fish will no doubt further stimulate worldwide demand.

The pressing problem is how to effect a transition from the present hunting approach to a cultivational approach. During their life cycles, from the fry to the adult stage, most ocean fish swim over vast distances. Many details about the actions and habits of members of the elaborate food chain, from plankton to large fish, are still imperfectly understood. Both the research required to clarify these points, and the management and supervision required after the cultivation of marine life becomes feasible, must be carried out on the basis of global international cooperation. What are your views on this issue?

HUYGHE: The sea is another battle field where, unfortunately, we see additional proof of the neglect characterizing contemporary civilization. There, too, with no thought of tomorrow, we exploit systematically. In addition, however, we inflict on the sea the ravages of pollution.

The problem of petroleum tankers is very serious. Ships of

this category already exceed capacities of 500,000 tons and are moving toward the million-ton mark. And it is impossible to say when an accident may cause a petroleum tanker to spill its cargo into the sea, causing a maritime disaster. It will be remembered that the tanker Torrey Canyon once spilled 110,000 tons of crude oil; and the amount was even greater in the case of the catastrophe of the Amoco-Cadix (1978). But what is even worse, greed and a total lack of conscience allow tankers to deliberately empty their tanks at sea to save money. A significant part of the surface and depth of the ocean has already been laid barren by practices of this kind and the subsequent destruction of marine fauna is certainly deplorable. But even more grave is the effect this sterilization of the sea has on the atmosphere. The source of oxygen in our air is not, as once thought, solely trees and forests: the plankton in the sea are its greatest producer. By polluting the sea and destroying plankton, we are allowing the atmosphere of the Earth to be irreversibly impoverished. Once again, a change in the way we think is our only remaining recourse.

Civilization must not permit the ceaselessly growing depredations, the childish pillage of the planet's resources, and the lack of consideration of the future to continue. Unless we pass from a stage of greedy exploitation to one of harmonious cohabitation, we will destroy our environment. This does not mean that we must blindly renounce technological methods but, rather, that these methods must be integrated in a larger system, where their harmful effects can be controlled and counterbalanced so that human beings may establish a new equilibrium with nature.

Once again we find ourselves facing the need to restore harmony in all places where modern aberrations have destroyed it. As we have said, we must begin with the human organism, psychological and physiological, with the aim of permitting all of its constituent parts to participate in a balanced fashion. The same thing is true in the vastly bigger organism of the natural world. In dealing with the organism of our environment, we must take the same kind of elementary precautions that medicine and hygiene recommend for our own individual organisms. If we admit the need to take measures to prolong our individual lives, it should not be impossible for us to apply the same mental approach on a vastly greater scale to ensure the survival of the human race.

PART THREE

Society Facing the Crisis

IKEDA: Of course, assembling the problems inherent in the current crisis and analyzing them to discover their faults are not enough. We must try to solve them, but this is a highly difficult task. Although the nature of the crisis is beginning to be appreciated, is contemporary society capable of combatting the issue and effecting a solution? What means are at our disposal for dealing with it? What is the nature of the reformation for which we should strive?

HUYGHE: Inherent in society are all the means of good social health. Instead of allowing them to fall into disuse, we must reinvigorate these means and establish balance among them. But contemporary society is intoxicated by and overestimates the new modes of action it believes itself to have created. At the same time, it despises and attempts to destroy the fundamental means that it has only perfected instead of replacing, as it believed itself to be doing.

Carried away with naive, radical modernism, society believes in its own ability to reform and rethink everything, to reconceive everything in accordance with rational structures, and to cast overboard the time-honored knowledge provided by experience. We have thus abandoned patient, natural development of data obtained from life itself for the sake of principles and arbitrary mechanisms deduced from logic alone. Although these principles and mechanisms have resulted in incontestable advances, they have also generated irrelevances contributing to imbalance.

It is, therefore, necessary to reestablish society by restoring the vital roots represented by the family and sound education:

those things that enable the gifts of sensitivity and the interior life to flourish. Through respect for the individual's life, we must imbue society with diversity instead of allowing it to ossify in arbitrary and abusive political systems. We must, in a word, enlighten humanity to its true destiny by awakening innate, essential aptitudes of love and yearning to transcend mortal concerns.

1

Social Tasks—Formative Action

HUYGHE: Manifestly, the principal lever in the process is education, in the broadest sense; that is, all of the means of pressure that society may use to mold the individual. It goes without saying that these means must not be used to enslave people or to inculcate in them systems of thought and convictions simply because society prefers them. In such attempts is to be found the source of all dictatorships—rightist or leftist—which grasp at education as the means of imprinting on children—and on adults—what I call ideological preconstraint. A truly rich education cultivates in each individual a sense of liberty closely connected with a sense of responsibility. It must prepare the individual to make good use of the fullness of all potentialities in that direction.

Often, though employing no authoritarian pressure, society involuntarily presses down crushingly on minds—especially minds at the formative stage—by means of general dominant ideas welcomed, disseminated, and popularized by society. Clearly members of a single generation may embrace, frequently without doubt, certain accepted intellectual attitudes in which they expect to find natural solutions to all life's problems. This approach represents a kind of contagion, a mental epidemic as it were. I am convinced that studying the mechanism whereby an idea or system of ideas invades and enslaves the human spirit, to the point where entire generations are compelled to think within the framework of its postulates, would elucidate many questions posed by the evolution of man.

Educating the Mind and the Man

HUYGHE: A program of formative action must rest on two points. First, it is essential to indicate the exhaustion of dominant but already outmoded and controvertible ideas in order to remove them from currency and replace them with compensatory tendencies made intelligible through striking formulas that can later assume directing force. This is tantamount to stimulating an inverse epidemic favorably influenced by the natural, regulatory play of life.

Second, it is necessary to rely on the kind of true education that sees in the child of the present the adult of the future. These two points must be treated in order.

The first task is providing access to new ideas. To do this, we must make it clear that the ideas we take as the basis of our lives and, therefore, consider normal and obvious are no more than the fruits of circumstances that, molding human beings in all epochs, transform concepts of things. These ideas are, therefore, both ephemeral and mutable. We must realize that, today, we live on the basis of a conviction born in about the seventeenth century. The continuing development of this conviction has been the source of the evolution of science and technology. In Descartes's expression, according to this idea, we are the masters and possessors of nature.

As we have already seen, the consequence of this way of thinking has been the replacement of the ancient idea of collaboration between humanity and nature and the resulting replacement of all natural potentialities with the contrary principle of exploitation, struggle, and aggression. With this new attitude, human beings saw that they possess the means of changing the world and compelling it to conform to their own will and desires.

From this way of thinking Marx derived both the dogma of

the predominance of history, in which human beings modify the world, and the idea of reciprocity according to which the world, transformed by them, conditions human beings. At this point, the idea of an immutable, static world, in which human beings have been placed to work out their destinies, disappeared. But, again having been reduced to means of acting on the physical environment, human beings turn from themselves and the molding of their personalities and interior ambitions and think exclusively of objective facts, their rational manipulation, and the science and technology born of these actions. The outcome of this obsession manifests itself in the preeminence afforded to economic life, which has become humanity's unique preoccupation. Man has forgotten himself in his exclusive concern with his own comfort.

It is now time to pay more attention to the lacuna—the void—human beings are creating within themselves. Already showing awareness of this problem, some of the most open spirits of the time resist being deprived of an interior life and of the opportunity to make use of it. Such people actually suffer because of the lack. Although still instinctive and confused, a protest is arising against an exclusively utilitarian, practical, and economy-oriented world. Thinkers must take stubborn corollary action to open the eyes of the masses to the disturbance occurring in the human condition and transform into clear, obsessive, and demanding ideas an emotion that is most apparent among the young as either dissatisfaction or a more or less obscure aspiration.

The second point is education. This need not proceed from a rekneading of current ideas. For even if their teachers are not, children are open to new ideas. It is necessary to prepare them to break out of the dictatorship of the quantitative and to give them both the experience of and the need for the qualitative. The evolution imposed on public education by people in charge is always a reflection of accepted, officialized teachings. These are the very doctrines that must now be surpassed and offset. Unfortunately, however, at the very time when it is essential to move in the opposite direction, educational programs become increasingly technically oriented.

Instead of subordinating teaching to practical efficiency, we must make it an instrument to awaken the inner life, lighten the load of the quantitative and measurable, which are rightly applicable to the external characteristics of the world, and stimulate appreciation of the qualitative, which is characteristic of the interior life.

We must make a clear distinction between the two interpretations of the word *qualitative*. In one sense, it pertains to the perception of the specificity of things on the basis of applied sensitivity. In another, it implies intuition, the awareness of a different scale of values opening the possibility of a progression to the interior life.

How is it possible to introduce the double experience of the qualitative into instruction? Instead of being based on ideas—that is, on abstract formulations accessible to everyone in the same way—instruction should develop interior perception and subjective appreciation. This means that we must reintroduce, on an even larger scale, those things that, as a consequence of pure aberration, we are now in the process of cutting out of our curricula.

Recently in France, in a rare example of ignorance of the prevailing situation, courses in philosophy have been half-abolished. Where they continue to exist, they have been reduced to the simplest forms. This is most lamentable since, whereas the sciences encourage a steadily expanding exploration of the exterior, concrete world, philosophy attempts to turn us toward the internal experience of reflection. I am speaking of true philosophy, which does not concern itself with formulas or doctrinal exposition, but opens the way to meditation.

Another characteristic of the currently prevailing mistaken approach is the steady reduction of the amount of time devoted to art—the chosen field of the qualitative—in education. To demonstrate the lack of awareness of the importance of this field among the highest responsible French authorities, I might cite a few figures. At the beginning of the school year in 1979, 200 teaching positions in the plastic arts and 216 in music were eliminated—in addition to the 356 that had disappeared on the occasions of the 3 preceding school-year openings. As a consequence, education in the plastic arts was eliminated from the curricula of 37 percent of all secondary schools (*lycées*) and 31 percent of all primary schools (*collèges*); music education was eliminated from the curricula of 70 percent of all secondary and 38 percent of all primary schools. Furthermore, to fill the positions remaining in the plastic arts, it was necessary to call on auxiliary teachers in 12 percent of all instances and in 35 percent of all instances in the case of music. Using auxiliary teachers is resorted to in less than 8 percent of all mathematics teaching positions. Patently scorned, art education is often limited to the study of historical facts or to the practice of such techniques as drawing faithful reproductions of models.

Much is said today of creativity. True creativity means more than simply stimulating a child to give random exterior expression to impulses. Inculcating creativity requires discovering, within the child, the things that deserve actualization and pursuing their best qualitative expressions. This is the sole basis for aesthetics, which, as cannot be repeated too often, is founded not on doctrines, theories, and transmittable ideas, but on effort, aspiration, and interior demand oriented toward the conquest of quality. Its basis is the will always to transcend self instead of falling back on things that are teachable and passively acquirable. The approach to art and the masterpieces of the graphic and plastic arts as well as of music ought, therefore, to find an increasingly prominent place in educational programs.

It seems likely that such an educational orientation would correspond to the recently growing public demand for contact with works of art. Increasing numbers of people are instinctively attempting to penetrate the secret of the source of spiritual rejuvenation offered by exhibits and art museums.*

We must pay attention to this sociological sign (as a certain kind of contemporary pedantry is fond of terming it), which demonstrates one of our epoch's pressing needs. We must

---

* A single example: In 1979, exhibitions at the Paris Grand Palais attracted nearly 1,239,000 visitors. Nonetheless, television makes practically no mention of art, which, according to the pronouncements of the augurs, "Holds no interest for the public."

understand its significance and attempt to satisfy the desire it obscurely manifests.

It would seem that Nichiren took a great step forward in regard to desires in the Buddhist sense. In the past, people have tended to believe too facilely that Buddhism requires the extinction of all desire. It should be noted, however, that the desire discussed in this context is directed toward the outside world, that is, concupiscence, greed, and appetite demanding satisfaction through material means. If I am correct, Nichiren perceived another interpretation of desire: aspiration or desire belonging to the interior life and conducive to its flowering and perfection. He saw that such desire is highly valuable.

Whereas occidental philosophies avidly seek perfection in a static state, like the one manifest in the Platonic spirit, Buddhism strives for projection in space, a duration which implies both life and lives. If this is true, how is it possible to ignore desire which, as aspiration, may also be impetus?

IKEDA: You have a good point. Tossed by instinctive desires on the one hand and dominated by reason on the other, humanity is in fundamental need of education in the broadest sense. I concur with your belief that we must break with blind faith—even worship—of the principles that have prevailed in modern society heretofore, and must shift emphasis in school education from science and technology to philosophy, art, and those things that cultivate interior riches and striving for high quality.

I am convinced that human education reflecting the goals of Buddhism and knowledge of the truths of life elucidated in Buddhist thought is of extremely great value.

Attainment of Buddhahood, the ultimate goal, means enlightenment to one's fundamental self. In the practical activities of life, such enlightenment assumes the form of the work of the bodhisattva. The basic meaning of the term bodhisattva is a person who works for the sake of enlightenment. In addition to such work, however, the bodhisattva undertakes practical activities, reflecting Buddhist enlightenment in human society.

Doing this means both realizing that the Buddha nature

exists in all human beings and, as a consequence, despising no one and respecting the personalities and lives of all. The parable *The Bodhisattva Named Never Despising,* in chapter twenty of the Lotus Sutra illustrates this point.

"Never Despising," the bodhisattva, earned his name from his habit of paying deep respect to the Buddha nature he knew resides in everyone. He never despised anyone because to do so would be to look down on a Buddha. But, for his pains, he was treated as a lunatic, stoned, and beaten with sticks.

As you have pointed out, human beings today regard themselves as no more than means for use in operating on the surrounding material world. As the attitude presented in the parable indicates, Buddhism considers the most precious of all things to reside in the human being who must not, therefore, under any circumstances be regarded as a mere means.

Modern human beings are perfectly willing to regard their fellow human beings as nothing but means to an end. The principle of the mercenary dominates all kinds of business enterprises, bureaucratic structures, and labor unions. Education has become no more than a mechanism for producing the kinds of people such organizations need. In my opinion, however, education ought to rest on the spirit taught by the bodhisattva in the parable just mentioned.

In all epochs, in both East and West, outstanding teachers have always adopted an attitude like that of "Never Despising" in dealing with students. Just such an attitude ought to be the foundation of education systems, structures, and concepts. Ensuring it such a place will demand an extraordinary revolution. But, if achieved, the revolution can change the way of thinking and living of individuals and of all society. As you have pointed out, people with open minds are already sensing the need for a change in modern society. That change must begin with our teaching methods.

The educational world today can be said to concern itself solely with producing human resources. In modern society, human beings, like mercenaries in times of war, are only means to an end. Education cultivates people who are useful only to the extent to which they fit into various slots in society.

Certainly a full life is impossible without goals. And sometimes it is permissible for human beings to serve as means for the achievement of high goals. Nonetheless, no matter what outside aims may exist, each person must be aware of the role he is playing and his reason for playing it. Not merely following orders like a soldier, he must act under his own volition and on the basis of his own decisions. Only then may he allow himself to become a means for the sake of attaining the goal of a fulfilled life. It is the responsibility of education to help its charges become capable of selecting the goals to which they wish to dedicate their lives, to cultivate the ability to discern the qualities of various goals, and to guide them in choosing correctly among the available alternatives.

Of course the scientific method of thinking, the acquisition of knowledge, and the mastery of techniques are all important. But the main prerequisite for all these is the ability to examine oneself and the cultivation of wisdom and strength to make acute observations of the interior qualities of things.

The attained goal and the fundamental content of the teachings of Buddhism are awareness of the basic human self. Shakyamuni became a Buddha, or Enlightened One, because he became enlightened to his basic entity.

Instinctive desires, love, and compassion can be called manifestations of the energy of life. Instinctive desires inspire intakes from the outside world for the sake of sustaining and strengthening one's own life, whereas love and compassion are outwardly directed dispersals of energy, oriented toward preserving and enriching the lives of others.

Both the intakes and the dispersals, repeated over and over, are essential to living. But ensuring that their effect is not destructive, but constructive and creative, requires respect for life force and a correct understanding of its complexities and subtle operations and functions.

Enlightenment to one's own life is the shortest, surest way to an understanding of the preciousness of all life and of the emotions and functions associated with it. This is true because, in attempting to understand the lives of others, we must rely on external knowledge which can penetrate only to superficial layers and cannot reach the profound world that remains unreflected in expressions, actions, and words.

The only way to know life truly and profoundly is from within. One must contemplate one's own life. A person who, after making efforts in this direction, attains perfect perception is called a Buddha.

There is a Buddhist legend about a demon goddess named Kishimojin (Hariti in Sanskrit) who, while having children herself, brought grief to others by devouring their offspring. Hearing of this, the Buddha concealed one of Kishimojin's own children. When she learned of this, the goddess went nearly mad searching for her child.

The Buddha called to her and said, "Even though you have many children, the loss of only one causes you great grief. Perhaps now you can understand how much others have suffered at the loss of their precious little ones." Thereafter, Kishimojin gave up her evil ways and became a benevolent deity, protectress of children, and helper of mothers.

This fable relates how, through understanding one's own suffering, one can understand how others feel and can wish to relieve their grief. A Buddha thoroughly comprehends with maximum breadth and depth the wonderful world of the life of the human mind, knows all the sufferings human beings encounter, and has the love and compassion to wish to save them. A Buddha not only wishes to bring salvation, but also has the capability of fulfilling his aspiration because of his perfect understanding of the truth of life.

Moreover, going beyond saving from suffering, a Buddha instructs and guides all sentient beings in the way to become Buddhas themselves. Buddhism is a system of teachings and practices for the achievement of this end.

To return to the topic of education, it is essential to remember that, in addition to the school, the home is, as it always has been, a very important place for a child's character formation. Indeed the home is the place where the most basic aspects of personality take shape because it is there that parents concern themselves not with enshrining in the mind special categories of knowledge, but with the molding of the child's entire being.

Consequently, as emphasis is increasingly placed on overall education, the importance of training in the home will deserve reconsideration.

Saving the Family

HUYGHE: The disintegration of the family and its incontestable loss of importance in modern life are extremely disturbing signs. Often-cited material causes are undeniably significant, but we must not overlook a deeper origin: the formidable tendency in modern society to efface everything essentially natural and instinctive—everything corresponding to the obscure conditions of our biological, emotional, and spiritual existence—and to substitute for them rationalism and its dogmatic principles. Thirty-five years ago, Arthur Koestler (1905–1945) clearly pointed out this dramatic conflict in his *The Yogi and the Commissar.*

Today, the family is regarded as something handed down from the past and, therefore, obsolete. People prefer to replace it with generalities, human categories, and groupings based on common activity and solidarities of a material nature, including everything from peer groups and pals to political parties and labor unions. Today, people confer on their duties to the labor union—the last refuge of otherwise worn-out moral obligations—the kind of importance once given to family duties. A substitution of this kind is very characteristic of the changes our world is undergoing and of the dangers they entail. Human beings today group themselves together only on the basis of ideas or common action.

The family is the biologically founded environment where emotional faculties are formed and brought to full flower. Our contemporaries never stop talking of "human relations" and how much they long to preserve or reestablish them. Can they fail to understand that, by definition, the family is the natural place for such relations?

IKEDA: As is indicated by the often-heard remark, "We have a house, but not a home," the traditional family spirit is fading. At the same time, the family's functions as a social element are being reduced. Nonetheless, the family is still the basis for the formation of human relations and, unlike artificial social organizations, cannot be modified easily. Its profound influence on personality formation, part of a system dating from remotest antiquity, cannot be ignored with impunity.

Though it is, in a sense, ancient and even primitive and though the bonds between parents and children and among siblings are less cultural than biological, the family fulfills functions beyond the capabilities of newer artificial relations founded on the rules of civilizations.

I interpret the family as performing two major functions. The first is maternal and all-forgiving. It brings peace and stability to human minds suffering from frustration and insecurity. The other is paternal. It stimulates cultivation of the intellect, emotions, and will and the development of sound human relations. The paternal function can be smoothly carried out only because of the existence of the maternal function. This assumption has all the more convincing power because mother-child relations significantly predate father-child relations and because this means the formation of the mother-father-offspring family unit must be comparatively new. In other words, whereas maternal functions are pronouncedly biological, paternal functions are strongly colored by social elements.

Although today society can, to a certain extent, compensate for the lack of paternal functions, the family cannot truly come into existence without maternal functions, the absence of which destabilizes children's personalities. Obviously I am talking of the paternal and maternal functions and not necessarily of fathers and mothers, per se.

In modern society, the paternal role can, to a degree, be supplied by education. In the past, education took place largely in the home, where traditions were handed down from generation to generation. Such a system sufficed in a time of few changes and limited fields of action. Today, however, fields of action have greatly expanded; and ideas alter rapidly. Under such circumstances, many of the ideas and traditions of the past have been abandoned as no longer pertinent. This is one reason for the diminution of family functions and part of the background against which the father has lost authority as the *pater familias*. I do not imply, however, that the family has lost its significance. And, in discussing the loss of paternal authority, it is necessary to try to discover the source of that authority.

In the past, paternal authority was the mainstay of the family. Founded in an ancient social system, this authority came into being as a way of instructing others about the nature of that system and of dealing with various problems arising in connection with it. Change in the old order deprived the father's teachings of much of their value and thus lowered the prestige of the paternal role. The outcome was a reduction in the value of the family as educator. But I believe that a reexamination of its educational responsibilities can restore the family to its old position.

Formerly, in ages when order was considered valuable, children learned how to live from family instruction. The value attributed to living according to the prevailing order was the source of the authority of the family and of the father as its nucleus. I am convinced that the family can be revived if it assumes the task of teaching its children a way of life that is immutable. Much of the distrust and dissatisfaction young people entertain in connection with the family arises from a reaction against the way parents live. It is not educational background, social standing or income that causes children to despair of their fathers. Instead it is a daily life style reflecting lack of self-assurance, indifference to justice, and lack of ambition for the future. This is why I agree with you that the only way to solve the problems threatening to destroy the family is to regenerate humanity by revolutionizing our interior lives.

Human characters are formed in relation with other human characters. Since the fundamental aspect of this formation is early parent-child relations, I believe that the attempt to regenerate humanity in the family is one of the most important issues of our time. Founded on Buddhist teachings, our human-revolution movement firmly believes that trouble in the family is one of the major sources of the problems confronting us today.

Diminution of the paternal element has inevitably accompanied the ascendancy in the home of the stabilizing maternal element. As a consequence, some children are spoiled, even debauched, to the extent that they actually reject the family itself. Nevertheless, the maternal function is vitally important because it provides emotional tranquility. In Japan, the pressing desire for tranquility is vividly illustrated by the many young people who, though having left rural areas for a life in Tokyo, ultimately return to the provinces, of their own free will, in order to find an oasis of spiritual peace. This phenomenon reflects the chaos of our times.

Since it is, as you say, a biological entity, the family is literally the womb from which each individual member is born. In going home, a person is doing more than going back to a house. Subconsciously, the return is made in the hope of rediscovering the familiar place of both birth and upbringing. This is why we must attempt to make our homes places where weariness can be eliminated and energy restored. The family must be neither passive nor exclusively biological. If it is to contribute to the total development of all its members, its very tranquility must be charged with the fundamental rhythm of life.

Urban Life

HUYGHE: It is impossible to overestimate the importance of urban life among the conditions causing the breakup of the family. Very few people are unaware of this situation, but what is to be done about it? Disarmed, we can only give in to it. Often, for economic reasons, large cities compel the laborer or employee to live at great distances from working places. Long commuting trips take hours that, as fathers of the family, they might better spend with loved ones. And today this is the lot of wives who work to supplement husbands' salaries. Once again, economic considerations take the place of the true needs of living.

The mass media—especially television—also contribute to

the breakup of the family unit. Television broadcasts into all living rooms, simultaneously, the same uniform and importunate lesson and, even in rural regions, substitutes its artificial, piercing pedagogy for the living contacts of conversation and for the personal education of the child by the father and mother. Exchanges at the family table are displaced by its hypnotic vision. What remedies can be taken against this danger? What countermeasures can we adopt against this state of affairs? As always, regulations and laws would only multiply the general, abstract measures that already alter the nature of life in contemporary society.

IKEDA: To add to the difficulty, whereas in the past human beings lived in collectives like villages and modest towns, today the individual finds himself alone in the crowds of urban centers. I should like to discover why this is true and to investigate the need for the collective for humanity in the future.

Of the two major functions I have enumerated for collective society in the past, one is the production function related to intensely close cooperation. This function might be compared to the role of a machine. I do not know what the situation was in Western agricultural villages in the distant past but, in Japan, whenever a large task had to be completed in a short time—for example, the planting of rice seedlings—everyone in the village joined forces. After completing the planting for one household, on the following day, the entire group moved on to plant for another household. In other words, the operation demanded collective action.

After modernization, however, the introduction of machinery to deal with such tasks rendered collective action superfluous in terms of pooling of labor resources. Although villages and towns persist in Japan, their inhabitants rarely have a chance to work together in a body as they did in the past. Now that mechanization has lightened the farm workload, both farmers and their wives often seek jobs in towns and, consequently, come to live urbanized life styles.

The weakened collective community has lost another of its

functions: education and assistance in the moulding of personality. The old-fashioned community played a major role in shaping the thoughts and emotions of younger generations by transmitting customs and manners that transcend reason. After obtaining intellectual and rational training in school, the rural child of the past learned from the collective community old-fashioned attitudes toward life, ways of dealing with human relations not imparted at school, and methods of conforming to the rhythms of nature. Modern society has lost this almost entirely.

As you point out, the cultivation of the authentic human personality requires a sense of unity with the rhythms of nature and the universe, and community bonds of the kind that cannot be fully explained rationally. These elements are essential to all human beings, no matter whether they live in the country or the city.

Believing that Buddhism can fill this need in terms of concepts, I consider essential the realization of a collective community, united by bonds at a profound level like those characteristic of a religion like Buddhism.

HUYGHE: The solution can be found only in a profound mutation in the interior life, a regeneration of the human being who has been separated by modern life from his natural state and normal functioning. Only a return to the interior life can increase the family unit's ability to resist. The human individual learns simultaneously how to strengthen and differentiate himself from contacts with close associates. By contrast, in artificial communities founded on nothing but abstract principles, the individual can only grow weaker.

In the case of living beings, imbalance cannot help becoming ceaselessly more evident; and death is always its end. Furthermore, in the natural course of things, a counter impulse always manifests itself. For instance, when in overemphasizing one of its aspects an individual or a collective throws human nature out of balance, it is the biological and psychological order of things for a balancing counteraction to occur. We must be on the lookout for the inception of such counteractions and must both point out the ossification of ideas standing in their way and propose other ideas that stimulate awareness of them.

Preserving the Continuity of Time

HUYGHE: First of all, we must battle the absurd, and as equally elementary as radical, principle requiring us to obliterate the past and all it can tell us. Aside from those episodic, inevitably ephemeral, ideas that each generation must revise, the past transmits to us the fruit of long, constantly enriched, human experience, maintained today by the family and the collective social body. In comparison with the reliable instincts of past experience, the abstract ideas hastily polished up by the reasoning machine are very lightweight. One can only wonder how our present age, hypnotized by the actual and utilitarian, can lose awareness of the heritage from the past. Our complaints about the evils of urban concentration ought to include sharp criticism of the progressive and unending elimination of our architectural patrimony—imbued with a sense of tradition, livability, and harmony—in the name of profitable, functional buildings.

IKEDA: The destruction of the architectural heritage is especially serious in Japan, where old buildings of historical value are often razed because they are outdated, functionally inconvenient, or economically unprofitable. By contrast, European cities like Paris and Rome seem to incorporate more historical architectural values in their urban life. Such architecture is extremely important for the spiritual depth it gives to cities and for the sense of stability it bestows on the human mind.

HUYGHE: Just as he finds himself situated in a certain place in space, so the human individual is located in a moment in the time through which his life journeys. The same is true, on an infinitely vaster scale, for the global life of all humanity. We ought to take our place in the time dimension just as we do in the spatial one. Duration of time exists only because it flows from something that has passed toward something that is to be; the present is an intermediate between the two.

This is why the notion of modernism, as we have already said, is one of those simplistic, pernicious abstractions that delight our epoch. This particular notion would have us think we belong only to the present moment and need do nothing but manifest its characteristics. To require this is to misunderstand the nature of time. We cannot separate ourselves with impunity from the past, which is the raison d'être of the present. To blockade ourselves up in the present is to reject the future, since it is impossible to submit only to present traits without interfering with the birth of what is to come. The grave danger inherent in this attitude is more obvious in cities than in the country, where nature keeps the farmer to the rhythmic flow of days and seasons.

Human beings must be aware of the continuity of time and of their manner of fitting into it. Understanding that activities of today differ from activities of the past is tantamount to understanding existence in a process of evolution. Tomorrow's events will be as fatefully different from today's as today's are from yesterday's.

Modernism can be neither defined nor determined, since it is and must be in perpetual mutation. Each generation has its own modernism, which is a negation of the preceding modernism. It is, consequently, more important to foresee the modernism of tomorrow than to lay claim to the modernism of the present, which is already senescent, if not moribund.

Preserving monuments and architectural ensembles inherited from the past gives the present a controlling sense of relativity and maintains a permanent confrontation among the generations. The future is born of this continuous dialectic.

After the great vogue of rural scenes in the nineteenth century, the West emerged from Romanticism with a respect for the historical monument. Logically, Japan should follow suit. Your nation has already, as you know, adopted and developed the idea of the museum.

IKEDA: Unfortunately, however, Japan is not pursuing the path this adoption might suggest. Not only are old buildings being torn down, but also the very traditional and meaning-laden place names of our towns and cities are being replaced with numerical or other insipid designations. The traditional wooden Japanese dwelling may be fairly short-lived in the humid climate of the archipelago. But today even houses sound enough to function for many years to come are torn down because repairs are too costly or because the buildings occupy too much land to be economically efficient. In very many cases, economic considerations result in the destruction of buildings in spite of their considerable historic value. Such was the fate of Frank Lloyd Wright's famous Imperial Hotel, which was important from the architectural-aesthetics stand-point and as a historical testament to the modernization and Westernization of Japan. It, too, was razed to make way for a modern high-rise hotel.

HUYGHE: I stayed at the Imperial Hotel on my first visit to Japan and remember being impressed by the way Wright had penetrated to the essence of traditional Japanese architecture without sacrificing any of his own modernism, which was in the avant-garde of his time.

IKEDA: In a world in which preeminence is afforded to economics, government policies are insufficient to deal with matters of this kind. For instance, in Japan, a building of histor-ical significance may be declared an official cultural property, but financial aid sufficient for its upkeep may not be forthcom-ing. Specification as a cultural property attracts increasing numbers of visitors with the occasional result that a heavy burden is imposed on the inhabitants of the building.

Economics is the prime object of attention of many Japanese, especially urbanites who are quick to see how much money they lose by persisting in living in spaciously generous, old-fashioned houses. To rectify the situation, they pull down the old and build multiple-dwelling apartment houses on space once occupied by single-family residences.

Efficiency, too, works to the detriment of old ways. The desire to lighten the labor load on city offices and post offices has inspired the changing of many of the familiar old local place names and the uniform restructuring of formerly complicated and intricately subdivided urban layouts. The new layouts are more convenient for use with computers, but the revisions make it impossible to identify the scenes of many works of literature or to follow the footsteps of the subjects of novels or biographies.

Perhaps most important of all, revised town plans destroy the familiarity and affection citizens once felt for old places. Replacing venerable place names with mere enumerations is like calling prisoners not by name, but by number.

HUYGHE: The same phenomena, engendered by the same causes, has led the French Postal Ministry to replace the old telephone-exchange names, which recalled the quarters of the city of Paris—like Éyseés, Invalides, and Odéon—with ternary groups of numbers. The sterile anonymity of the number is being imposed everywhere. We have only to wait until, one day, registration numbers replace family and given names.

IKEDA: Common to all these phenomena are the modern concern with nothing but profit and an underestimation of the past and its spiritual depth. The spiritual aridity of contemporary urban life is a constant source of stress for the urbanite. Nor is the urban characteristic unrelated to the large numbers and high frequency of crimes in our cities.

As you say, in addition to the present spatial setting, human beings live in a continuity of time flowing from the past to the present and on to the future. Both space and time are related to our bodies and our spirits; but it seems to me that, if space is related mainly to our physical aspects, time is connected mostly with our spiritual aspects.

The material supports of our physical lives come from the present world. But the supports of our spiritual lives come principally from the past. Although the various kinds of information made available by the present enrich our spiritual lives to a considerable extent, our true spiritual sustenance is information and intelligence reaching us after passing through the selection process of time.

The environment in which human beings are born and bred is all the more spiritually enriching and stabilizing for having been the place where other human beings—simple forebears or celebrities—once lived and worked. In hard times, great encouragement is to be had from realizing that many others have shared similar experiences in the same locality.

People are proud to live in the same town, to look at the same houses, and to walk the same streets as a great person from the past. This may be why in Europe, and especially in France, many streets are named after famous people. Though they exist, examples of this kind of thing are limited in Japan. Perhaps this is as it should be, since the Japanese have their own characteristics and do not need to copy the French in these matters. They should, however, prize connections with the past more enthusiastically than they do.

HUYGHE: More often than not an acknowledged principle instead of true understanding has been behind the respect for, or even the cult of, historical monuments established in the West since the eighteenth century. This has made it possible to venerate and care lovingly for, even at great cost, a celebrated cathedral and, at the same time to erect on the same courtyard a totally modern steel-and-glass edifice. Amiens is a case in point.

The historical monument must not be treated as an abstract, like something in a show window. It is a unit with an atmosphere of human life, an atmosphere capable of being evoked only in its proper natural environment. Each generation has the right and the duty to create anew but not in brutal clashes with contradictory tendencies from different epochs.

It is often said that people in the past ceaselessly combined elements from diverse eras. As evidence, it is possible to point to a medieval cathedral to which the eighteenth century had no compunctions about adding a choir in the baroque style. But this argument is specious, since none of these variations breaks the unity of either the baroque (to which, in the larger sense, as Heinrich Wöfflin (1864–1945) points out, the Gothic belongs) or the agrarian civilization.

But we have now entered the industrial civilization, and the agrarian civilization is no more. Consequently, the task is no longer to modulate phases lending themselves to combination. We are confronted by a violent contrast, a rupture separating our civilization from its predecessor.

The transition from one civilization to another has transformed the role of the architectural monument. In the agrarian civilization, sensibility and a sense of habitation nourished architecture. In the present industrial civilization, however, architecture is dominated by practical, abstract preoccupations. This is why in our time a functional art theory, called Functionalism, has been evolved and often taken to blind excesses. This, too, has become a kind of mental epidemic.

In places where once it was possible to follow variations within a continuity, our epoch substitutes conflicts of incompatible elements. And this is why it is always desirable for manifestations of the spirit of our time to occur in distinct ensembles, forming wholes in themselves, instead of making breaches in old regions and brutally dissipating their own atmosphere. This evident truth has, however, had a difficult time finding acceptance in our urban designs.

Nonetheless, little by little, the idea of an urban fabric deserving respect in its homogeneity is advancing, although only among the most advanced spirits. Other more limited people who, unfortunately, too often occupy positions of authority, have not yet come to understand and, under the pretext of modernism at all costs, daily do irreparable damage. A typical case is to be seen in Paris, where some misguided people obstinately insisted on destroying the Saint-Germain markets, the sole survivor of an old urban function, and substituting for their ancient stones the glass and steel of the Pompidou Center.

This is an example of a major characteristic of our age: the sin against harmony, both exterior harmony in connection with our environment, and interior harmony in relation to the equilibrium of our faculties. We wish to regulate everything according to principles, dogmatic definitions, and even recipes inspired by the laws of physics but inapplicable to the diverse and compensative richness of life. Our own interior jurisdiction perceives and tests harmony, which is not only a blossoming, but also perhaps self-protection for the individual. If and when appreciation of harmony, experienced in and by each individual, is eliminated, nothing will be left but rules stifling all possibility of humanity, which will finally have become mechanized and monstrous. It seems likely that, should this happen, humanity will have lost the capacity for diversity that defines the individuality of a person just as, on a larger scale, it defines the principle of everything living.

We will have to return to this topic. But we cannot discuss social problems without considering first national and political problems, with which social ones are closely connected.

2

Social Forms

HUYGHE: Modern man is confronted with many kinds of societies corresponding to the political options offered by contemporary history. Most of the kinds are, however, to different degrees—whether rightist or leftist—menaced by an administrative intoxication with regulation and by repression of individual initiative. Far from remedying it, these kinds of society seem ready to accentuate this fault, which is basic to our times. Do you agree that this constitutes a serious threat?

Complexity or Uniformity

IKEDA: The French seem to understand things of this kind instinctively. French thought is characterized by a tendency to regard human beings, and especially the individual, as the center of everything. French respect for art is famous throughout the world. Since art is the product of individual creativity, I regard respect for it and the tendency to center thought on the individual as intimately connected.

In totalitarian societies, art tends to be suppressed or regarded lightly as a means to totalitarian ends. I should be very interested in hearing your ideas on respect for the individual and the question of art.

HUYGHE: The interior life is always enriched by overcoming contradictions. Confronted with opposed elements, weak souls capitulate by adopting one of the two antagonistic viewpoints. By contrast, obstacles stimulate strong souls to seek to go on (this is the only way in which they make progress). They are enriched by the harmony they attempt to create between two disparate aspects of reality.

Perhaps it is in this way that France has made a contribution to the Western world. France is in a geographically and historically favorable location, on which have converged antinomic elements cast into the space destined to become Europe. First, the Loire River divides France roughly into northern and southern halves, which belong to two different civilizations.

Southern France belongs to the Mediterranean world, which represents the agrarian type of world par excellence. After initial impulses provided mostly by Egypt, this world came into being as a consequence of Greek and then Latin developments. It embodies a spiritual attitude dominated by peasant tastes for stability, lucidity, and rational generality. By contrast, the northern part of France was settled by waves of nomadic peoples from the great Euro-Asiatic plain. The founders of the Germanic, Scandinavian, and Anglo-Saxon worlds, these people settled in France as the Celts and Franks. The spirit they inherited is different from that prevalent in the south and is much more deeply penetrated by impulses from the life of the senses and much less profoundly rooted in the life of abstractions. Thus the French have, through their ethnic origins, received and combined two profoundly different mentalities.

This situation exists in no other European country. The great majority of Italy is Latin: Nordic and Arab invasions have done no more than affect its peripheral zones. Italy remains fundamentally Mediterranean. The Scandinavian lands, Germany, and England, on the other hand, depend more exclusively on the Nordic world. Confronted with a duality from the very beginning, France has been subject to the beneficent necessity of conciliating opposites.

Moreover, the gradual process whereby France evolved has further accentuated this fundamental diversity. For centuries, the monarchy strove to exercise unified control over extremely different provinces, each of which had its own propensities, traditions, and language. The need to assemble divergent elements compelled France to find a way out of the difficult situation facing Europe, and patient and fruitful effort made possible exceptional success. Instead of succumbing to contradictions leading finally to parcelling and diffusion, France was able to forge a large unit, from which has emerged spiritual wealth. The fanatic revival of separatism among, for instance, the Bretons and the Basques, is a mark of modern disarray.

In the complex ensemble that France has, by ability and duty, created, it is possible to discover both a masculine and a feminine side. Throughout the history of the nation, the masculine side had been represented by brilliance in arms, military preeminence, and rational thinking. This is the combative, the soldier aspect of France. The other aspect is represented by the priority women have been afforded in both society and the life of the emotions from the time of the Courts of Love of the thirteenth century to the salons of the eighteenth century, and including the digression represented by the so-called *Precieuses* of the early seventeenth century. In other words, France has made optimum use of, and has melded into a common spirit, contrary aptitudes and has played them in compensatory rhythm according to the needs of changing generations. France has combined these elements as two sloping surfaces combine to form one roof.

Another duality that France has always found itself prepared to overcome and employ is that between the individual and the group. No doubt, because France is subdivided and very rich in dialects and local cultures, the Frenchman cannot avoid being a separatist always disposed to affirm his own particularity. He is, by definition, an individualist.

At the time of his Gallic conquest, Julius Caesar noticed this national characteristic and the difficulty with which the Gaul was bent to follow a general rule. But the exact contrary was also evident. It may be because the Frenchman saw at an early stage the need to overcome this defect—which is at the same time an excellent attribute—that he created a cult of rationality and, at the time of the Revolution, went so far as to erect in Christian churches altars to the goddess *Raison*.

The rational approach despises sensitive and emotional characteristics. It strives to extricate general ideas convertible into laws from living complexity, and always wishes to establish a communality founded on universal principles. In this instance, too, the combination of resources and individual independence with the ever-present demands of an abstract, universalist way of thinking has enriched French culture. Instead of slicing human diversity and embodying one of its aspects, even perfection, French culture has welcomed everything and has been highly conciliatory. This is perhaps why it has assumed an extremely human form.

The French have still another resource called taste, that is, the sense of high quality that they have always spontaneously required. It is difficult for a Frenchman to say such a thing without running the risk of being criticized for nationalist conceit. Nonetheless, it is impossible to deny the many cases in which people defer to French taste, which is evident in the feminine fashion industry, where France has an assured global preeminence. The French are sufficiently aware of their faults to be able to afford themselves supremacy in this field. No doubt this is what accounts for the important role art always plays in French culture.

Notably in art and literature, France is less distinguished by exceptional geniuses and blossomings affirming racial particularities—like Shakespeare in England, Dante in Italy, Cervantes in Spain, and Göthe in Germany. Instead, France is more often represented by a multiplicity of artists of different tendencies. For instance, France is one of the rare countries that has been able to evolve an exemplary classicism, while at the same time experiencing entirely baroque phases. This duality exists practically simultaneously in the art of several epochs. For instance, French Gothic of the thirteenth century obeys the general norms of classicism, whereas the flamboyant Gothic of the fifteenth century is baroque in nature. In other words, the course of development of a style that itself did not survive for more than three centuries successively reveals both tendencies.

Incontestably, the seventeenth century is the triumph of French classicism. Nonetheless, various foreign scholars, stamped with their own national predispositions, unhesitatingly class that age in the baroque and justly discover in it baroque characteristics. In the eighteenth century, the summation of classicism in Louis XVI architecture by such men as Gabriel and de Soufflot can be juxtaposed with furnishings representing an almost frantic excess of the rococo. In the nineteenth century, too, France is divided between the neoclassic vein of such painters as David, his disciples, and Ingres and the romantic vein of painters like Delacroix and of composers like Berlioz.

IKEDA: The French way of allowing many different artists to share the scene instead of producing single epoch-dominating figures seems to be an important factor in solving the dilemma of whether art should exist for the sake of human beings or human beings for the sake of art.

When a single school of art exercises controlling sway over its age, populations are more likely to deify individuals, whose artistic or literary works are lauded as supreme. Under such circumstances, ordinary people feel grossly inferior and practically enslaved to art.

When diversity reigns, however, the supreme representative of one school can be the object of criticism and even ridicule on the part of adherents of another school. Although in themselves undesirable, even antagonistic clashes in the worlds of art and literature are preferable to deification of individual artistic figures.

The possibility of choosing among diverse approaches preserves and strengthens the human sense of the importance of the role of the individual. Although artists and writers must serve their muses, the rest of us are free of this duty. Consequently, it is for art to serve humanity and not for the general populace to serve art.

The attitude of the people either permits single schools of art to monopolize the field or prevents them from doing so. As long as the individuals in society protect their own self-awareness and make their own choices, the very diversity of human personalities and tastes will inevitably require corresponding diversity in art. It will be impossible for any one artistic view to dominate to the exclusion of all others.

The domination of the field of art or literature by single schools of artists indicates that individual human beings are not exercising their own choices but are following the opinions of others or public opinion in general. And this, in turn, suggests the loss of awareness of the central importance of the human role in such matters.

Certainly the production of superior art and literature is important to the glory and honor of peoples and nations. Nonetheless, I believe that such a role should be secondary to the service of individual human beings. Consequently, a society ought to ensure variety and diversity of possibility, permitting large numbers of people to give total and hopeful manifestation to their talents and personalities and thus to savor both the happiness and satisfaction of living under such circumstances.

HUYGHE: It is true that diversity, united with liberty, multiplies possibilities for creative work. This is why the French who, while eminently rational—sometimes to the point of enslavement to a doctrine, or an aesthetic, flattering their own intellectualism—have been open to all kinds of experiences. In this connection, inveterate French individualism counts for a great deal. But it is necessary to take into consideration the consequence of an innate French feeling for quality and devotion to taste.

The two things go together. The individual is distinguished by quality, and all the more so for being submitted to a common order. In France, rich artistic diversity and ample humanism arise, no doubt, from this dualism which is able to employ both the creative and unexpected (to the extent of being subversive) resources of the individual and the organizing, stabilizing resources of rational order.

IKEDA: What you have to say about French cultural characteristics is food for thought on the issue of creativity and the social framework. But the need to relax bonds and limit standardization for the sake of freer individual creativity can result in the danger of weakening and impairing the functioning of the collective social organization.

Thus, to enhance the power of that organization—and probably because of the violent conflict among national units throughout the past few centuries—modern states have tended to impose extreme standardization on their own internal diversity.

In the case of Japan, in the middle of the nineteenth century, pressures applied from without, by such nations as Russia and the United States, and from within, by the Meiji government, terminated more than two centuries of isolation and initiated a rapid program according to which the structure of the state was strengthened in the hope of catching up with the West. This program received further impetus from increasing contacts and competition with other nations and, as you know, ultimately led to the development of totalitarianism.

An emperor-centered governmental system, Shinto as the state religion, and Confucian morality were tools employed to reinforce Japanese totalitarianism. They were abandoned or allowed to ossify after the nation's defeat in World War II. But the fundamental desire for a strong national framework has never altered. Indeed, Japan's current success as an economic power can be said to have come about because that attitude remains alive and well.

In the Japan of today, expansion of the blessings of material wealth and development of transportation and communications organs, not raw power, restrict diversity, standardize living styles, and destroy traditional culture. The numerous regional dialects of the Japanese language persist now only in the speech of people of more than middle years. On even slightly formal occasions, young people invariably speak what is called standard Japanese. In the past, local color enlivened Japanese cities and towns. Now, however, at least in their business and shopping districts, they all look exactly alike. Regional costumes are to be seen mainly in television folk-music programs.

In my opinion, however, the age has passed when nations

were justified in suppressing internal diversity and sponsoring uniformity in the name of a strong social structure, which is useful in international competition. Such an approach belongs to the barbarity of military might. A truly creative society must prize both diversity and individuality.

Perhaps France cannot justly be called ideal in this connection. I fully realize that your country faces many problems. Nonetheless, I do think France is unique in the way in which it has remained a strong Western state while preserving the diversity of its various districts, prized individual creative abilities and, through creative culture, achieved much in, and made great contributions to, the modern world. This is why I believe that Japan, which is still unable to divest itself of totalitarian tendencies, has much to learn from France.

The cultural background of the Japanese people is diverse. Although numerous points about our origins remain unclear, undeniably the Japanese people have evolved as a result of the complex interweaving of Japanese native inhabitants with two basic stocks, one entering from the Asian continent to the north and another from the southern seas. Furthermore, although a unified national state was developed early, local regions have developed and maintained distinctive cultural traditions until relatively recent times. In terms of religion and philosophy, too, the Japanese tradition embraces not only the indigenous Shinto, but also Taoism, Confucianism, and Buddhism, all imported from China. Though on a limited scale, Christianity, too, has its place. Surely a background of this complexity should enable us to generate a rich culture in the future.

Totalitarian Societies

HUYGHE: Our digression on France and Japan is not superfluous because it allows us to understand better why totalitarian societies of either the right or the left constitute an immense danger from the human viewpoint. Totalitarian government— the adjective itself is sufficiently significant—arises exclusively, even furiously, from one direction only. Highly regulated and rationalized into a system, it controls and enslaves the individual and goes so far as to proclaim these actions. The rational expression of the collective law is deprived of its natural collective, which is the individual representing the variety inherent in biology and, especially, in psychology.

Rule by collective law, which is by definition immutable and indubitable, has the additional drawback of resulting in immobilization. The law of time, which carries us along with it and is the law of life, demands that all things evolve and transform themselves ceaselessly. Because they are implacably fixed in orthodoxy, totalitarian governments lead to desiccation that entraps, as would the stunted carapace of a crustacean. In the world of nature, if the carapace fails to grow, the living animal inside is stifled to the point where it degenerates and perishes. It is impossible to deny the law of life with impunity.

Oddly enough, public opinion is divided into two apparently radically opposed tendencies in this connection: the right, which in its extreme forms, leads to fascism and dictatorship, and the left, which passes over into Marxism. In spite of their differences, one can perceive at once that both agree when it comes to crushing the individual.

What can be the outcome of a left that, in the nineteenth century, fought passionately for human liberties, if it ends up on the dead-end street of negating its reason for existing?

IKEDA: This interesting point raises the question of the future of Marxism. I believe that, since it is fundamentally incapable of breaking with totalitarian methods of control, Marxism must inevitably be profoundly shaken by upsurges of a popular demand for freedom. Do you think it is possible to maintain a totalitarian system and guarantee popular freedom at the same time?

HUYGHE: You are correct in saying that Marxism poses the question of individual liberty. In the nineteenth century, it represented a new and promising position. At the time, human progress required a correction of the position of servitude of the weak (the poor) in relation to the powerful (the rich).

Although this relation had always existed in various forms, it deteriorated because of the rise of the bourgeoisie. Having come to a power founded on money, on the precedence of the rich, the bourgeoisie felt licensed to exploit the labor and output of the popular classes to generate money. Marx perceived, and wished to exorcise, this threat of capital.

He proved unable, however, to escape from the law which he himself had enunciated of social environment and education. He was of bourgeois stock. His thought had developed at the time when, at their apogee, bourgeois convictions enthroned a materialism entirely supported by the dazzling recent triumph of the physical sciences. At the time, nothing was as understandable as matter and nothing as valuable as its technical exploitation. Social reality could be expressed only in economic terms. With August Compte, philosophy became a new religion supplanting older ones.

Even though Marx dedicated himself to the generous spirit of socialism which he intended to apply to the happiness of the people, he was unable to free himself of the ideas governing his times and environment. He could not disengage himself from the materialist and economics-oriented vision that obsessed the bourgeoisie. His inability was such that, when borrowing Hegel's brilliant idea of the dialectic and the contradiction envisioned in it, contradiction that does not negate but motivates reconciliation of opposites, he stripped it of its original idealism and imposed dialectic materialism on it.

At the birth of his philosophy, Marx was still mentally fecund. His thought itself entered into the mold of current ideas and was all the more convincing to his contemporaries because it dressed itself out as "scientific," although it was based on notions that had ceased to be scientific.

Nonetheless since it presented itself in this light, thanks to the way in which it conformed to already accepted conceptions, his philosophy had an impact contributing to its prodigious future fortune. It awakened the proletariat and gave them ideological arms that both assured their rise and triumph in certain countries and stimulated the social progress that has since then become a preoccupation of great priority.

But things that were valuable and effective in Marx's day could not escape the law of time and became outmoded later on. Marxism should have been reworked and allowed to evolve. The dreadful thing, however, is that it has become a dogma with the rigidity and authority of the religions it fought against. And, following a destiny like theirs, it has isolated itself from its initial drive to become sclerosed and locked into rational constructions of the kind dogmatism erects. The overflowing, bubbling fountain has ended up a hot spring managed by politicians and confined in rigid canals. In defiance of wind and sea, in violation of the evolution of the world, codified Marxism wishes to defend "scientific" materialism at a time when both science and evolution question it. This is one of the most striking paradoxes in history.

To explain this strange fixation, it is important to remember that Marxism succeeded first in Russia, where established society, at the time among the most backward in Europe, was on the verge of collapse. Almost a medieval state, Russia passed without transition from the adoration of Byzantine icons to the worship of new ones. The nation became congealed in immobility because the authoritarianism of its new rulers followed patterns inherited from the autocracy of the tsars. Russia seemed to have believed that the movement carrying humanity toward freedom could be petrified in a manner resembling that in which saintly images are represented. The world today finds itself confronted by, and incapable of escaping from, this drama.

Ideas take a long time to take root and sometimes, when rooted, are already dead and outmoded. Today, the Marxism which a century ago was rejected by its contemporaries as too innovative and audacious, has become material for instruction by large numbers of university professors. As is often true in such instances, acceptance by the spirit of academe can be a sign that Marxism is already an established relic of the past. In an epoch that pretends to be modern—devoted to the avant-garde—is it not already time, after a century of use, to break from its most petrifying element?

Consideration must be given to some recent signs. For a number of years a certain ebullition—that of life refusing to allow itself to be dammed up—has been audible. Soviet youth is allowing its impatience to break out, as has been corroborated by the insurrection of the most liberal and courageous Soviet thinkers—including Solzhenitsyn and others who, when they have been able to escape repression, have been obliged to go into exile to express their independent views. We must note well, however, that these people do not reject a socialist or communist Soviet Union. They wish to defend the rights of life against doctrinal petrifaction reinforced by a repressive administrative system. Bureaucracy is always a means of immobilization put to the service of established, but arrested, ideas. The drama breaking the Soviet Union asunder at the present time is only a new phase of the eternal dialectic, in which Marx more than anyone believed and which leads to the awaking of immobilized, oppressed, and stifled forces reclaiming their natural play against adverse, self-satisfied, and rigid powers.

IKEDA: Your interesting comments about Russian Marxism as being the worship of new icons in place of old ones indicates what happens whenever new thoughts are introduced to a society. Unless people reflect profoundly on, and revise, past ideas, newly introduced philosophies inevitably must find places for themselves within preexisting structures of thought. This was the case when democracy was introduced into Japan after World War II ended .

As you say, new doctrines are long in taking root. In my opinion, democracy has still to take firm root in Japan. Furthermore, Marxism may not yet be truly well established in either the Soviet Union or China.

Resistance to inherited systems may take various forms. At first, only a limited segment of the population will take part in the struggle against an establishment. The power of the established system may seem to quench the revolutionary fire for a while, but the embers will continue to smoulder in the minds of the people and, sooner or later, will flare up again. If the elements of the movement are in accord with essential human needs and desires, the revolution will repeat itself over and over until, ultimately, it changes all of society. This is why I put my trust in the triumph of the better aspects of human nature and look hopefully toward the future.

Ordinary people are sensitive to changes occurring around them and are, in a sense, eager for renovation and change. Nonetheless, when a set of ideas is very far ahead of its times, ordinary people often seem conservative or even reactionary by comparison. But, when events bear out the truth of a line of thought, these same ordinary people can adopt an even more decisively reforming course than that advocated by philosophies that once seemed too advanced.

In such instances, leaders and intellectuals who, while proclaiming reforming ideas and slogans, act in the spirit of conservative systems and are most eager to preserve their own power find themselves unable to keep up with the revolutionizing zeal of the ordinary people. Rivalry then arises. Solzhenitsyn and the other critics you mention do not reject a communist Soviet Union, but represent resistance against an old-order, dogmatic ruling class on the part of people truly awakened to the fundamentals of the Marxist revolution. Though Solzhenitsyn is now compelled to live in exile, I feel certain that some day his thought will find acceptance in the Soviet Union.

HUYGHE: You underscore the singular situation Marxism finds itself in: doubly rigid first, because of being adopted as an iconology in an undeveloped Russia and, second, because of having been converted by intellectuals into a static system marked by nineteenth-century philosophy and incapable either of adapting to twentieth-century thought or of preparing a new philosophy for the twenty-first century.

A few years ago, a striking example of this incapacity to adapt to reality was evident in the scientific domain. Supported by state power, the Soviet agronomist Trofim D. Lysenko asserted an outdated, antigenetic scientific theory, which elsewhere had already given way before experimental scientific evidence. Nonetheless, Lysenko, who was president of the Soviet Academy of Sciences and enjoyed Stalin's support, imposed ideas so forcefully that his opponents were eliminated by repressive means.

In totalitarian countries, experience—the oxygen whereby science breathes—must give way to blind doctrine. In the case of Lysenko, everything demonstrates that hereditary factors genetically transmitted determine the basic facts of our personalities. But this runs counter to the dogma of the equality of all human beings and to that of determination exclusively by exterior social pressures. A double blasphemy! Where would the doctrinaire communist be if we admitted that some people are innately more gifted than others (although, undeniably, some are borne blond and some brunette or some are afflicted with congenital illnesses or infirmities and some are not)? Such an attitude represents the sin of elitism! Where would we be if we stopped affirming that the environment molds the man?

In spite of this, however, I had witness from French scholars and friends who, having attended conferences in the Soviet Union, admitted that many Soviet scholars were fully aware of the obsolete and paralyzing nature of the "official" Lysenko doctrine. They were willing to speak, secretly, in this fashion to foreign colleagues, but did not dare affirm their convictions in front of established legal authority.

But the pressure of the evidence has grown too strong. The dike had to give way and the Soviet Union has now abandoned Lysenko's biological theories.

In a parallel, but inverse, situation, the Nazis supported the incontestable action of genes for the sake of forming an equally monolithic and aberrant, though contradictory, doctrine of racism. To demonstrate the soundness of its foundations, Hitler had millions of human beings massacred. Thus, impervious to all evidence contradictory to their own principles, rational systems admit only partial truths and, because they refuse to integrate these truths into the living complexity of reality, are transformed into devastating errors and aberrations.

Let us not do the same. If assuming, in principle, that social and historic developments alone determine the nature of the human being runs contrary to all certainty, let us realize what weight this can have. Let us attempt to work it out, not to constrain human spirits, but to develop in human beings the awareness and application of responsible freedom.

It is by a similar historical paradox that, in doing battle against capitalism, Marxism unwittingly borrowed the same mold that suffocated its adversary, materialism. Marxism and capitalism thus now find themselves at the same impasse.

China

IKEDA: And what about China? Though both are Marxist nations, a clear line demarcates China and the Soviet Union. I believe that China is fated to play a large role in international society and world civilization. At present, however, the Chinese are not in a condition to assume that role. Do you see elements today permitting us to hope that China will be important for humanity in the future?

HUYGHE: At the present moment, it is difficult to say more than we have already said in the first part of our discussion. We have remarked that, with great clairvoyance, Mao Zedong was determined to spare his nation a brutal and radical passage from the agrarian to the industrial era. On all other points, however, even Mao was obedient to Marxism and conformed to its structure. At the head of one of the world's oldest agricultural civilizations, he obviously had difficulty maintaining certain fundamental realities which, with great lucidity, he always considered sound. Nonetheless, the size of the masses he directed inclined him to submit to collectivist directives and to crush the individual contemptuously.

Although the Chinese population has increased by half since the advent of Mao in 1949, it seems that serious famines have stopped and that sufficient food is now ensured.

Thus, very wisely, agriculture has not been sacrificed to industrial growth and efforts have been made to avoid massive concentrations of factories, and rural dispersion is observable.

Nonetheless, the urban proletariat is still in a favored position. The city worker's actual mean income is three times that of the peasant, who participates in the work of the agricultural commune and cultivates his own private patch of land as well. Experts claim that the average life expectancy of the Chinese will grow by from 12 to 16 years. The per-capita gross national product is evaluated at 4 percent of that of the United States, with a population reaching more than eight billion. We can only wonder what course Mao's successors will pursue.

IKEDA: I have a number of reasons for believing that China will play a vital role in the future of humanity. One of them is its unique history of thousands of years as a unified nation. Of course, dynasties have fallen, but the idea of unity has always persisted. And new dynasties have always restored unity.

In the inevitable future task of evolving a global unifying system, the experiences of the Chinese in governing a vast, multiracial nation are certain to be a valuable reference, especially since they have traditionally preferred to rule through righteousness rather than through military might.

Certainly military force has been used in China in attaining unity but, once unity has been achieved, government has generally been based on ideals of justice and on as equitable an enjoyment of the blessings of unification as possible. Each dynasty has stressed the compilation of histories in order to demonstrate its own legitimacy and to prove that it attained authority and maintained stability not through force, but through the manifestation of harmony based on ideals.

The invariable appearance of an irrepressible desire for unity during times of confusion following dynastic collapses represents a deeply ingrained tradition. The mere eruption of personal ambition would have been unlikely to enjoy sufficiently popular support to make nationwide unification possible. Furthermore, ambition can scarcely explain why unification has always followed, even though dynastic downfalls have been numerous.

A second important aspect of Chinese experience is the current interest and effort the government is devoting, in spite of the worldwide tendency to identify modernization with industrialization, to supporting the agricultural tradition while stimulating industrial development. In this I sense a similarity between the French and the Chinese approaches. I am convinced that harmonious coexistence between industry and agriculture—in other words between humanity and nature—is an issue of maximum importance to the survival of our race. Although at the present time it is impossible to assess the success the Chinese may have in this connection, I deeply respect the way they have avoided the trap into which many industrialized nations have fallen, of sacrificing agriculture to industry and have striven for harmonious coexistence between the two.

Although, as these comments show, I believe China can be a model to mankind in fields like government, economics, and industry, as far as the dignity and freedom of the individual are concerned, we must seek patterns in Europe, especially in France, and not among the Chinese.

HUYGHE: The important question of Sino-Soviet relations remains. China is too competitive with the Soviets not to be on the lookout for Soviet weak points and is too traditionally practical not to prefer adapting to circumstances rather than being blindly doctrinaire. These are China's trump cards in the rivalry. But even if more fragile because of its intellectual rigidity, the Soviet Union has considerable advantages in material forces. These brother-enemies keep a sharp eye on one another.

Certainly the Soviet Union would like to benefit from her current advantage but fears that, if she enters an armed conflict, the capitalist nations will outflank her. The Soviet Union is, therefore, tempted to deal with Europe first, and it is not impossible that preparations to this end are steadily going ahead. At the same time, the Soviet Union is restrained by the fear that China would seize the occasion offered by a Western engagement to attack from the east. What will be the deciding factor? The Soviet Union's future and ours depend on this and the day of reckoning may not be as far away as many people reassure themselves by imagining.

It is insufficient to leave everything up to the profound propensities—which I call regulatory—that will play a part in fashioning the future. In our forecasts, we must take into account issues that might distort the anticipated course of events and that depend on politics and the calculations and decisions of men of state, who are much more concerned with the immediate interests of their own nations than with the great problems of humanity.

The most brutal of those events is war, always written like a filigree in our future. Whether war will occur probably depends on the options taken by the Soviet Union or, more precisely, by the parties and groups that come to power at the hour of decision following Leonid Brezhnev's death. Should the Soviets strike Europe in order to free their hands to deal with the contentious Chinese, or should they strike China before their oriental neighbor can organize her growing powers?

The disquieting passivity of the United States—an important piece on the chessboard of the the Soviet Union—which has, we must remember, produced inveterate chess champions— will play a major role at the decisive moment.

IKEDA: During my numerous trips to the Soviet Union and China I have met with leaders and, of course, with young people and ordinary citizens who were no doubt hand-picked for the occasion. This aside, however, I felt that the people are happy at least with the material welfare and relief from the former regime that the Marxist revolution has brought. Both Chinese and Soviet Marxists are to be praised for having relieved their peoples from the suffering of poverty.

Nonetheless, both governments suppress creative work in the fields of philosophy, scholarship and art and impose especially stringent restrictions on expression of thought and on public assembly. Authoritarian control of this kind is on the increase even among free nations and is perhaps necessary to save the wretched from the excessive competition laissez-faire principles generate between capital and labor and among ordinary citizens.

The liberal approach limits authoritarian control to the correction of errors. Marxism, however, thoroughly controls material production, labor, and all other aspects of society. This is why Marxist political policies cannot help employing totalitarian methods. But a Marxist government is certain to be shaken to its roots when the majority of the people it controls, although satisfied with the material aspects of their lives, come to dislike regulatory systems and demand spiritual liberty. As you point out, Marxism would deserve high historical appraisal if it were to cease being dogmatic, conform to the changing times, and create governments that satisfy peoples' needs. Though it seems to differ drastically from the kind of doctrinaire Marxism evident today, such a system would probably closely approach the ideal Marx himself had in mind.

A Liberal Society

IKEDA: What is your forecast for the future of liberal societies? In various countries today regulatory measures are being taken to establish order and protect the weak from the jungle-like confusion that results from the free competition on which liberalism rests. What is most important in ensuring order without infringing on human liberties within a liberal society?

HUYGHE: Probably the inevitable and always complimentary rhythm of life will lead us beyond the stage and the impasse of authoritarian societies to return to a liberal society. We must not expect this to be merely a return to the preceding kind of liberal—that is, capitalist—society, the deficiencies and excess of which authoritarian societies have, in their time, attempted to correct. The flaw of the capitalist liberal society is, as you have rightly indicated, that it leaves the field open to the talented and to constraints imposed by the powerful who, with the support of money, are licensed to devour the weak. Thus, paradoxically, it is the producer of work who is exploited and reduced to barely sufficient ration. It must be realized, however, that such things are now forbidden and that the inadmissible abuses of the nineteenth century have been eliminated, in principle, by social laws imposed progressively since the beginning of that same century.

Societies that are free to develop as they like tend to pass from one abuse to another compensatory abuse, and are sometimes compelled by their own "socialist" conversions to prize formerly despised manual labor to the detriment of management and the liberal professions. This leads to still another excess witnessing to the same materialism that has passed from the bourgeoisie to its adversaries.

We are witnessing an aggressive reversal of opinion against the employer, who, having imposed his yoke too rigorously since the triumph of the bourgeoisie, has now been made the culpable scapegoat of society. Responsible for enterprise and performing a difficult task, the employer is as indispensable as a ship's captain. Of course, the ship's boilers will not function without stokers, but good navigation demands a captain on the poop.

Perhaps this indicates the weak point of contemporary liberal societies: they permit the strong—that is, the capable—a bigger portion than is actually his due. An intermediary, the double of the speculator, has stepped in between the laborer, who actually produces, and the employer responsible for management has arrogated to himself a share of the profit that is always growing and always out of proportion to his own usefulness. Too often this intermediary recalls the medieval manor lord who, owing to his own fortification along the highway, imposed abusive passage tariffs. Certainly, with the multiplicity of taxes it levies authoritatively at all stages, the state sets the example. The flaw in liberal societies is the opportunities they provide skillful exploiters to take the lion's share, which, in Marxist nations, goes to politicians.

The working people—that is, the creating element—including all echelons, from laborers to planners, and directors no longer enjoy the major benefits derived from the products they turn out. The speculator drains them off himself and, all too

often, fraudulently escapes the increasing and crushing imposi-
tions society has established on income. As a result, the effective, controlled laborer is penalized and hit hardest; and people
who contribute least and take most from society occupy the
most-favored position.

Although evidently socialist measures are required to correct
liberal society, it must be realized that socialism as it exists
today has succumbed to the vices characteristic of our times.
Too often it serves as an instrument of rationalized and excessively dogmatic organization opposing abstract ideas to living
realities. Fundamentally, it has undergone a course of evolution
analogous to the one undergone by religions. Socialism has
replaced the now lost generous initial force of its creator spirit
with the kind of thing that destroys churches. It has immobilized itself in abstract doctrine and the ritual of the administrative regulations it conjectures for society. It no longer sees
anything but economic profit which, however, it distributes
according to the demands of the state.

All social solutions are compromised if they fail to assure
improvement for both the spiritual and the material aspects of
humanity.

3

A New Kind of Society

IKEDA: I, too, regret that both socialist and capitalist societies have fallen into materialistic ways and, therefore, run the danger of suppressing elements that are essential and basic to humanity. Which of these two social forms will be first to realize and correct its own mistakes, thus finding a way out of the current impasse? Or will the emergence of a third kind of society prove essential? If so, where will such a society originate?

HUYGHE: One of the most discouraging facts of our time is the lack of a truly fruitful opposition between the two confronting factions of capitalism and Marxism, which actually represent competition on a common basis of materialism. Since materialism is the profoundest fault of our civilization, it is impossible to expect a solution from two social forms that, although in different and opposed ways, reflect and consolidate the same utilitarian position.

The gravest problem of our era is the fundamental lack of a truly revolutionary force in the sense of a rolling back from a general acceptance of the positivistic approach imposed by the nineteenth century. The difference between the two social forms consists solely in determining who shall be the beneficiaries of technical exploitation of actualities. How can we put hopes of regeneration or a way out of the dilemma in either capitalist or Marxist societies when both presuppose the preservation of a concept that is the cause of both our present crisis and the suffocation it brings about?

Where can we look for a possibility of regeneration? The pieces are not on the chessboard of present politics. Nonetheless, it must be admitted that a liberal society offers more hope than any other since authoritarian systems—fascist, communist, or any other form of Marxism— posit the principle of imposing themselves by constraint or force. It is relatively unimportant that the options are contradictory, as long as they refuse to countenance anything but total, unreserved obedience and threaten to annihilate everything that might be an obstacle.

Only a liberal society permits a free play of individual initiatives. Obviously, awareness of the major faults of an epoch cannot be, at first, collective but must arise from the most lucid and advanced spirits of the time. Such awareness must result from individual, more or less isolated cases, which generate aggregations only after having attracted a following. A liberal society, through its principles of initiative and permissiveness, is the sole kind that permits the implementation of ideas contradicting accepted notions and indicting failings.

In short, our one hope is the emergence of a third, indispensable force, the program of which will be not division of wealth gained from material exploitation, but orientation of humanity in another, complementary direction, and thus stimulating the reemergence of such dormant and stifled aspects of humanity as conscience and spiritual appetite, both of which fiercely reject materialism.

In the past, such movements have emerged only with the support of religions. Apparently, in world history, religions have been given the task—the mission—of recalling humanity to spiritual truth and awakening spiritual orientation. Consequently, I consider very important work for the sake of such an enlightenment on the part, for instance, of Buddhism, which maintains its religious foundation. Something similar might be expected from other religions.

Unfortunately, it must be realized that a whole militant wing of the Catholic Church—as was once the case in the Protestant

Church—seems willing to curry favor with the public by making overtures toward materialist doctrines like those of Marxism. In wishing to conform to and following the so-called modern spirit, the Church intends to modernize. Actually, however, in adapting in this way, the Church shuts the doors on a future that looks to religion for salvational openings. The misunderstanding is tragic.

The Role of the Sacred

HUYGHE: In other epochs, no doubt, a regeneration of the kind required now to pull man from the morass in which he is mired possibly more deeply than ever before would have been evoked by the appearance of a new religion. But the reign of the positivist mentality is so absolute in our time that it seems virtually impossible for a religion to penetrate this opaque obstacle in order to come into being. Still, this is an enigma of the future, and no one can predict what lies ahead.

I consider the name of the French Nichiren Shoshu newspaper—*Troisième Civilisation* (Third civilization)—excellent and pertinent. With you I believe that, to win the masses and restore to them a calling to the spiritual life, we must strive to bring into being a third civilization, which must be religious in nature. Even the nonbeliever André Malraux has condensed the situation in a striking phrase: the twenty-first century will be religious or it will not be at all.

IKEDA: You mention the way in which, as time passes, philosophies and religions tend to lose the vigor and intensity they demonstrate during the lifetimes of their creators and founders. Foreseeing the likelihood of such a fate for itself, Buddhist philosophy deals with this problem in a perspicacious fashion that offers caution to people in future times.

The teachings of Shakyamuni, like those of the many other Buddhas who are said to have existed before he came into this world, must pass through three phases after the founder's death. These phases are called *Shobo* (the Former Day of the

Law), *Zobo* (the Middle Day of the Law), and *Mappo* (the Latter Day of the Law).

During the Former Day of the Law, the Buddha's doctrines are vibrant and alive. The people to whom they are taught accept and practice them in their essential truth and pass them on to others. During the Middle Day of the Law, however, external forms are imitated, abstract teachings are put in good order, splendid temples are built, and solemn ceremonies are conducted. But the true spirit of the teachings is in the process of being lost. In the Latter Day of the Law, the spirit of the teachings has been lost entirely; and only its ruins remain.

More than a theory of the stages of transition in the history of Buddhism, this extremely interesting analysis is applicable to all religions and philosophies. The establishment tends to react with stern repression against religions and philosophies in the early stages of their revelation, when the founders are still alive and when the teachings themselves, handed on by disciples, still have not reached a wide audience. The severity of the repression increases the more revolutionary the ideas expressed in the new religion or philosophy. Followers must accept this as their lot.

The motives of people who brave such circumstances to serve a religion are pure and totally free from the desire of gain, power, or fame. In other words, in their minds, the teachings are just as vibrant and active as they were in the mind of the founder. This is the nature of the Former Day of the Law. In their early stages, faith of the pure-minded was the mainstay of Christianity and Islam as well as of Buddhism.

The situation changes when the religion or philosophy triumphs over virtually entire societies. In the hope of obtaining blessings and grace, people of authority and wealth vie with each other in making rich donations of fine chapels or temples, land, and other property. This in turn creates the need for an ecclesiastical organization to manage both property and believers. Ultimately, the ecclesiastical hierarchy becomes entangled in worldly fame and wealth.

The desire for social fame and material possessions adulterates original faith and discipline. As a consequence of human weakness, these secular desires gradually get the upper hand and, although its external trappings increase in splendor, the religion runs an increasing danger of losing its original spiritual basis. This is the meaning of the Middle Day of the Law. Once the process has run full course and the spiritual content of the religion has been totally lost, the Latter Day of the Law will have begun.

In the case of Shakyamuni's teachings, the Former Day of the Law and the Middle Day of the Law lasted a thousand years each before the Latter Day of the Law began, according to Japanese reckoning, in 1056 of the Christian Era.

Buddhism explains these periods not as indications of the declining efficacy of Shakyamuni's teachings, but as a warning against changing attitudes and objective conditions on the part of those who hear the teachings. The Buddhist believer who preserves original purity of faith can maintain lofty ideals without being perplexed by exposure to desire for wealth and fame. A ceaseless process of self-revolution and renovation is absolutely necessary to preserve human beings from degradation and to help them maintain a noble spirit.

Since it establishes independence and tolerance on the basis of profound human truth, I am convinced that Buddhism contains elements that can be the source of a way out of the present world crisis. By *independence* I mean the ability to resist being controlled by instincts and impulses and therefore the power to withstand materialism. This is done, not by fleeing from or destroying the physical life, which is subject to instincts and impulses, but through greater spiritual strength. By *tolerance* I mean respect for the right to live of all other humans and nonhuman beings, reverence for their spiritual values, and willingness to assist all of them. This is the meaning of the Buddhist term *compassion.*

Profound enlightenment to one's own inner truth is the way to maintain balance and further amplify two important forces: the centripetal force of independence or self-determination, and the centrifugal force directed outward toward others. Such is the core of Buddhist teachings and discipline.

A Buddha is one who is enlightened to wisdom (*bodhi*),

which means awareness of the fundamental universal truth permeating all living beings and all other phenomena. Buddhism does not attempt to deny or flee from materialistic reality. Instead, it strives to awaken human beings to the inner spiritual truth that guides reality. This is why I believe it can become the source of the strength required to create a brighter future for human society.

The Human Revolution

HUYGHE: We have now returned to the fundamental problem, the issue that preoccupies us above all others. The present crisis demands that, in order to reestablish our equilibrium, humanity—both proletarian and capitalist—turn away from exclusively materialistic aims. Objectivity requires us to say that, owing to the deterioration I have just denounced, socialism in all its forms is in grave danger: far from having elicited a reevaluation of the people, it is about to transform them into a new petite-bourgeoisie. The farther the people deviate from their origins, the greater their loss of profound qualities. Rural humanity is a blend of living, authentic forces that must be preserved. Proletarian humanity progressively deviates from these forces.

Moving, as people today do, solely in the direction of concrete, material aims and assuming that mere comfort and a taste for it constitute progress, human beings impose upon themselves the same way of thinking that ruined the bourgeoisie. Contrary to Marx's prediction, the bourgeoisie is feeding itself continually on its own base and is absorbing new strata as it teaches its own positivist and utilitarian way of thinking. Any observer who refuses to be duped understands that the class struggle is transforming itself into an internal rivalry between a new bourgeoisie, eager to gain terrain, and an old bourgeoisie wishing to hold on to already acquired ground. I do not consider this an enviable goal.

We must hope—as is no doubt consonant with your preoccupations and spiritual ambitions—for the creation of a liberal society based on a profound spiritual transformation. Humanity must be reeducated and turned away from obsession with the concrete. A spiritual source conjoined with a creative source must be reestablished in the human mind. As we have already said, far from favoring the necessary awakening—or reawakening—the diffusion of stereotyped information media develops an increasing mental passivity and standardizes ways of thinking. The conditions of life and those of information and culture unite to extinguish self-effort and striving oriented to outside goals. Reduced to the commercial level (to increase the value of the publicity they carry), owing to their base ambitions, television networks contribute greatly to this deterioration.

We must simultaneously develop the willpower for self-constraint that makes our energy efficacious and deflect our energy from appetites and petty satisfactions fed by elementary pleasures and comforts.

Energy, the principle of life, must be kept on course. It must not be allowed to lose itself in the swamps of material greed as a river is swallowed up by sand. Applied to discipline and self-control, energy can be oriented toward its true ends. I cannot say too often—and shall say again—that the great current of energy traversing all Creation asserts itself in rising from the initial sleep of matter and in acceding to the direction progressively stamped on it by conscience until the spirit, its summit and guiding point, reveals its true finality, opening itself up to the search for high quality and, thus, helps human beings conquer themselves through constant improvement.

I believe that I agree entirely with your concept of a human revolution, which I envisage as moving in the same direction and based on the same foundations as you do.

IKEDA: I consider the human revolution indispensable to overcoming the current crisis as well as an essential theme imposed on us as human beings. Among all animals, only the human being is capable of carrying out such a project. Indeed, I consider coming to grips with the human revolution, for the sake of raising the self to a loftier level, proof of humanity.

The term *human revolution* seems to have been coined by

Professor Shigeru Nambara, president of the University of Tokyo, shortly after the end of World War II because, in those times, he realized that, more than changes in exterior political systems, the people of Japan required the adaptability and support that self-revolution could provide. At about the same time, my mentor Josei Toda, second president of Soka Gakkai, employed those words in his explanations of the practice of Buddhist teachings.

Before World War II, Toda had seen his duty in his work as a man of business. Later, when the militarists gained power, both Toda and Tsunesaburo Makiguchi, the first president of Soka Gakkai and Toda's revered mentor and fellow believer in the Buddhist teachings of Nichiren Daishonin, were imprisoned by the government. Through his experiences in prison, however, Toda came to understand the great power of Buddhism and the profundity of its truth and resolved that spreading its teachings would be his life mission.

Taking his awakening to his own mission as one example, Toda employed Alexandre Dumas's *Le comte de Monte Cristo* as an illustration of the meaning of the human revolution. In the novel, a pure young man named Edmund Dantes is wrongly imprisoned for a crime he has not committed. His life is revolutionized but in the wrong direction, since his sufferings convert him into the demon of revenge called the Count of Monte Cristo. Toda's own revolution converted him from a man of business affairs to a man of religious faith and a missionary whose fundamental belief was in the spirit of Buddhism. He insisted that Buddhism makes possible, and even requires of everyone, the same kind of revolution that he underwent for the sake of manifesting a nobler self.

Buddhist teachings divide the conditions of life according to its goals and posit ten different states or conditions, into which I shall go into detail later (these are the Ten States and the Six Ways). Suffice it to say here that the states are of two kinds: those arising from self-oriented living, that is life for the sake of one's own well-being and happiness; and altruistic life, that is life for the sake of the well-being and happiness of other human and nonhuman creatures. In Toda's case, the human revolution led from the relatively self-oriented way of life of a businessman to the altruistic way of life of a man of faith devoted to spreading the Buddhist teachings.

Obviously, Buddhist missionary work is not the only way a person can lead an altruistic life. Any work can be done in such a way as to extend beyond one's self and immediate family to render service to others. Work undertaken with such an understanding is a source of deep happiness and great strength of will.

I have written a novelized history of Soka Gakkai from the standpoint of an organization of people awakened by President Toda's call and forming a great current for the sake of the human revolution. I believe that people in all realms and all walks of life must strive to carry out their own human revolutions, since this is the only way to bring about a transition from selfishness and obsession with one's own instinctive desires and emotions to altruism and, thus, to eliminate the causes of the suffering of our time.

More than this, however, the human revolution is the way to find a true reason for the existence of humanity.

HUYGHE: But before humanity can undertake this self-reformation, this interior correction, whose principles and modalities we have yet to study, society must ensure peace. Our tour of the horizon has given us a glimpse of the threats of war, not only between capitalist and Marxist societies, but also between such Marxist societies as those of the Soviet Union and China.

Peace

IKEDA: What do you consider most essential to the realization of lasting world peace? Do you consider eternal peace possible? Of course, this question involves political and structural elements, but I should be especially interested to hear your views on it in connection with spiritual aspects.

HUYGHE: Obviously I believe we can and must strive for the establishment of world peace. At the same time, however, I entertain a fairly profound skepticism about the possibility of maintaining it permanently. Actually, realizing global peace means that humanity must assume a higher position in the scale of beings and that the distance separating human beings from animality must be less abbreviated.

If I am not mistaken, the Austrian zoologist Konrad Lorenz quite accurately terms one element shared by human beings and nonhuman animals as aggression. Of course, he uses the word in the widest possible sense and it is this very amplitude that leaves room for hope. Ultimately, in human beings and other animals, aggression is the propulsive force stimulating the extension and affirmation of the self in relation to others and sometimes in relation to the world of nature. The notion of trying to eliminate this essential motivation is unthinkable. As psychoanalysis teaches, however, it is possible to sublimate it: aggression can become simple ambition or may be transformed into a desire to emulate. In short, the important thing is to try to defuse the destructive potential of aggression by altering its orientations.

In modern life, sports are an excellent example of this kind of transportation. The aspect of sports that attracts the public is the possibility of dissipating physical tension by watching one's own team overcome its opponents. Sports contests ought to be encouraged as catharsis, to borrow Aristotle's term, and as a way of discharging aggression.

In addition, sublimation is possible in the direction of creative activity. The projection of the self into a creative work arising from the self and intended to be shown to others is an expansion of aggression in the large sense in which Konrad Lorenz employs the word. Development of art, literary creativity, and wholesome competition among philosophers can supply outlets for fundamental aggression, which, in human beings, must assume forms infinitely more highly evolved than is the case among nonhuman animals.

We must remember that, since the advent of life, tension between opposites has governed practically everything. Humanity is endowed with one pole, aggression. It is also endowed with the compensating pole of love, which is as innate as aggression, although it manifests itself in precisely the inverse fashion. The double action of these two poles was seminally present at the time of the appearance of the living cell and its pulsating functions of rejection and attraction. Anything that can be done to reverse current trends and deflect humanity from purely material greed and its pragmatic satisfaction in order to develop the interior human life and stimulate its fulfillment favors the faculty of love (the application of which is not apparent in the technological domain). The program for the sake of peace must, therefore, be included in a general program for human evolution oriented toward inner growth.

The society of the past offered a graduated series of groups conducive to the development of a feeling of human solidarity. You have mentioned the family as a nucleus favorable to the development of love. Beyond the family were immediate friends, the circle of relations, neighbors, and then the locality and the city, which was still on a human scale. Next came the province and, finally, the national state. Even though it might prove necessary to expand this series of successive, inclusive orbs, each must be permitted to preserve its own way of life and not to lapse into abstraction imprisoned within the autonomy of concepts. Should they become only categories, they cease complementing each other, clash, and espouse the intransigence of discussion of ideas. Far from facilitating a connection and progressive movement to a more comprehensive collective, categories cut reality piecemeal and suppress the nuances characteristic of emotional life. They have the aridity of logical definitions.

Our civilization prefers groupings based exclusively on such categories. The "social classes," an idea invented in the nineteenth century, offer a striking example of my meaning. Having been elevated to the rank of absolutes and having become obsessive, the social classes offer nothing but a principle of antagonism and combat. Political parties are another example of categories based on abstract doctrines admitting nothing but confrontation.

In religions, the past has known analogous phenomena. But, as religion in general has fallen into an eclipse in the modern world, conflicts among religions are on their way to extinction. The mood of appeasement among them is indicated by the ecumenical movement. Similarly, it is possible to argue that the entity of the nation is in the course of passing away. But alas, supernations in the role of trusts in economic life, add to localized conflicts (which have died out only in a Europe which is already exhausted by wars) the threat of gigantic clashes that could engulf the rest of the world.

Nonetheless, modern life has two unprecedented elements that tend to create an international awareness. One is the increased number of people who travel and the other the immeasurable growth of information now reaching the majority of people, especially in the form of television with its evocative images. Although modern technology seems to have nothing but polluting and degrading effects, used well it can strengthen awareness of the human community.

As has already become a commonplace, the terrible danger represented by the increased destructive power with which science has endowed weapons has actually had a beneficial counter effect. Since the development of the atomic bomb, the menace has become so fearsome that leaders in positions of responsibility are terrified to provoke an unleashing of the fury of the weapons at their disposal. This is no longer an abstract notion, but a working force, the neutralizing effect of which we have already observed on several occasions. This effectiveness will, no doubt, persist until the day when another fool like Hitler emerges.

Ultimately, everything depends on human nature which, as we know only too well, regresses more than it improves. Our final recourse must be to think of and work on human nature. Once again, we confront the truth that tomorrow's task must be to exert ourselves in connection with human nature and the restoration of its inner fullness.

It is necessary here once again to emphasize the regenerating effect art has on sensibility. Art can support the power of love, which is the sole salvation for humanity and the continuous exercise of which art itself implies. If the artist's work represents the completion of an act of love, transport, and giving, the spectator who acquires and attempts to find access to that work of art can communicate with it only by means of an act analogous to love. This is because such an act must be founded in understanding and fusion.

I return to the importance of giving the greatest possible place in education to the awakening and application of the sensitive activities inherent in literature, poetry, and art. Each of us is endowed with the faculty of love, which naturally provides equilibrium by counterbalancing aggression. As always, nature furnishes the riposte to its own dangers. Our epoch has discovered the immense role played by antibodies in physiology. Psychology too is gifted with analogous resources.

Art and Love

HUYGHE: I should like to add that art seems to me to play an especially large role because, while the linguistic differences inherent in literature underscore the isolation of nationalities, art, which manipulates primarily images and sensations, is available without translation to all human beings. For this reason, it demonstrates the communality of humanity and does away with the differences that human beings set up as a result of the categories within which they enclose themselves.

I realize that politicians frequently incorporate this theme in the perorations they deliver at inaugurations of international expositions but, so far as I know, they rarely go as far as to put their words into practice.

We must not neglect to observe that religion has been a great motivating force in the name of communality among peoples, by offering a new outlet for the spirit of aggression. My statement is, of course, subject to the condition that, in order to serve this role, religion must not limit itself to the ritualized category of a given church and must not allow itself to become the source of struggles—often bloody—with other churches. It is only fair to say that Buddhism has escaped this danger because it is essentially based on progress in the inner life and the development of the love implied in it. At the very beginning, Christianity gave love a position of first preeminence. But it allowed itself to be invaded by ritualism and theological doctrines from which have resulted sometimes atrocious discords.

One of the novelties of the modern world is to have stifled the religious sense. As a consequence of its unavoidable materialism, our age has turned humanity away from religion. To see this, it is only necessary to refer to Marx and the pages he wrote on the need to eliminate religion. Marx's antagonism is all the more deplorable because it comes from a man who deeply cared about human generosity and remedies for social imperfections and cruelties. In addition, it shows how heavily the materialistic society born in the nineteenth century weighed on the spirits even of people who revolted against it. The twentieth century has only aggravated the imbalance.

IKEDA: In relation to the things necessary to achieve peace, you have concisely explained many of the thoughts that I entertain. I certainly agree that enriching the inner human life is of the greatest importance and that we must strive to strengthen the power of love as a counterbalance to aggression. I suspect what you call love is what I mean by respect for the dignity of life and concern for the well-being of all living things.

This is the sense in which Buddhism lays the greatest stress on love. As an illustration of this emphasis, one of the stories about his former lives relates how, as part of his own self-discipline, Shakyamuni once gave his body as food to a starving tigress incapable of feeding her young. The famous Indian King Ashoka, who reigned from 268 B.C. until 232 B.C., strove to carry on the Buddha's teachings by instituting hospitals for the care of wounded animals. The Japanese empress Komyo, a devout Buddhist, is said to have established a hospital for sufferers of leprosy and to have washed the bodies of lepers with her own hands. Nor were these people abnormally fond only of certain special categories like animals and lepers and negligent of ordinary, healthy human beings. They were attempting to apply the Buddhist spirit of universal caring that extends to all living creatures.

But maintaining balance between ceaselessly destructive aggression and the force of love that respects and seeks to protect life is not enough: love must be given preeminence. And this must be done on the widest possible scale. The fiercest murderer gives preeminence to love when he himself or those close to him are in question. Fundamentally, such a murderer is in no way different from national leaders who, while affording first concern to the interests of their own people, unhesitatingly take up arms in belligerence against other races or nations.

Furthermore, people who, while regarding human associates with love and care, experience no conscience pangs at killing nonhuman life forms are dangerous. This is true because sometimes one race regards other races as subhuman, as Hitler did non-Aryans in general and Jews in particular.

Giving precedence to love over aggression in relations with all forms of life removes the danger of such a mistake.

Human nutritional needs require sacrificing other beings for the maintenance of life. Nonetheless, if love is given precedence at all times, meaningless killing can be avoided; and we will feel profoundly grateful for lives that must be sacrificed for our food. Moreover, realizing the precious price that must be made for our sustenance, we will strive to live so as to be worthy of the sacrifice.

I do not insist that becoming a Buddhist is the only way to practice the spirit of universal love. I do believe, however, that no one who fully understand the law of life as taught by Buddhism can fail to be awakened to the spirit of love.

Buddhist doctrine teaches that our lives extend from the world of the past to the world of the present and then continue into the world of the future. In all three of those worlds we are constantly creating good karma and bad karma that determine our conditions. Owing to karmic causation, an individual may be reborn in the future in a nonhuman state. Perhaps a life that is human now was nonhuman in some preceding existence. The ultimate meaning of this doctrine is that there is no difference and no barrier between human and nonhuman life forms.

Giving in to aggressive desires and senselessly harming and killing nonhuman life forms produce the kind of bad karma that causes a being that is human now to be reborn in a more constrained and limited form in a later existence. It only stands to reason, then, that a human being who is truly concerned about himself will not run the risk of such a thing by despising and injuring nonhuman life forms, but will strive to accumulate good karma by affording all life forms a maximum degree of care, protection, and assistance.

Obviously, it is all the more important to avoid injuring and killing other human beings. War must be shunned because it causes both immense loss of life and happiness and the destruction of civilization's achievements and because it impoverishes inner human life.

HUYGHE: No matter from which angle we approach the problems of the world today, we always return to the central theme: rehabilitating and harmonizing the inner life.

IKEDA: That is true. There can be no doubt that the fundamental evil of our times is the shrinking of the subjective as the objective increases and the undervaluing of quality as quantity is overvalued. The source of the problem is to be found in the way human beings have neglected to revolutionize themselves while seeking to revolutionize their surroundings, including other human beings and material conditions. Indeed, civilization to the present can be characterized by its striving to revolutionize the environment.

HUYGHE: This must be the conclusion of the examination we are conducting. The great stage achieved by the civilization we call modern has given man mastery of the exterior world, from which he has extracted natural resources and which he has transformed in conformity with nothing but his own convenience. In doing this, he works toward the destruction of that world by exhausting and polluting it.

The result is an environmental revolution that absorbs all human care and has as a corollary, namely, the negligence of the inner life which is reduced to the utilitarian practice of rational faculties. We can only wait, and hope, that the eternal compensating balance will bring about a return to the needs of the inner life. Man has taken a great step in conquering the world but, in exchange, is in danger of losing possession of himself. Engrossed in sordid material greed, he has forgotten his own vocation and his own reason for existing. He must reconquer his authority and rediscover an awareness of his own fulfillment.

PART FOUR

Rediscovering Humanity

IKEDA: In examining contemporary problems, we have reached the conclusion that the source of the unhappiness afflicting humanity today is spiritual modifications brought about by our epoch and manifested in two outstanding trends: domination by instinctive desires on the one hand and subjugation to the exclusive control of reason on the other. The pressing issue is finding a way to rectify the situation.

You insist on the need to harmonize humanity's diverse characteristics by sublimating instinct and cultivating love. Buddhism teaches that enlightenment to the inscrutable ultimate nature of life itself leads to the establishment of harmony in one's own inner diversity.

HUYGHE: What you say is a recapitulation of one of our aims: the human revolution. We cannot expect novelty to provide a miraculous solution. Instead, we must recover our own natural state and our position of equilibrium and cease making something unnatural of ourselves. To achieve this, we must cause all our diverse faculties and potentialities to converge toward a common, global enrichment. Instead of extending in single directions, where our very conquests can become unbalancing factors, we must strive to protect and develop the power of harmony, which is the fundamental support for both life and the spirit.

IKEDA: Just as games must be played according to rules, so there are rules human beings must follow if they are to survive on Earth. I do not believe that science and technology, oriented toward "the facts," are immoral in themselves. But, we must discover rules for the application of technology in ways consonant with the true place of humanity within nature's overall operations. Wholesome development, conducted with respect for such rules, can stimulate a great soaring of the human spirit.

1

The Key to Harmony

HUYGHE: Harmony is the keystone in the arch of balance, without which nothing can ever be accomplished. Harmony appertains as fundamentally to the human interior as it does to exterior relations. Within himself, man must allow harmony to control his various possibilities and capacities without stifling any of them. In addition, he must reestablish harmony with the environment in which he develops, that is, essentially with nature and the world in which we find ourselves.

Unfortunately, modern civilization fails to realize this. Our civilization's sole vision of its ends and tasks is both imperfect and partial because it is too directly and narrowly utilitarian. It is founded on facts, each of which must be isolated and defined in order to be understood and analyzed. (The English language exhibits this dependence on facts in a striking way in its frequent use of the expression a matter of fact.) In our day, nothing seems valid unless it is envisioned within limits as a concrete object and not as something living and connected to the depths of an entirety. Nature lies before us like an animal spread out on a dissection table to reveal secrets to be exploited for the benefit of humanity. Recent reforms in French mathematical education have attempted to advance the fundamental idea of unities. But we must apply a sense of unities to all aspects of our lives.

It may be that a scientific, positivist civilization like our own differs from its predecessors largely in that older civilizations were founded on religions. The role of religion is to offer a vision and a global explanation harmonizing physical reality with moral reality, the interior world with the exterior world. We moderns are lost in the diversity of the concrete, where we think of things in terms of logical connections between facts and not of the connections of harmony that give balance to the whole.

IKEDA: Yes, but connections established between humanity and nature in the past were not always the same everywhere. Eastern and Western primitive religions taught that humanity should be subordinate to the gods they perceived in nature. By contrast, Judeo-Christianity evolved the teaching that humanity is the lord of nature. I consider both ideas—that man is subordinate to and lord of nature—essentially incorrect.

The Buddhist approach to the relation between the two is certainly preferable in all respects. While emphasizing the dignity of human life and setting forth ways to realize it, Buddhism teaches that humanity and the world of nature exist in a relationship of interdependence requiring mutual assistance. How would you compare this interpretation with those of other religions, and how do you evaluate its significance for the future of humanity?

HUYGHE: Your principle of balance strikes me as extremely judicious. If a religious conception of the world must afford humanity both maximum dignity and responsibility for its achievement, it must at the same time develop the knowledge that man is only a part of the world of nature in which he participates. And, when through this concept, he understands the whole universe, man will come to experience a certain humility and, I might add, a certain submission.

Humanity and the Universe

HUYGHE: To its merit, Buddhism is especially devoted to

uniting humanity and the universe, to integrating the one with the other, and to underscoring the common constitution of the two. It insists on the principle of harmony that can unite the two and that modern civilization offends in a dramatic fashion. Perhaps you would be good enough to explain the theory of the elements that is fundamental to Buddhism.

IKEDA: Buddhism, which certainly considers union with nature very important, posits five major elements composing everything in the universe, including, of course, human beings: earth, water, fire, and wind plus a fifth called *Kū* in Japanese, or *Shūnyatā* in Sanskrit. Though often translated as air, this word is better thought of as meaning void replete with all potentialities. Discord in the five elements of the universe and the world of nature naturally generates discord in human beings, who are composed of those elements, and can, eventually, lead to their annihilation.

An outstanding Buddhist doctrinal treatise called the *Abhidharma-kosha-shāstra,* by Vasubandhu (thought to have lived in the fourth or fifth century), describes the first four of the five elements as constantly undergoing change and breakdown as they occupy given spaces and hinder the invasion of these by other elements. In other words, these physical elements change in time and occupy certain spaces. The fifth element, *Shūnyatā,* however, must be treated differently. In contrast to the four material elements, it is a concept of a spiritual order and represents an inclusive totality of the others. But I shall treat this topic in order as I progress.

Buddhist thought provides for a set of four true elements and a set of four provisional elements. The provisional elements manifest themselves in the phenomenal world and are provisional because the phenomenal world is ceaselessly changing. The true elements are the qualities of solidity, liquidity, heat, and motion.

In addition to being the compositional constituents of all things, the four elements are the fundamental expression of all actions. To each is assigned a characteristic role. For instance, the role of fire is to burn things; that of water is to cleanse things; that of the wind is to blow away dust, and that of earth is to promote plant growth.

Since, as has been said, the material, phenomenal world is in a constant state of change, the elements of which it is composed are subject to vicissitudes. As long as harmony is preserved among the operations of water, fire, and wind—the most vigorous of the four—life is assisted and promoted. When that harmony is broken, the world is destroyed and life is transformed into death. According to Buddhist theory, when the world is destroyed, tremendous disasters caused by fire, water, and wind will occur.

In contrast to these three elements, earth is firm and solid. It not only stimulates the growth of plants, but also supports all animal life. Metaphorical Buddhist teachings hold that when a person has amassed truly bad karma, the earth becomes unwilling to support him and trembles (that is, an earthquake occurs). A person named Devadatta consistently hated and tried in many ways to harm Shakyamuni Buddha, his cousin. Ultimately, refusing to support him any longer the earth split open, plunging Devadatta, alive, into a subterranean hell. Although apparently mythological, this story clearly illustrates the role Buddhist thought attributes to earth.

The four elements have immense significance for life itself and for human existence in particular, because disruption of natural harmony not only brings about horrendous disasters caused by fire, water, and wind, but also leads to total annihilation by wiping out the earth, the very foundation on which our lives rest.

The fifth element, *Kū* or *Shūnyatā*, is simultaneously the universal space that includes and encloses the other four elements and the place that serves as the source of energy generating the other four. While itself lacking form and color and incomprehensible in space-time terms, it is the original and true existence from which earth, water, fire, and wind manifest themselves in the space-time world. The four elements that form the phenomenal world arise from the infinite energy sea of *Shūnyatā*, to which they must ultimately return. Universal energy comes into existence as phenomena, grows, and finally goes out of existence to become energy again. In my view, the Buddhist philosophy of the five great elements arises from observation of harmony and rhythm in the interrelations between material existence and the energy that is its source.

HUYGHE: In explaining the way Buddhism indicates the harmony between humanity and nature you lead me again to underscore how the Orient and the Occident have been predisposed to distinct attitudes reflecting in their different conceptions of material reality. At first glance, the Eastern and Western traditions seem nearly to coincide. The West, too, distinguished four elements—earth, water, air, and fire. It did not, however, envision the fifth that is found in Buddhist thought.

The four elements that distinguish philosophy as the good sense of the West correspond to the states of matter as set forth scientifically by physics. Earth must be interpreted as inert, solid matter, like the Earth itself; that is boulders or, more generally speaking, crystalline formations. This form of matter occurs at low temperatures. At higher temperatures, matter passes from the solid to the liquid state, which the Greeks called water. When temperatures rise still further, molecular cohesion decreases correspondingly. The resulting state is even more fluid than in the case of liquids: it is gas, or what the Greek symbolized by the word air. Raising the temperature still further brings us to fire, or light. We have passed from one extreme to the other, from solid, compact matter to that something immaterial that is the phenomenon of luminosity.

In the West, this division has been endowed with great stability. The very term states of matter is significant. Etymologically, state derives from the Latin verb *stare*, to stand, that is, to be immobile.

The idea of the breakdown of elements that Buddhism asserts is not part of the Western notion of states. Among the classical philosophers, only Heraclitus—whom the Greeks themselves called the Obscure—insisted that "everything flows" just as he rejected the intellectual tendency to fix and immobilize things in unity. Indeed, he affirmed the existence of contradictory elements. In the West, only philosophy nourished by the latest discoveries of modern physics—like that of Stephane Lupasco—can arrive at this concept, which has been pushed aside for twenty-five centuries. Those same modern physical discoveries were necessary to make people understand that the so-called states of matter are actually no more than diverse aspects of energy which can, it is true, stabilize itself in forms but is, at the same time, a force capable of acting and transforming. This kind of thinking did not exist in the West earlier.

Until our time, the worlds of solid matter and movement were distinct and capable—so people thought—of acting on each other but not of mingling. Aristotle, for instance, made a clear separation between form and impetus.

In the West, this distinction of solid matter, conveyed in forms, and of the impulse of motion facilitated the invention and development of mechanics.

What is a machine but a logical and repetitious system arriving at an imitation of movement by analyzing time and cutting it into small pieces? Henri Bergson used the clock as an illustration of this. In progressing from minute to minute, the clock cuts time into slices, thus providing a transposition or a spatial caricature of duration which, since it is in continuous evolution, has nothing to do with such fragmentation. In effect, the clock is a machine attempting, to the best of its ability, to imitate time through spatial means. It transcribes time's continuity but, in order to do so, must cut it up on the divided circle of a dial.

It was to exorcise this separation and remedy this division that Einstein turned physics upside down by introducing the concept of space-time, something Western thought had previously conceived of only with difficulty and, often, with reservations.

In asserting that all things flow, Heraclitus contravened the tendency, which he sensed all around him, to envisage everything in terms of the immutable (sub specie aeternitatis). The obsession of classical thought represented by this tendency has been inherited by science in the ways it attempts to evolve immutable laws behind the fluid appearance of reality. Chemistry defines and extracts components (once again etymology is informative: component derives from Latin *cum* and *ponere* or to put together) that determine substances which, no matter what changing appearances they assume in time, are considered unvarying. The West always strives to discover the permanent behind perceptible motion. According to this view, air is, by definition, a composition of oxygen and nitrogen. In the terminology you have just used, air would be equivalent to wind, or the movement of air. This is why misunderstanding results from translating the term *Kū* as air.

First, I should like to comment on the essential difference in the four elements, which as you say are "constantly undergoing change and breakdown"—a difference that you yourself have aptly noted. Solids, symbolized by the Earth, do not change except when broken down, that is, when they lose their form, which defines them as objects. But the other elements, which are ill-equipped to form objects, have the constant capacity of free movement in space through time. This motion signifies, not breakdown, but transformation made possible by the elements' mobility. This is why Western tradition has concentrated on solids, represented by the Earth, to the point of attempting to conform thought to them by articulating thinking in terms of neat, defined, stable ideas resembling solid objects. As I have observed, this is what has driven the West to take mechanism to such great lengths. The machine deprives movement of its natural fluidity in order to transfer it to combinations of fixed, geometric pieces mounted together in such a way as to transmit impetus without losing their own determined forms.

If I understand the term correctly, I should prefer to regard *Kū*, not as a fifth element, but as something apart from, and antedating, the formation of the other four elements. You yourself point out how different it is from the others because it is "a concept of spiritual order." I consider *void* too negative a definition. But, then, how are we to be expected to understand something that can exist outside space and time? Perhaps *original reality* is the most adequate expression. By it, I mean Being in its primordial detachment, before it has assumed form or appearance. In other words, it is energy in its pure state before it has been embodied and materialized in the elements of the physical world.

Such precise terms might seem too meticulous. But they are highly relevant to two mentalities for which, owing to different tendencies, linguistic equivalences are hard to establish. Pointed out in this way, the differences between them strongly indicate the complementary nature of the two spirits, each understanding the world from a distinct viewpoint. It is necessary for us to borrow both viewpoints just as we require two eyes to see things fully, in the round.

IKEDA: Now that we have clearly stated the five elements as set forth in Buddhist philosophy, I should like to return to an earlier point. These five elements, which make up everything in nature, correspond to the five elements composing human beings. Loss of harmony between the world of nature and the world of humanity threatens our race with annihilation.

HUYGHE: This is an essential point. There is great wisdom in the conviction that, if a single organism in itself—for instance, man—requires harmony, the need is all the greater in the vaster organic system including that organism. Insufficient in itself, the harmony of man is united with that of the universe.

From antiquity—and all the more persistently in the Middle Ages and the Renaissance—Western thought has entertained the idea that man is the microcosm and the universe the macrocosm and that, in spite of their dizzying difference in size, the two reflect each other.

Astrology, an ancient belief that appeared when Mesopotamian shepherds first observed nocturnal skies and that enjoys a curious revival in our own times, is founded on the postulate that the human lot depends on the cosmic whole. And if our epoch, which is narrowly submissive to scientific development, enthusiastically revitalizes beliefs contradicting experimental evidence, it is yet another sign of a secret revolt and a thirst to break out of the mental prison of modern civilization. And, by an amusing paradox, astrology today dreams of nothing so much as of being recognized as scientific. The same can be said of Marxism.

IKEDA: From ancient times, astrology has played an important role in Japan and China. During the Nara (646—794) and Heian (794—1185) periods in Japan, times when institutional systems were based on Chinese models, the astrologer was a governmental official.

The sun, moon, and stars were thought of as virtual mirrors capable of reflecting disorder in human lives, the state, and society. But divination was more often used in connection with national and social phenomena than with the fates of individuals. Some Buddhist texts say that when countries or societies violate the correct law, there occur strange heavenly phenomena, like the appearance of two or three suns or disorderly movement in the constellations.

From the standpoint of fundamental Buddhist philosophy, however, reflections of the movements of the heavenly bodies in human society occur on only the phenomenal level. On the profoundest level of the vital force, each life is the universe itself. In other words, Buddhism teaches that, on the ultimate level, each human life is not a microcosm but the macrocosm.

Metaphorically speaking, individual lives are like waves on the ocean. Each has its own shape, but all are produced by the waters of the ocean. The waves and the ocean are inseparably one. Enlightenment (*satori* in Japanese) is attainment of the ultimate level at which this truth about the nature of life becomes clearly perceptible.

In its deepest recesses, the human mind always wishes to return to nature. At the same time, however, we are always afraid of nature's fathomless powers. This is why humanity has drawn a line between itself and the natural world and has created civilization as an intermediary environment and a buffer zone between itself and nature's might. In spite of this separation, human beings persist in wanting, occasionally, to come into contact with nature and to give themselves up to its forces. The more the civilized environment has expanded, the stronger has grown the human desire for reconciliation with nature, just as a spring rebounds with greater force the farther back it is pulled.

Expansion of civilization not only puts increasing distances between humanity and nature, but also destroys and thus greatly reduces the scope of the natural environment. Available space on the planet is limited and each time additional land is put under the plough, less is left for pristine nature. Destruction is the inevitable outcome when steadily reduced in scope, the natural environment loses the resilience to absorb mutations caused by human action. For instance, every year the damage caused by landslides in Japan increases as more and more suburban wooded hills and mountains are cleared for housing developments. Hills that could withstand torrential rains when their green cover was intact crumble after having been stripped to make room for human habitation.

As long as they had abundant room, the five elements of earth, water, fire, wind, and void preserved balance and harmony. Cramping them and working other transformations, human encroachments have tremendously weakened the elements' capacity for maintaining harmony.

Humanity has violated the natural environment on the surface of the globe. But still untouched subterranean vastnesses and the immensities of cosmic space continue their rhythmical operations, enclosing mankind, whose scope of control is limited largely to the surface of the planet. As the earthquakes and typhoons that strike Japan many times each year vividly illustrate, in spite of all our boasts of mastery, in comparison with the mighty forces of nature, we are no more than chaff before the wind. Ecologists and specialists in other scientific fields are making it perfectly clear now that human beings can expect to lead wholesome lives only as long as they preserve harmony with the eternal universal rhythms and protect the ecological spheres that have taken billions of years to evolve.

The natural world consists of a multilevel, miraculously dynamic structure including human life and extending from particles and atoms to the moving galaxies. Each harmoniously operative level is enclosed within the structure of a higher level, and each, while forming part of the overall order, preserves its own identity.

Laws govern the region of matter composed of particles and

atoms. New characteristics and regulating factors not observed in the world of atoms obtain at the molecular level. Characteristics are still different at the level of such complex substances as proteins. This is true because a higher degree of harmony is maintained in complex substances than is to be observed in the world of the simpler substances that go into its composition. Beyond the world of inorganic matter and the organelles of complex substances is the world of cells, where at last we come upon something clearly identifiable as "life" in the biological sense of the word. Finally, beyond cells, tissues, and organs, we arrive at the biological life form called human life.

Each of the echelons of this structure has its own laws. With all of the other living entities, we human beings contribute to the composition of a biosphere. Furthermore, since that biosphere is the support of our own lives, we run the risk of self-destruction when we upset the order prevailing within it.

While conscious of being essentially a part of this universal harmony, human beings manifest awareness of their individuality and, to protect their individual entities and satisfy their desires, revise the total harmony by creating societies and civilizations. Indicating that the human being has transcended the status of a mere biological entity to become a spiritual entity, this development is nonetheless always pregnant with the threat of destroying the total harmony.

In extreme terms, the lofty human spirit tends to threaten both universal harmony and the foundation of its own biological existence. Preventing the realization of this danger requires the establishment on a high spiritual plane of a different power capable of controlling dangerous propensities. In other words, it is necessary to realize harmony and order on the spiritual plane. I believe that religion that is the product of the highest spiritual development is the force capable of performing this function.

Buddhism clarifies the complex, multilevel structure supporting all things and explains the subtle operations of its mechanism in terms of causal determination. According to this teaching, all phenomena arise as a consequence of a cause. This, in turn, means that all beings are interdependent. Incorporating this teaching into the human spiritual world provides great power for the suppression of egotistical impulses and stimulates harmony and balance that cannot help generating similar harmony in all human life and in our environment.

Harmony—a Law of Life

HUYGHE: Harmony becomes increasingly essential in nature the higher the echelon and degree of perfection of the entity. It becomes especially vital with the appearance of life, the development and even the simple prolongation of which it assures. In the purely physical world—the world of matter—things are constituted as the result of combinations of elements, atoms, and molecules. These elements group themselves or agglomerate simply according to modes or orders that, while diverse, are fixed, that permit substances to differentiate; and that obey certain laws. Crystals illustrate this point. They differ among themselves only in geometric composition, the symmetry of which indicates harmony.

With the appearance of life, as is essential according to the principle of finality, functional organization must be added to coherent juxtapositioning. In other words, in a living body, matter is no longer merely agglutinated or even ordered but participates in a common operation and a common destiny. Of course, the material universe, too, obeys the principle of harmony, which is manifest in everything from the coherent structure of the atom to the immense systems of the stars. But its neat combinations are applied to types that ceaselessly repeat themselves, identically and eternally.

As soon as it appears, life is confronted with the future and the unknown, where it must map a course to follow, although the destination—while certainly existing—is unforeseeable. The closer life comes to perfecting itself in the higher echelons constituting spiritual activity, the more indispensable becomes harmony among parts. When harmony is disrupted in the living body, illness results. If this rupture occurs in mental life, psychological illness or madness occurs. A process of destruction sets in.

The concept of harmony is as essential as that of energy or dynamism. Anything deployed in time must have harmony in order to exist. Matter is inevitably subject to attrition and destruction, as is evident in the law of entropy. With the appearance of life, struggle with this negative process begins. And on what does the struggle depend? Obviously on the harmony on which the organism is founded—a whole in which all the parts exist, not merely in themselves, but also in collaboration in a common operation. The word operation implies ideas of dynamics and projection in time.

Nothing lasts that relies solely on juxtaposition or position in space. Time demands collaboration, meaning, or convergence toward a common goal. The law of equilibrium and balance, which reaches fruition in the living, feeling, sensing being, supposes both contradictions and the capacity to overcome them.

In the physical world, things are what they are and obey rules of established coherence. They suppose a principle of unity and constancy in a formulateable unity. This is why reason and logic—born of the application of the human spirit to the physical world—are founded on unity. The relation between them is merely a kind of symbiosis between the world of matter (application) and the world of thought (understanding).

In the living entity, everything clearly results from contradictions and oppositions; and life realizes itself and comes to full bloom only when it establishes a collaboration—or in the fuller sense, harmony—among disjunctive impulses. Most often harmony assumes the form of rhythm, and opposites requiring reconciliation emerge in succession. Each opposite would be negative if deployed by itself, but becomes fruitful because it is accompanied by an equivalent from a continuing principle. Contradiction, which is sterile and destructive in static juxtaposition, can when it becomes roughly equivalent to symmetry, prove efficacious the moment it moves into time, with life, in the form of rhythm—from one alternative to the other alternative as is natural to rhythm. In this way is established a play that successively fills in lacunae.*

The whole problem may be resolved into the difference between the straight line—incarnation of the rational, logical spirit and its constant unitariness—and the sine curve. This curve has inverse curves but becomes the great revealed law as soon as movement is present, as soon as time has been admitted. The straight line and the plane are seen in crystals, which represent matter in its most perfectly accomplished static state. In the world of vibrations, even within the heart of matter, the rhythm scheme is found in the play of waves.

The law of equilibrium is sufficient for static matter. When applied to time, where it continues to play an increasingly fundamental and essential role, once energy begins operating, the law of equilibrium is transformed into a law of rhythm. As a consequence, the importance of harmony becomes steadily greater as the level at which it is applied moves from simple life to mental life, and markedly more so as it advances to spiritual realities.

The progression is easy to follow. First, harmony may be established among isolated—or contradictory—elements. All contradictions imply opposition on a plan of encounter, a common ground. Thus, at the level of matter constituted in space, harmony assumes the form either of symmetry forging unity between two similar but rigorously isolated parts or of a discreet agreement of two isolated fragments. When motion animates matter and projects it into time, rhythm comes into being in the form of waves—the regular succession of phases with opposite curves describing a sine curve. It comes to flower with the appearance of life, which adopts rhythm as the basis of its behavior and, through it and its successive play of compensations, finds equilibrium in time.†

In the presence of consciousness—and all the more as

---

* This process is valid at the macro-level. In the infinitely small that we cannot perceive physically, the principle of contradiction can be observed in the positrons and negatrons in the nucleus of the atom.

consciousness advances to higher levels—accord becomes love, the need to form the highest unity of which we are capable in attaching ourselves to that which is not "the self." For hate, which is the affective form of contradiction, and greed, which strives to reduce and absorb things exterior to us, love substitutes a sense of harmonious completeness.

From static symmetry localized in space and mobile rhythm located in and annexed to time, harmony rises to the level of lucid consciousness, eager to cooperate with "the other." Upon reaching the spiritual plane, it flowers as ambition for peace throughout the universe.

At all levels of harmony, and especially at the level of love, may be observed the indistinct desire to rejoin with the primordial unit that is the source of all things.

IKEDA: In connection with your comments, I am reminded of the ideas of the Austrian physicist Erwin Schrödinger, who proposed the interesting notion that living creatures are nourished for growth by negative entropy. For more than 30 years, I have regarded this idea as a correct expression of the distinction between material entities and living entities (biological life).

As your illustration of crystals indicates, structure and order exist in inanimate matter. But the order observed in crystals is always static. The living entity, on the other hand, has the capacity to generate and maintain its own high-level order. To paraphrase Schrödinger, currently existing order has the innate power to sustain itself and to bring forth new, ordered phenomena.

The living entity runs counter to the law of increasing entropy of the natural world and develops its own order. But to

---

† For several years, increasing effort has been devoted to the study of rhythms. In France, the group entitled Groupe d'étude des rhythmes biologiques includes eminent research workers in both laboratory experimentation and practical medicine. The group has its home at the l'U.E.R. des Science exactes et naturelles, Clermont-Ferrand.

this end, to increase inevitably growing entropy, it must cease-lessly interpose a negative entropy. I believe that Schrödinger's originality lies in his having evolved this idea.

HUYGHE: Please allow me here to state a fact in order to exclude a possible objection. Recently, certain biologists have been brought up to reject the idea of the negative entropy attributed to life. It is true that each living organism contradicts the principle stated by the French physicist and engineer Nicolas Carnot (1796–1832)—the second law of thermodynam-ics—according to which, in each isolated system, as long as energy remains constant in quantity, it decreases in quality until it approaches an anarchic, undifferentiated uniformity. Clearly because of its constant efforts at further organizing itself, life represents an effort to climb back up this decline. It must be said, however, that life does this only through the aid of the resources it consumes from the environment in which it partici-pates and the entropy it accelerates. In this sense, the law of entropy is not violated. That is certainly true, but the radical novelty in this instance is the effort to reverse the decline. This effort appears with and virtually defines life. Although, in totali-ty, it must end in defeat, this does not debar the attempt, without which nothing would exist. It can, therefore, be said that in principle, life tends to be negative-entropic.

It would be interesting to discover whether if, in the move-ment toward perfection as it rises from level to level—from the physiological to the psychological and from the psychological to the spiritual—life confirms its initial orientation. The spiritual life escapes the laws of physics and represents pure improve-ment in quality.[‡] But science is far from attaining this domain.

IKEDA: Developments in modern biophysics, which have much to teach us about the details of the phenomenon of life, are gradually clarifying the mechanism whereby the order

---

[‡] Here I can only skim the surface of the problem, the significance of which I have already stressed in my book Ce que je crois. (Ed. Bernard Grasset, Paris, 1976, p. 147.)

prevailing in life is formed. Cooperation of its internal structural elements and the process of forming a dynamic order characterize life. I agree with you that another of its characteristics is the existence of shared operations and goals.

Within a constantly flowing dynamism, a harmonic rhythm is observed. And, the higher the level, the broader its amplification and the freer its amplitude. But, unless a high level of harmony and order capable of tolerating these great amplitudes is maintained, the living body in question must face destruction.

Illness is the outcome of disruption and breakdown in harmonious rhythm. As was true of ancient Western medicine, the medicine of the East was founded on the concept of harmony within the living body. Speaking broadly, traditional Japanese medicine derives from two sources: Chinese medicine and Buddhist medicine (which can be thought of as including ancient Indian medicine).

The basis of Chinese medicine—the doctrine of Yin and Yang and the five natural elements—deals essentially with the problem of harmony and its absence. The healthy condition is one in which Yin and Yang, vital energy (*qi*) and blood (*xue*), and vacuity and repletion, as well as the five natural elements (wood, fire, earth, metal, and water) are all in a state of equilibrium. Their being out of harmonious balance produces illness.

Consequently, the major aim of therapy is to discover and remove elements throwing these forces out of balance and, in this way, to enable the living body to return to its original dynamic harmony. To achieve this aim, it is essential to eliminate external disrupting conditions. Still more fundamental, however, is realizing equilibrium and harmony by, for instance, complementing Yin elements if they are insufficient, reducing Yang elements if they are in excess, and adjusting the balance among the five elements.

Practically the same principle of harmony is to be found in Buddhist medical theory. In this instance, however, therapy concentrates on restoring harmonious balance among the four great elements of earth, water, fire, and wind. To this end, various regimens—breath control, physical control, and mental control, for example—are prescribed. Many of these systems are of great interest to modern specialists in psychosomatic therapy.

The great Chinese Buddhist philosopher Tiantai Zhiyi (538–97) considered illnesses resulting from disorder in the four great elements to be the most superficial and said that the most serious of illnesses are those arising as a consequence of karma. In this way he revealed the characteristic of Buddhist medicine that transcends human psychology to illuminate the depths of life itself. The profound Buddhist investigations of the Nine Consciousnesses is the theoretical aspect of therapy designed to combat these illnesses which are psychosomatic.

The many delusions to which we are subject arise as a consequence of the karma lying at the foundation of the lives of all individuals. For instance, Buddhism interprets schizophrenia as self-bifurcation caused by various delusions. Manic-depressive psychosis develops when the operation of delusions makes maintaining harmony between the rhythms of the individual life and those of the surroundings impossible. In Buddhist medicine, determining and eliminating the causes of these delusions must be accomplished through the practice of faith.

Practice of faith, in this context, is identical with what you call a return to the primordial unity from which all things are created. In Buddhist terms, this primordial unity is expressed as the teachings of the Lotus Sutra itself (or *Myōhō-renge-kyō*). The act of returning—or devoting both the physical and spiritual aspects of one's life—to it is expressed in the word *namu*, which is derived from Sanskrit and means to revere in the ultimate sense of becoming one with *Myōhō-renge-kyō*.

The doctrine of the Unification of the Three Truths, which demonstrates the unity of the fundamental law, is a philosophical statement of the perfect union of the three aspects of life: nonsubstantiality (*kūtai* in Japanese), provisional existence (*ketai*), and the Middle Way (*chūtai*).

Though this doctrine is subtle and difficult, the natures

of the three aspects can be generally indicated as follows:

Nonsubstantiality means that nothing has a fixed existence of its own and that all things are fundamentally *Kū*, or undifferentiated potentiality. This *Kū* might be explained as the energy that causes the blossoming of flowers or human verbal expression.

Provisional existence means that, although all are *Kū*, things do have a temporary existence and that harmony prevails within and among all of them.

The Middle Way, in this connection, means that in their truest form, all things are characterized by being, but are neither nonsubstantial nor provisionally existing and that all depend on the universal force of life for support, existence, and controlling rhythms.

Life has all three of these aspects, which are perfectly united and none of which can exist independent of the other two. In other words, harmony among phenomena pertains solely to provisional existence, but this cannot be considered without reference to both nonsubstantiality and the Middle Way. The concord prevailing among provisional existing life phenomena must, as you have pointed out, exist in the face of ceaselessly occurring contradictions and oppositions. Elements for the resolution of contradictions occurring in provisional existence are to be found in nonsubstantiality. And elements for resolving contradictions between provisional existence and nonsubstantiality are to be found in the Middle Way.

The principle of the Unification of the Three Truths applies not only to the world of human life, but to everything in the animate and inanimate worlds as well. Among inanimate phenomena, provisional existence is paramount; and nonsubstantiality and the Middle Way are latent.

Although the Unification of the Three Truths applies to them, vegetable and nonhuman animal life forms lack the ability to be aware of their actions. Human beings, on the other hand, have the will and the individual power to grasp and understand the principles of life in an active fashion and can observe themselves as examples of harmonious vital life force. Indeed, the capability to be aware of the true nature of life is the element distinguishing human beings from vegetable and nonhuman animal life.

Most important of all is self-awareness regarding the operations of the Three Identical Truths. As you have noted, people created capable of recognizing the eternal rhythms of life manifest awareness in the form of the wonderful wisdom of love. By the same token, however, human beings have such negative aspects as the delusions called hatred and greed as well. Buddhism takes the view that delusion and wisdom are ultimately the same thing. *Delusion* is a general term for anything that causes human beings to suffer or be perplexed mentally or physically and includes the Three Delusions of greed, anger, and folly. If they come to prevail in human society, these delusions destroy harmony and lead to destruction.

This is why Hinayana Buddhism teaches that the first goal of self-discipline is to escape from delusion. But, even with the most assiduous effort, this is impossible because eliminating delusion must mean eliminating the human mind where delusion is born. And this, in turn, means the destruction of the human life form.

Among Mahayana scriptures, the Lotus Sutra most clearly sets forth the unity of delusion and wisdom, that is, the oneness of perplexity and enlightenment. Wisdom cannot exist apart from delusion, within which it is actually included.

From the viewpoint of actual practice, instead of being at their mercy, human beings must clearly perceive the true nature of delusions and apply their own wisdom to overcome them. The wisdom to perceive and overcome must be derived from the origin of life itself by constantly striving to direct consciousness toward fundamental unity, the mother of all things.

Many episodes in human history vividly show that ignoring the force of life and attempting to deal with delusion on the plane of consciousness only is a very imperfect method. The doctrine that delusion and wisdom are one harmonizes contradictions because it looks directly at delusion, illumines the situation with the light of wisdom generated by the force of life and, in this way, transforms constricting delusion into wisdom.

Harmony in Mental Operations

HUYGHE: Harmony, the persisting thread throughout our inquiry, must regulate relations between humanity and nature and must be the foundation of the organization of life and, consequently, of our mental activities, which are life's loftiest expression.

In *Die Wahlverwandtschaften* (Elective Affinities), Göthe summarizes this continuity in the program he assigns to humanity: "To be in harmony with one's self and with the world."

Restored to mental life, harmony provides the key to the human revolution, the necessity of which becomes more apparent daily. We have already posited the principle; the moment has now come to specify the modalities. This revolution must turn us in another direction, as the etymology of the word itself indicates. This direction must be toward restoring harmony among disjointed elements within man. A renaissance of subjectivity must balance hypertrophy of objectivity. We must balance the pride of rationalism by turning a humble ear to those inner voices that we no longer heed because we have stifled them.

If it is the natural state of man to do battle on two fronts, we must harmonize them too. We must stop occupying ourselves exclusively with the exterior front, which obsesses us because we live solely to conquer our environment, and devote ourselves to the interior front, which we neglect excessively and where we encounter disaster.

Let us limit our discussion of the exterior front to two, in some ways diametrically opposed, human faculties: sensation and abstraction.

The life of the mind is nourished by sensations. Eighteenth-century psychology—that of the French philosopher Etienne

Bonnot de Condillac (1715–80), for example—believed that the entire human interior life is nothing but combinations of, or the end product of, sensations. The very partiality of this extremely simplistic view reveals the grievous decline in thought that has led to the contemporary crisis.

Granted that the sensory life is an essential source of nourishment for the mental life; the human being still must put information provided from without to work and make it usable or, in the strict sense, intelligible. This is how the intellectual faculties, the faculties of logic and reason, are formed.

These, then, are the two extremes, one a point of departure and the other a destination, but the two are valid only as long as the interval between them is nourished and filled. This interval is the life of the emotions. Clearly applying sensations directly in intellectual work, as positive information destined to be ordered and made profitable, deprives them of a whole part of their necessary task. Harmony requires that sensation first come into contact with and fertilize sensibility. The linguistic proximity of the words sensation and sensibility reflects this close correlation and play of harmonics. Sensation leads to sensibility; that is, to an interior echoing of an initial impression. This initial impression liberates in us a vibration that confronts sensitive tendencies concealed by the subconscious but manifest by our emotions. This interior substance is essential to us as the only way the intelligence can intervene to clarify and codify experience.

Our civilization tends to forget this because, as we have said, the physical sciences have instituted a method proscribing the subjective, which they designate as anything depending on the subconscious, the intuition, the imagination, or sensitivity without being controlled by rational intelligence. In other words, these sciences have created a system that is strictly necessary to their own practices but that, by an unjustifiable extension, pretends to tyrannize over all physical life and has ended up producing a veritable mental distortion. Following the example of the physical sciences, human beings have felt compelled to reduce themselves strictly to exact perceptions and their reasoned, organized applications.

This is the source of the threat of imbalance and suffocation that you very correctly say hangs over us. Man today is reduced, on the one hand, to desires, propensities responding to sensations, and an almost animal sensuous life (after all, this is what we have in common with the other animals) and, on the other hand, to imprisonment within an arid intellectualism. This is where everything converges; but, of the entire intermediary field, humanity preserves nothing but the utilitarian residue. And this is substituted for the emotional life, which is no longer permitted to operate fully.

The contemporary crisis leads us again to the conclusion that life and the living human being create an organic ensemble, all the parts and all the functions of which must be coordinated and work in conjunction in a mutually enriching and—to use the word yet again—harmonious fashion. We must react strongly against the schematic view that gradually turns human beings into superior machines and almost into caricatures of electronic brains. With the understanding that normal development of all parts is essential to the ensemble, we must allow man to employ all his faculties to the full.

As we know, when man shall have recovered his full, balanced functional abilities, it will become essential for him to use them by engaging in action in time. The human mental organism is destined to live, to last, to evolve, to transform itself, and to achieve something during the course of a lifetime. The only word for this is aspiration.

Well-perceived and well-founded, aspiration is the ultimate that human life contains. Such a goal, which every human life pursues (and the word pursues is well-chosen since the goal constantly draws us on), develops the individual's quality, as we have seen stressed in the case of the arts.

Perhaps this goal, the attraction to the "best," which is alive in each individual, reflects a great collective movement leading humanity in the same direction—a movement to which each of us must contribute according to his means. Only under such circumstances can life be truly harmonious. And the reward for living it will no doubt be true, profound happiness, that is, the satisfaction of existing.

The Question of Happiness

IKEDA: Believing the fulfillment of material conditions essential to a happy way of life, human beings expend maximum energy on the satisfaction of their desires. Indeed, pursuit of such satisfaction can be called the driving force behind the development of human culture. Reason, too, has developed and proved its efficacy within this same pursuit.

Today many people have come to regard reason and the satisfaction of desires—essentially means or conditions for happiness—as ends in themselves. Consequently, as you point out, they either allow their ways of life to degenerate to virtually animal sensuality or permit arid intellectualism to dominate them. I believe people mistake means for goals because they have no clear understanding of the nature of the essential goal, true happiness.

The nature of happiness is too complicated to be described simply. It can be said, however, that happiness depending solely on sensual fulfillment is fragile and fleeting. The knowledge that physical satisfaction is not everything and that a happiness resulting from deeper spiritual satisfactions exists puts life on a firmer footing.

Furthermore, a life embodying knowledge of the expansive happiness coming not merely from spiritual satisfaction, but also from bringing gladness and joy to others, is free of obstructions and stands on very solid ground.

Each individual must determine the kind of happiness to pursue, but lack of awareness of deeper, more durable fulfillment hinders freedom of choice. At present, in spite of assurances of individual liberty, too many people are deprived of true freedom by being, without their realizing it, forced into uniformity on fundamental issues.

For example, although enjoying freedoms in connection with choice of occupation and domicile that would have been unimaginable to our forebears, people today are, without knowing it, deprived of freedom of thought by being semi-compelled from childhood into an educational organization based on uniform knowledge and thinking patterns. Under the old apprentice system, a child was thoroughly taught a skill but was not instructed about how to sell his own work at the highest possible price or instructed in believing happiness to lie in economic well-being. Today, on the other hand, before being instructed in a skill or trade, children are taught that poverty is the worst possible misery and that generating wealth is the best way to contribute to society.

The actual choice of occupation today is free. No modern child has his life's work determined for him before he understands the nature of society. All may wait to make up their own minds after the education process has been completed. Furthermore, it is possible to change occupation later if something more desirable turns up. Nonetheless, young people gradually become increasingly deeply dyed with the notion that pursuit of economic profit is a goal in itself. And this has the effect of limiting freedom of choice.

This is why I feel that a reordering and reappraisal of our thoughts on the nature of happiness are of compelling significance and value at the present time. You speak of a multilevel structure in human life entailing a shift from the sensuous to the sensitive and from there to the intellectual life. This approach is extremely important in connection with making the happiness human beings seek deeper and more enduring.

Interestingly, the Buddhist doctrine of the Three Worlds corresponds with the three levels you establish and with your view of happiness. According to this doctrine, the world filled with rapture, called the Heavenly World, is divided into three echelons: the Heaven of Desire, the Heaven of Form (or physical being), and the Heaven of the Spirit, or the Formless Heaven.

The Heaven of Desire, in which satisfaction of desires brings happiness, is subdivided into six orders, in the highest of which, namely, the Heaven of Desire for Power, the will to control and dominate is gratified. The Heaven of Form is explained as being filled with happiness though the beings in it have no desires. I interpret the happiness of this realm to be like the joy derived from beholding a beautiful scene or like happiness derived from participating in sports for its own sake, with no desire to win.

The happiness of the Heaven of the Spirit arises from speculative thought and the discovering of truths.

But Buddhism teaches that all these happinesses are shallow and ephemeral and that human beings should strive to attain a still deeper, more enduring kind of joy. The happinesses of the Three Worlds depend on relations between the constantly changing external environment and the equally constantly altering mind of the perceiving self and cannot, therefore, endure long. Moreover, they are selfish joys often built on the sufferings of others.

Lasting happiness as taught by Buddhism is derived from giving oneself fully to immutable truth perceived beyond ceaselessly changing phenomena. The process whereby this happiness is achieved can be thought of as the search for the truth within the self, or self-revolution. In different terminology, it is overcoming selfishness by devoting oneself to something.

Hinayana Buddhism views happiness as attainable through rejection and isolation from changing phenomena and the self. In contrast, Mahayana Buddhism teaches first that we must seek a fundamental basis transcending phenomena. When our inner beings rest steadily on this base, we acquire power to control life and phenomena. Then we must devote ourselves to the happiness of others and, in this way, justify what you call our raison d'être.

Even the happiness we experience from relations between ourselves and our external environment is more abundant, expansive, and enduring if our inner beings are well-cultivated and unwavering. The situation can be compared to mountain climbing. For the sickly individual with no skill or knowledge of the peak in question, mountain climbing is both difficult and perilous. The healthy, skillful, informed person, however, discovers greater joy from climbing and mastering mountains the more craggy and dangerous they are.

Similarly, relations with the external environment are a series of hardships for the person whose inner being is insufficiently developed. Hardships become causes of pleasure for people who have the power of life force and are strong and wise within. The joy they experience increases and deepens from the knowledge that, instead of revolving around their own concerns, their lives are a source of strength and profit to other people.

No one can escape the issue of life and death. But by making us aware of the eternal, immutable universal force of life, Buddhism shows the way to conquer the issue, which otherwise is the most basic of all causes of suffering. Understanding this involves a principle pervading all human existence and providing the key to true happiness. Admittedly, it also involves the concept of enlightenment, which is difficult for non-Buddhists to comprehend.

In their search for happiness, which they seem to look for only in external, material conditions, people today often enter unawares on a path of degradation. Observing this makes me all the more certain of the importance of attempting to analyze the nature and source of happiness and to discover ways to make it deep and enduring.

The Psychological Synthesis

HUYGHE: The search you have in mind can succeed only when we are fully aware of the diverse and multiple elements of which our nature is composed. Happiness does not reside solely in the possession of the object of material desires. Human beings can find true happiness only in the full use of all the faculties with which they are endowed and in the growing awareness of the direction in which humanity is being driven, each of us being only a single participating element in that drive. It is natural for happiness to take the form of the knowledge that we have fully satisfied our conditions, accomplished our task, and justified our reason for being.

Nor is this necessarily a matter solely of spiritual aspects. Recent discoveries in psychophysiology have proved that, to work as it should, our physical organism requires our mental life to be active on all the different levels offered to it. As biology demonstrated long ago, by definition an organism is composed of organs that, to thrive and expand together, must function in symbiotic harmony. Our cerebrospinal system, the foundation and support of our psychical activity, conforms to this fundamental law.

Each of us is made up of a superimposition of elements where all the stages of evolution leading to Homo sapiens are inscribed and preserved. This structure retains the series of functions that have appeared during the course of evolution and that indicate the successive complements that have enabled mental life to attain the richness and variety of human psychic activities. It has taken no less than two hundred million years for this slow gestation to advance from reptiles to Homo sapiens. But it must be clearly stated that new faculties have not replaced and invalidated their predecessors. Instead, they have extended their functioning and made possible better adaptation to circumstances. They form an ensemble of increasing richness in which each contributes to the total balance. The older faculties ensure fundamental functions; the more recent ones, extensions of capacities in the face of the tasks of life. To examine them in chronological order, it is necessary only to observe their stacking in the anatomy of our central nervous system.

The human nervous system preserves elements that first appeared and were successively perfected in the chain of nonhuman animal life. In addition, the fetus recapitulates those stages in the course of its own development. This course begins with a tube-shaped rudimentary medulla possessed by the embryo. This closes to form the spinal marrow and the cerebral vesicle destined to evolve into the brain. The spinal marrow, which corresponds to the primitive link in the embryonic chain, is missing in protozoans but already present in coelenterates and insects. In man, as in lower animal life, its realm remains that of elementary stimuli and automatic reactions. It represents a rough summary of psychical activities still limited to pure mechanisms.

The medulla oblongata, which the nineteenth-century French

physiologist Flourens called the "vital knot" and the "keystone of the arch," controls metabolism and nervous activity limited to vital internal functions. Finally the cerebellum appears to control relations with space, particularly equilibrium, and, in its most recent zones, voluntary movement of the body members.

At this point, true psychical life begins to manifest itself and grow from the subconscious to the conscious. The paleencephalon, which will later be enveloped by the neencephalon, regulates activities corresponding to those of primitive animals. The R-complex, the so-called reptilian brain near the hypothalmus, controls only visceral regulation and elementary pulsations of primitive instincts. The group of subcortical structures known as the limbic system of the brain and already present in primitive mammals receives sensations—initial knowledge of the outside world—and transmits them to the cortex. Memory begins with the hippocampus, and at this stage we have arrived at what is called the raw material of consciousness and initial emotional behavior. With the surpassing of simple mechanisms, an elementary capacity of choice manifests itself.

In superior mammals, the cortex appears at the moment when amphibians metamorphose into reptiles. And with its appearance, the operation of a clear consciousness, later increasingly better organized, becomes possible. Once again the composition is of six superimposed levels representing different kinds of nerve cells. These levels are connected with preceding centers, the material of which they organize. The paleocortex is coordinated with the reptilian brain. The mesocortex, which combines with the paleocortex to form what the late-nineteenth-century French anthropologist Paul Broca (1824-1880) described as the limbic brain, or the old brain, furnishes the emotional raw material of consciousness. But the neocortex, which envelopes the paleocortex, is necessary for symbolic and verbal capacities. As a result of its capacities of inhibition, elaboration, and intellectual organization, the neocortex makes possible intelligent behavior and rational control. With this development is accomplished the passage between—to paraphrase Arthur Koestler on the work of Paul MacLean—"what one senses" and "what one knows." In other words, homo sapiens, with his faculties of abstract thought, has appeared on the scene.

The process manifesting this much evidence of stages leading from an indefinite organism to an intelligence capable of mastering itself amounts to what Piveteau has called an ascent toward consciousness and thought. In humanity, however, the ascent attains not only the intellectual, but also the spiritual level, where it finds its culmination.

The necessity for close collaboration among these parts, which must remain coherent among themselves, is perfectly apparent. Modern life has upset this coherence, especially since positive science has gained control of mental life and has tended to emphasize exclusively certain elements that, from the scientific viewpoint, seem more efficacious than others. These are the elements making possible objective, exterior information from which to draw knowledge of facts reduced to quantities by measurable signs and put into operation by a system of abstract and logical association. If isolated, as it is today, such a system trammels the operation of the intuitive and emotional, in other words of all those things called subjective. Ultimately the subjective becomes inactive; and, without its assistance, we can attain abstractions but not spiritual fruition. As a consequence of this state of affairs, human fullness is blocked and bound.

Intelligence is reduced to cultivating its own mechanism. It becomes exclusively functional and too autonomous. It ceases to be the sharpest and most keenly perceived point in the ascent from the material to the spiritual.

An aspect of our brains, revealed not long ago, offers a second proof that complementary functioning among our associated parts is indispensable. The very positive experiments undertaken in about 1950 in the United States by Dr. Sperry and his associates clearly distinguished the roles of the two hemispheres of the brain. Until then, the left side of the brain had been considered superior in terms of commands—at least among right-handed people—because, owing to the chiasma or intersection of the nerves at the level of the cerebellum, it controls the right side of the body. This is not, however, the case at all. The functional asymmetry of the brain confirms the necessity of complementary operation since the left hemisphere is linked with rational comprehension, language, speech, and thought. The right hemisphere perceives first of all qualities of sounds and the sense of intonation (more than abstract thought) and musical melody. In a general fashion the right hemisphere is connected with audio and visual images and, therefore, more to symbolic meaning than to geometric structure. One half of our brain is partial to the conceptual and measurable. This is the half more closely bound to practical manual action. The other half experiences primarily the particular and qualitative. Surely this relationship should stimulate us to strive to maintain balance between objectively oriented faculties and faculties born of subjectivity. Our very cerebral structure warns us against the aberration that has led us to violate nature by directing our psychical activity in one direction only instead of allowing it the fullness of harmonious functioning.

2

Re-forming the Inner Life

IKEDA: The principal evil of our civilization is a lack of willingness to examine steadfastly and then to rectify the inner life. The higher religions teach that we should lend an ear to the inner voice, which, in Christianity and Islam is that of God. Buddhism, on the other hand, delves into the inner world of the force of life, from which the inner voice is believed to emerge. We have just been speaking of balance and equilibrium in psychical activities. Certainly the time has come for human beings to cease devoting all attention to the exterior world and establish equilibrium between their considerations of it and the inner world. Under existing conditions, in which normal balance and harmony have been lost, true progress must take place in connection with both the exterior and the interior world; and neither must be sacrificed for the other. I consider the teachings of Buddhism the clearest guide in achieving this kind of balance.

If, as you say, the only true progress is inner progress, for its sake each of us must cultivate the inner strength to control and correct impulsive desires and karma-determined partialities.

HUYGHE: The evil you mention has already struck the West full force and, unfortunately, is spreading eastward now that, as you have said, Japan is being drawn into the same cycle as a consequence of accelerated transformation into an industrial society. With its predilection for action and efficiency, the West is at fault. The West invented science in order to increase its hold on the exterior world. And, in recent centuries, the West has called the game and conquered the world.

As a consequence, the West has been compelled to give priority to developing faculties facilitating exact representations of the exterior world and its facts. Essentially intellectual, these faculties make it possible to use sensations to perceive exactly, to control resulting impressions, to transform them by giving them general values, and to make them pass into the category of ideas or abstractions. The etymology of the word *abstract* is significant: Latin *ab* (from) plus *tractus,* past participle of the verb *trahere* (to draw). In other words, in abstracting, we draw from the confused mass of particular sensations the permanent, general facts enabling us to unify phenomena that otherwise would be experienced autonomously.

This leads to progressive desiccation, as our psychophysiological constitution confirms. The neocortex, which is unique to the human race, establishes among the images we experience connections, liaison, and assimilation making it possible to gradually replace what is experienced by means of the thought. In this way, the experience is deprived of emotional qualities but gains in its place a generality that the sensation cannot have because it is always localized and attached to the phenomenon provoking it.

The excessive development of our neocortical—that is, essentially intellectual—faculties has created a kind of localized congestion, if a comparison may be made with the vascular system. As long as the total amount of blood in the body remains constant, congestion in one organ deprives the other organs of their due supply. Similarly, concentrating the psychical life in intellectual faculties, by a natural reaction, impoverishes the rest of those things that are directly experienced and lived, in other words the emotional faculties.

The characteristic of the intellect is to take us out of the directly-lived in order to project before us, as in a picture, an abstract representation. It is rather like a mathematician who writes on a blackboard figures that have been running through his head. The mathematician may disappear, but the written figures remain.

The intellect operates in the same way. It plunges into the boiling, changing, constantly flowing stream of the experienced and extracts elements from which it creates ideas, the symbols of which may be either numbers or words. Then it inscribes those ideas on the screen of thought, where they acquire the characteristics of the objective world. Once constituted, an idea can repeat itself in the most diverse brains, just as the most individualized spectators with the most distinct and irreconcilable subjective lives are obliged to see in a cube the same geometric figure subject to but one definition.

The Westerner conforms to this mechanism more than anyone else. He turns his attention constantly toward the exterior world first because of his predilection for action, which must by definition take place in the outside realm. He is always looking forward toward those things that stand opposed to each other in front of him. Moreover, by means of intellectualization, he projects his own mental life into those opposites as if it, too, were part of the exterior world.

In the strictest sense, science requires this process of objectification. At least science, unless conceived by extremely open and humane men of wisdom, demands objectiveness exclusively and displays suspicion of, and even profound scorn for, subjectivity. But the interior life remains essentially subjective.

When I extract from something I sense deeply, though obscurely, an idea that explains the issue, I have objectified my subjective life. But, from that moment, the idea is fixed and determined. It no longer moves. I have transformed into an object of thought something that earlier participated in life and, ceaselessly nourished by new contributions, ceaselessly evolved.

The Westerner is thoroughly accustomed to looking ahead of himself. To be aware of himself, he needs to see himself as if in a mirror—the mirror of thought. Illustration of this need is seen in the development of the self-portrait in the history of Western art. But I know myself, not so much from seeing my image in a mirror, which gives me objective information about myself, as from closing my eyes and attempting to experience and find out what I am within myself.

The Westerner's error is to introduce into his civilization an increasing impoverishing of the inner life. In *Drinkers of Infinity,* Arthur Koestler has shown admirably how this deformation, this mental sectarianism, pushed to extremes as in Marxism, for instance, can end up in the elimination of the individual and his own resources. "We differ from others in the purity of our logic. . . ," says the old People's Commissar Rubashov. "We do not admit the existence of any private sector, not even within the skull of an individual . . . We have replaced vision with logical deduction. . . ." Actually this excessive standpoint is only the twentieth-century extreme and rationalized conclusion—together with new convictions in the name of the "objective"—of a position adopted by the West in the nineteenth century.

All the same, it is a mistake to generalize, as some Eastern people have tended to do, and attribute to this Western tendency, no matter how widespread it is, an absolute value. To do so is to forget that some Westerners have always been aware of the danger incurred. Movements and eminent individuals have struggled to preserve the inner life. Had this not been the case, the West would have had no art, no poetry, no mysticism, and no religious life since all these activities depend on the interior life and subjective consciousness.

With Westerners of this kind, the East can establish connections on an equal footing. Conflicts have arisen because the East has usually been confronted with the West and its objective, military, administrative, and commercial actions.

Degrees of Consciousness

IKEDA: As you clearly point out, the Western intellect has generally been directed to the exterior world in an attempt to objectify the subjective operations of life. In contrast, Oriental wisdom has consistently concerned itself with the operations of subjective awareness and has made profound investigations of the inner life of the individual. Most of these attempts have been cursory, however, and, just as some Westerners have delved into the inner world, so some Easterners have devoted themselves solely to the outer world and to technological inventions. Nonetheless, Eastern spiritual culture has no doubt made a greater contribution to the elucidation and fulfillment of the inner life than has Western civilization. Furthermore, I am convinced that the Eastern philosophy of humanity and life is fully capable of making up for the shortcomings of, and rectifying distortions in, Western civilization. Through their speculative thought and practical activities, Buddhists have been especially active in evolving detailed theories about the structure of life itself.

Among Buddhist doctrines, that known as Consciousness Only (*Vijnapta matrata*) is deeply related not only to Western philosophical cognition, but also to modern psychoanalysis. Going farther than mere consciousness, however, this doctrine is a theory of existence dealing with the force of life that performs acts of consciousness. In other words, it deals with both the operations of consciousness and the conscious mind carrying out those operations. The indivisible oneness of both consciousness and existence indicates that revolution in the conscious mind can open new vistas and worlds in the operations of consciousness.

Buddhism teaches that the workings of human life are possible because of the coming together of Five Aggregates (*panca skandhah*): *rupa,* form (the physical being); *vedana,* perception (sensation); *samjna,* mental conceptions and ideas; *samskara,* volition; and *vijnana,* consciousness. The principal element in the series is consciousness, which means both the act of subjective consciousness and the life performing it.

Focusing on consciousness, this doctrine deals with the process of life operations and elucidates the inner regions of life. Information received through sensual—visual, aural, olfactory, gustatory, and tactile—perceptions are only partial. To compile, synthesize, and assimilate them and to determine ways to respond to them, another kind of consciousness is necessary. This consciousness, which operates in the cerebral cortex, is called thought-consciousness (*mano-vijnana*).

Thought-consciousness, considered sixth in a series including consciousness depending on the five sensory organs, conceptualizes information gathered from those organs and determines ways of adapting to them. It is, consequently, a fairly lofty kind of spiritual activity. But, since it always depends on information gathered by the five senses from the exterior world, it is impotent in relation to the inner world of the conscious being. The tendency you mention for the Western intellect to be oriented always to the exterior world arises, no doubt, from a halting at, or an overemphasis on, this sixth consciousness.

Buddhism, however, goes farther toward understanding the inner world by positing a seventh consciousness independent of sensory perception. Called *manas-vijnana,* the seventh consciousness is reflective, meditative thought directed to the inner world. It is, in addition, the being engaging in the meditative thought. Since it is the source of extremely self-centered impulses and emotions, Buddhist thought provides for an eighth consciousness, called the *alaya-vijnana,* which is an accumulation of the karma that can be called the seeds of such impulses and emotion. In addition, there is a ninth consciousness (called *amara-vijnana*), which represents the life force of the whole universe.

I shall go into detail about these consciousnesses later. Here I should merely like to call attention to one point: whereas up to the eighth, all of the kinds of consciousness relate to the individual life, the ninth has entered the realm of the ubiquitous self in union with the universe. Buddhism places maximum emphasis on enlightenment to this ninth consciousness and, through its manifestation, control of the individual fate as embodied in the eighth consciousness.

I believe that the artists, poets, mystics, and religious leaders you refer to as having struggled to protect the inner human life must have had presentiments, or have glimpsed the profound world, of the eighth and ninth consciousnesses of Buddhist teaching.

In East and West alike, profound human inner reflection and acute intuition have enabled people to behold the inner world, with greater or lesser degrees of clarity. I believe that it is on this deep level of life that ties of human love transcending differences in ideology and culture can be formed.

Mastering the Self

HUYGHE: We agree that, confronted with the present crisis, both the East and the West must understand the need to add to the currently obsessive awareness of the exterior world, a consciousness of the self, which you call the seventh consciousness. But unless mastery of the self parallels mastery of the exterior world, such awareness runs the risk of being sterile or, at any rate, unrewarded. What good is self-knowledge without the ability to influence the self?

Desiring to interpret psychical reality exclusively on the basis of models of physical reality, our epoch tends to imagine that the same determinism controlling physical reality actually governs psychical reality, too. All our thoughts, feelings, and acts originate in and are explained by causes exerting pressures on us. Material and social pressures are exerted from without; psychical pressures arise from our subconscious. The least-experienced lawyer knows perfectly well that all judges saturated with these contemporary convictions are powerless to condemn crimes excused as resulting from reputedly abominable social oppression or from hereditarily inherited impulses or impulses acquired during the developmental stage. Everything is explainable. All is fated and, therefore, excusable.

The liberty claimed by our contemporaries is first and foremost liberation from legal and moral rules and is quickly reduced to nothing but the freedom to give way to impulses. Liberty becomes license.

But the freedom human beings truly need arises from self-mastery. We can obtain such freedom only by struggling against the fatalities oppressing us. These fatalities are of two kinds. It is as if man were caught between the jaws of a vise.

One jaw is the exterior world, which is a given, imposed fact. It is possible to act on it and take part in its activities, but it remains what it is. The second jaw is man himself. He, too, depends on the physical world and is represented by all the fatalities resulting from the bodily constitution that is the fundamental support and conditioner of psychical life. This basis is enormous and, like the tip of the iceberg, the perceptible, above-surface part is much less important than the part submerged in the depths of our physiology and subject to all the fatalities of heredity, temperament, and physical limitations plus all the other fatalities acquired from education, development, and environment.

Humanity is subject to these two influences both of which are, in a way, equally objective since, in addition to the objectivity of material facts outside and before me, which I understand with my senses, there exists an objectivity of material facts within me. These are imposed on my personality with all the weight and demands of my body. Both objectivities—that of the outside world and that which constitutes my physiological composition—imply a constraining determinism. For animals, subject to natural instincts and to such artificial instincts as conditioned reflexes, the second determinism is total.

Although animals are powerless to combat these forces, in the struggle with them, human beings have recourse to the interior part—that is, the spiritual—aspect of their lives. A light illumines the fate inscribed either by heredity or acquired by habit in our physiology. And that light is what, in the strict sense, I call the spirit. It begins at the point at which consciousness ceases being a mere registration of information. The spiritual life is the zone beyond the determinisms that try to control humanity, namely, the place where human freedom starts.

Exterior facts, by and large the same for and equally imposed on all human beings, confront this zone. They are the raw material of science. At the same time, however, the zone is confronted by other pressures rising from our physical constitution and influencing our psychical operations. But the zone surmounts these pressures, transforms them, and uses them to feed its own light. Like the flame shooting from the pinnacle of an oil-well rig, that light transforms the matter of the organic strata that are its food and fuel into a fire that struggles against the night.

Escaping from the jaws of a fate striving to command it, the spirit resides in this zone, which is the center of its liberty and its spiritual consciousness. The development of this spiritual consciousness permits the human spirit to strike back in such a way as to influence both physiological reality and psychophysiological facts. In this zone, the human being takes cognizance of his instincts and receives impressions in order to submit them to his own will. Similarly, he takes cognizance of appeals from the exterior world to awaken his desires which, however, he teaches to obey his own laws.

Interposed between the instincts commanding our appetites and the exterior world offering to satisfy those appetites, the intellect proposes effective measures for bringing the two together. The spirit, on the other hand, directs our energy toward other fulfillments appearing only in its own lights. It attempts to control forces born of the body and the physiology toward other goals. At the same time it attempts to avoid making the world it observes only an object of the extension of human appetites and instinctive drives.

I like to compare the spirit between these two attractions to the ridge tiles surmounting the two sloping sides of a roof. Descending either side of the roof leads to the fatality that dominates humanity. Climbing either side, however, leads to the crest, the ridge, the most elevated part emerging from and dominating the whole roof. Similarly, the spiritual life equally surmounts facts imposed on our own interiors and those imposed on the exterior to lift itself above the two possibilities for weakness.

IKEDA: Buddhism attempts to account for the inner constraints in human life by examining karma in the eighth consciousness (*alaya-vijnana*) and delusions in the seventh consciousness (*manas-vijnana*), that is, in both hereditary and acquired impulses. Since it is the latent source of the energy from which the delusions of the *manas-vijnana* arise, the *alaya-vijnana* is considered the realm possessing the greatest fate-power for influencing human life. Since it is the source of both its physical and spiritual aspects, the eighth consciousness is inseparable from the structure and characteristics of the individual life. What you call the totality of destiny resulting from the physical composition corresponds to the physiological level of karma latent in the *alaya-vijnana.*

In the light of what I have just said, it should be apparent that the karma inherent in the life form from its birth includes both physiological and psychological karma. Physiological karma forms the hereditary characteristics that manifest themselves in physique and other bodily traits. Psychological karma generates the latent elements producing the foundation of psychological characteristics. As you say, there is a determinism in physiological constraints. In addition, Buddhism teaches that there is equally a determinism in the constraints of psychological karma.

Though it may not manifest itself at the time of birth, karma, which is imprinted deep in the force of life, may emerge either physiologically or psychologically later as the consequence of some accidental and apparently unrelated occurrence. In its explanation of both physiological and psychological karma, Buddhism explains determinism on the basis of karmic causes and effects. Once implanted in the eighth consciousness, karma resulting from the actions of the life form remains, never to be obliterated. Karmic causes are stored as a kind of latent energy to be activated in the future by the emergence of a karmic cause, that is a manifest force. Although the life entity cannot break from the bonds of cause and effect, it is not therefore impotent.

Free Will

HUYGHE: We have now come to the problem of free will, which is one with that of willpower. Distinguishing within the human the being that perceives (the objective extrovert) and the being that experiences (the subjective introvert) is not enough. A great deal of place must be given to the being who, informed of what he knows abstractly and of what he perceives with all his sensibility, is gradually led to orient his actions and make decisions. At this point, a new faculty is brought into play: the will. And the issue of the will is connected with the issue of free will. Are our decisions determined, are they the inevitable consequences of exterior and interior conditioning? Or are they free, even if only in part, depending only on us and our own autonomous choice? In these questions, philosophers have found material for a discussion that has been pursued throughout the centuries. Perhaps, by the light of what we have been saying, it is possible to try a new approach to the question.

Actually, determinism and free will are not as mutually exclusive as some simplistic philosophies would like to think. We have in us a part that is determined, our destiny. Our free part must take a stand and revolt against this destiny, for it is this free part that has the capacity to brave and bend, to direct fate. This is the problem of self-mastery.

IKEDA: This would seem a good occasion to recall the biological evolutionary process ending in Homo sapiens that you mentioned earlier the process from the spinal bulb to the reptilian brain, then to the paleencephalon and neencephalon and, finally, to the neocortex of the modern human brain. I say this because I see a parallel between this biological development and the expansion of freedom. Do you agree?

The human being has the freedom to become either incomparably excellent or utterly fearsome and vile. In other words, freedom is instability. Whether human beings make something valuable of it depends on whether they have the wisdom to know themselves accurately and to regulate and control themselves. People who have developed this kind of wisdom can make use of karmic effects in such a way as to create a better future. They can even overcome physical defects.

Karma is deterministic. But human beings have considerable latitude in dealing with it. No doubt, being born with this kind of freedom indicates some good karmic cause in a past existence. Most important of all, the ninth consciousness (*amara-vijnana*) is the source from which flows the power of life and independence to cope with the constraints and dominance of karma.

Of course, both good and bad karma exist. Bad karma is the seed from which spring delusion and suffering. When it has germinated and developed, the seed of bad karma manifests itself in delusions and impulses, including the instinctive drives of psychology, which are active in the seven lower consciousnesses. Conditioned reflexes, which are founded in innate karma, come into being after birth as an outcome of life experiences.

HUYGHE: The principal role to be assigned to the individual and to all humanity, if it is to fulfill its destiny and avoid floundering in the present crisis or other crises, is to develop the spiritual zone that you refer to as wisdom. Therein lies a characteristic of humanity not to be found in other animals. It is by means of this spiritual zone that human beings have passed the other animals in following a rising course of which humanity is the summit and which has required the degree of perfection to which humanity has attained.

The raison d'être is to be found in what can be called the spiritual transport, which is inseparable from the moral drive. The spiritual transport indicates the direction we are to take. The moral drive develops in us means to take that direction and provides us with the power to follow it. The spiritual transport is one with the moral drive. In a sense, it is preparation of the resources whereby the moral drive accomplishes its mission.

The moral drive is put to work in all religions worthy of the name. Believing in nothing but social morality is denying the facts, though it is true that the moral codes of certain primitive religions are dictated by society and its needs. To the same extent as the spiritual transport, the moral drive is apparent among human beings, among Christians as much as among Buddhists. Here our views coincide, though we approach the issue from opposite and distant coasts.

IKEDA: Practitioners of Buddhism have striven to pioneer a higher level of spiritual life in order to triumph over the constraints of the exterior world and the power of their own inner destiny. As I have already said, the most extensive and powerful basis for this spiritual life is the ninth consciousness (*amara-vijnana*). This consciousness is present in all human beings, but becoming aware of it is difficult. A person who is enlightened to, and fully manifests, it is called a Buddha.

Since it is present universally in all human beings, however, the ninth consciousness can be called an internal law. Scientists elucidate universal laws in the external world. Similarly, a Buddha manifests and elucidates the laws existing in the depths of life in order to transmit them to others. The very word *Buddha* means one who is enlightened or one who has attained wisdom (*bodhi*). The truths taught by Buddhism reveal the nature of the profoundest facts of life. The practical regimen advocated by Buddhism is a system of self-development enabling all human beings to be enlightened to the truth, just as a Buddha is.

This is a topic that I should like to treat more deeply when we discuss humanism. But, at this stage, I shall merely say that Buddhism divides life into ten states, the highest of which is that of Buddhahood and the lowest of which is that of hell. The criterion determining the difference between these two opposites is degree of freedom. The Japanese word for hell, *jigoku,* means a hell inside the Earth, a prison where people are deprived of liberty. And Buddhism explains hell as a place of bondage and total lack of freedom.

By contrast, the Buddha state is one in which enlightenment and wisdom have been attained. Though, on the surface, these two might seem unrelated to wisdom, as the French philosopher Simone Weil has clearly pointed out, wisdom is the subject element leading to freedom, and true freedom is won through wisdom.

For example, human beings have won freedom in the external, material world through scientific wisdom. But concentrating exclusively on the external world offers no help in coping with the maelstrom of delusions and karma that keep the inner world in fast bondage. Practice of Buddhist philosophy can, however, show the way to ultimate freedom in this inner world.

Desires and Aspirations

HUYGHE: In designating as karma the totality of fated elements constraining us—as long as our moral drive, armed with our will, fails to revolt against these fatalities to lead us to the way that our spiritual drive recognizes as better—to my surprise you, nonetheless, make a distinction between good and bad karma. This enables you to circumvent the problem.

Let us stop systematically opposing the two contrary conditions of determinism and free will, and give in to the temptation of a doctrinal, cut-and-dried position that is easy to adopt. In 1800, in his *The Vocation of Man,* the German philosopher Johann Gottlieb Fichte said that doubt is the result of the conjunction and contradiction of our objective thoughts, which must be deterministic, and our subjective feelings, which are evidence of our free will.

The best way to approach the problem is to employ psychology to condense reality in its many diverse aspects, which seem irreconcilable only to minds stifled by logic. In doing this, it becomes apparent that two diverse, fundamental forces are at work within us. One is immediate and impulsive and leads us to obey what, in order to excuse ourselves, we call fate, or all those things that you have lumped together as instinctive drives and experientially acquired instincts. This is where we encounter the two jaws of the vise closing down on us and representing, in my metaphor, injunctions from the interior and exterior worlds, the totality of which is determinism.

Yet another force emerges from our most profound nature or perhaps from the ascending current of all evolution. This force is like an instinct, urging us to perfect and transcend ourselves.

The first force is that of desires; the second, that of aspirations. Here again we observe the law, fundamental to life, of tension between opposites. We are subjected not to fate but to the attraction of two powers. Our task is to regulate this double attraction. We must satisfy the desires that push us toward such gratification or disengage the force whereby we take part in evolution and its foreseen conclusion. Either we choose to abandon ourselves to a weight that tends to drag us to the animal point of departure, or we triumph over it by joining the ascending current, which gives meaning to creation and opens the future to it.

Concupiscence limits us because it enslaves us to our senses and desires. Aspiration, on the other hand, liberates us because it is an initiative. It is apparent, then, that physical matter is the natural field of operation for concupiscence, whereas only the quest for quality explains aspirations. Concupiscence is directed toward the existing and present; aspiration, toward something that as of yet does not exist in the mundane order. Dissatisfied with what exists, aspiration demands more than ourselves. We are required to produce a *more* that completely excludes the quantitative and has entered the order of the qualitative to become one with the *better*.

As their very name suggests, the physical sciences have taken as their only domain the realm of physical matter and quantities. Naturally and almost fatally, they have clouded awareness of the interior way of the idea of quality. Concupiscence desires more; aspiration desires better. Verbal distinctions have been created only to respond to the demands of reality. Had it not been for the irrefutable obviousness of this duality, there would have been no need to invent the two terms.

Aspiration tends to establish things that do not yet exist but that people would like to introduce into the world. It leads to creation, which is located at the beginning of the road to liberty.

Aspiration of this kind occurs in artists when they conceive projects for certain works. Partly this is done to realize and give concrete form to something dwelling if only latently, in the artist who wishes to reveal these things to others. It is for the sake of introducing into reality a quality that has been missing in it. The artist takes up chisel or brush in order to create in the exterior world an object that he finds wanting.

In addition, creative acts may take the form of invention or deliberate additions to things that already exist. Such initiatives, which modify the established order of things, are manifestations of liberty inherent in human beings. Only the human being has the power of adding to the world something that he foresees and wishes but that neither exists nor enters into the determinism of the physical universe. Instead of being the object of pressure, the human being delivers a thrust. The moment he becomes a creator, the expert, acts in the same way.

Confronted with the desire for something real, the human being becomes submissive and enters into the play of determinism. But, when he aspires to make an addition, to reach a level of quality unanticipated by others, he initiates preparations for a creative, free act. Certain modalities may, it is true, influence the act but not its quality. The essence of human liberty is to be found in this transport, which, I repeat, belongs only to human beings. It is a human characteristic distinguishing us from the nearest nonhuman animals to at least as great an extent as reason.

And what is true of human works of art is equally true of human existence. The practical end may be determined and foreseen but not the moral quality animating it. It is because liberty has two paths at its disposal that the good and the beautiful, in the terms of traditional philosophy, are corollary and, in a sense, parallel forces.

IKEDA: I am surprised to see that what you say agrees completely with my own frequently entertained ideas. The expansion of human liberty must take place on two fronts: control of phenomena in the exterior world and control of the various forces at work inside, within the self.

The development of the scientific-technological civilization has brought a certain degree of freedom in relation to the exterior world with the result that human beings now suffer less intensely from some natural disasters and famine has been eliminated in some societies. This same development in civilization has had the adverse effect of liberating those inner forces requiring control—especially the instinctive drives and desires that can have a degrading influence. Expansion of our control of the outside world has been won at the price of submission to our desires. Or, it might be said, our civilization has flowered as we have been made slaves of our desires.

This progress of modern human history reminds me of Doctor Faust, who promised to sell his soul to the Devil in return for youth and wealth. In Göthe's version, in the end Faust is saved by God through the Virgin Mary, much to the chagrin of Mephistopheles. We can only ask ourselves if divine power will be equally as accommodating in offering to save modern humanity from its present predicament.

In my view, the current situation is more severe than the one Faust faced, since we are confronted by a law and not by the tender and forgiving Virgin Mother. Through the operation of our own willpower we must strive to rectify the mistake we have made in bartering our priceless souls for the gratification of fleeting desires and must initiate the struggle to control our innermost lives.

Although often regarded in the West as meaning fate, the Buddhist term karma actually means action and refers to the effects produced by the actions performed by an individual. The Buddhist belief is that all aspects of an individual's current state of existence—both interior, as in the nature of his personality, and exterior, as in the environment in which he finds himself—are karma-determined. No third party, like God, is responsible for deciding and manipulating these conditions. Consequently, all the interior and exterior forces binding us depend on karma, the struggle with which is interpreted by Buddhist thought as the issue of free will or liberty.

As you have just mentioned, some Buddhists regard karma as fixed and immutable. The Lotus Sutra, however, teaches that, by manifesting the essential life that is the source of all things, we can freely make use of our karma.

To take a homely example, some people are determined by karma to be short-tempered. This is generally regarded as a failing. Conversely, however, a short temper can be interpreted as a sign of liveliness and readiness to act. Realizing that he has such a karma-determined characteristic, a person is free to make use of it by suppressing his short temper when its effects are likely to be negative and making full use of it when it can be of genuine value.

In the broadest sense, education is an attempt to give individuals the power to expand their own freedom. But, in order that freedom may relate not merely to the external world, but also to the deep, subconscious, vital power, Buddhism teaches the need for a revolution of human life.

HUYGHE: The concept that we have been attempting to extract from humanity throughout our dialogue takes form: it is necessary to strive to develop the full and complete human being. I should like to call our approach humanism but in the largest, not the limited historical, sense. This complete human being may be compared to a carriage drawn by three horses. The first horse is sensibility, the receiver of messages relayed by external reality through our sensations. It is in addition, however, the perceiver of our inner reactions to those messages and of profound aspirations rising, originally, from our subconscious. The second horse is the intelligence, the capacity to be aware of the meanings of external and internal messages and to explain them in clear, intelligible, logically organizable notions. The third is the will or the power to choose freely among the various appeals attempting to subdue us and the aspirations born within us at the stimulation of our sense of responsibility. With the combined assistance of these three powers, the human being can be in full possession of his capacities and his destiny, which is partly, but I believe not entirely, determined and which is partly created in the fashion of a work of art. The greatest human nobility abides in this last.

Liberty and Morality

IKEDA: In all societies, human freedom has been recognized

as simultaneously desirable and fearsome. This is why societies have both limited freedom and established severe systems of social ethics to bind it psychologically.

Too many past restraints on freedom were employed in connection to the advantage of people in authority and have been removed in the process of modernization. While a necessary condition to it, freedom alone cannot ensure the manifestation of human dignity. Doing so requires constant application of human will, ideals, and powers of self-control. Of course, the value of freedom in ensuring human effort and self-restraint is great. In our time of greatly expanding liberty, the need to maintain correct relations between freedom and human dignity is all the more important.

HUYGHE: Desires rise from the depths provided by our physiology, character, and subconscious. They are drives that must be controlled in order to be directed or restrained. Aspirations reflect our fumbling attempts to improve ourselves and transcend the imperfections of human nature. This is where moral rules, established by society for the sake of its own sound development, can become stifling because they are moderate. Aspiration sometimes must go farther than social law.

This is the problem with morality. Society fully realizes that impulses born of our most instinctive desires can express a possibly depredating egoism that could damage social equilibrium. Society is, therefore, obliged to keep an eye on and shackle those impulses when necessary. It has established rules to be imposed on each person so that individual needs do not upset global balance.

But the case is entirely different with aspiration. Through the particular individual case (*me*), aspiration transmits a voice from the depths that, within us, obeys the law of evolution mysteriously imposed both by Creation and by man—Creation's most lucid part—for the sake of improvement. Since it inspires us to want to go beyond what exits, it must at the same time compel us to go beyond the practical means represented by established law. As the source of our free initiative, refusing to be limited by the framework of a fixed order, aspiration can find itself restrained by law, on which it must, however, exercise pressure in the name of perfection.

Our epoch has eagerly challenged rules, which it has found established by a secular society no doubt rigidified in ideas that are too narrowly formulated. It first of all perceived the limitations such rules impose on the exercise of freedom and, therefore, rebels against and tries to deny and eliminate them. Our epoch thus obeys the compensating rhythm that is the natural behavior of life but, in going too far along this path, may stimulate an inverse movement, against which we must be on our guard.

Even if ceaselessly perfected by an inventive opposition to cope with its narrowness, morality would nonetheless remain necessary. It is born of the human aspiration for something better. Armed with rational thought, human beings attempt to legislate aspirations and to cast them in molds of fixed ideas in the form of commandments and codes. But, according to an eternal dialectic, eventually aspiration for something better leads us to interpret moral codes as restrictive and oppressive and to wish to make them more supple, larger, and more perfect. Reaction against it is justified when moral law becomes a stifling formula. And all abstraction immobilizes and imposes fixed formulas.

Thus the offensive waged in our time against morality might have been justified in its initial drives. But such an offensive becomes dangerous when it begins extolling not only the liberty of the better, but also license. It is unwholesome to oppose an imperfect law that society attempts to impose by means of simple abandon to instincts. Doing so invites regression to the point at which the need for law originated.

In an eternal effort, liberty must always be exercised in the face of all laws, which can never be more than a single stage attained and, therefore, a threat of atrophy. Liberty must perform its creative role against such stagnation. It must be maintained as a progressive instrument and must provide moral law with new openings toward superior quality. History must continue to be a continuous, progressive dialectic. Awareness of the collective laws required to perfect society must always restrain instincts. But, the minute such laws have been established, an inverse dialectic is legitimately installed between it and aspiration, requiring that we go still farther and higher. In morality, as in art, there is a creative power.

IKEDA: Whereas nonhuman animals develop almost exclusively according to species, human beings are born with so many different possibilities for development that education is of decisive importance. After birth, the nonhuman animal progresses along a rectilinear path. Human beings, however, have a very broad choice of paths to follow. The liberty afforded us can be grounds for the growth of nobility or it can make demons of human beings. As the old Japanese proverb says, "Education counts for more than clan."

The philosophical argument persisting from ancient times as to whether human beings are innately good or innately evil bears witness to the freedom with which we are endowed to manifest either of these two poles. I believe that human beings are innately neither good nor bad but a neutral blank, yet capable of becoming either good or bad.

You seem to characterize the power for good as aspiration and the power for bad as desires. If I were to borrow your terms, I would say that desires represent the animal and instinctive energy in human beings, and aspiration the humane and creative energies. We are capable of manifesting either kind of energy and, under their influence, of becoming any kind of person. Since we are given the freedom to choose which of these forces will control us, we are in the painful position of constantly being compelled to make the choice.

Since their lives are determined by instincts, animals escape both the pain of having to make a choice and the danger that accompanies freedom. Laws and unwritten codes of social behavior are the rules that have been evolved to relieve human beings of the pain of choosing and the perils of freedom. In a sense, they represent restrictions on freedom and heteronomous control, sometimes imposed to serve the advantages of the ruling classes and sometimes generated by distrust in human nature. Ultimately, people become aware of these sources and react against them. Controls and regulations geared to the advantage of people in power fundamentally suppress general human dignity. Rules reflecting distrust in human nature despise the dignity of humanity and seem to endorse the idea of innate evil. Both kinds of rules represent negative and defensive, instead of positive and progressive, thought and, therefore, cannot help human beings manifest those aspects justly deserving of respect.

Action to break from some constraints is proof of human inner evolution and, as you say, reveals the manifestation of the power of aspiration. Undeniably, however, conscious reaction against the bonds of legal and moral codes, though justifiable at the outset, can lapse into license. This is why I feel it necessary to think of freedom from a somewhat different viewpoint.

In the broadest sense, freedom is freedom to act. Without such freedom, of course, all other liberty loses meaning. Nonetheless, the freedom to act alone does not enable us to perform in ways consonant with the dignity inherent in human life. We must realize in fact that apparently untrammeled acts are often bound by invisible constraints. Unless this problem is solved, freedom of action remains a two-edged sword.

As part of an attempt to illuminate the issue, I should like to cite a passage from chapter three ("Simile and Parable") of the Lotus Sutra: "(He) will constantly dwell in hell, strolling in it as though it were a garden, and the other evil paths of existence he will look on as his own home." The word hell means the most painful, suffering-filled state of life. The "other evil paths of existence" are the paths of authoritarianism in which the well-being of the self is elevated while that of others is despised. Persons traveling these ways egotistically lack consideration for the unhappiness of the weak. They are in a reprehensible state of subjugation to their own instinctive desires. As the passage in the sutra points out, such people are unaware of being in this condition and believe themselves to be happy and secure and have no thought of reexamining their position. Thinking themselves at home or amusing themselves in a garden, they are free to act as they choose. In this sense, they undeniably enjoy freedom of action. But the fundamental issue is this: can people who remain unaware of being in so inhuman a condition be called truly free? Similarly, is a person consumed with hatred and obsessed with revenge truly free? Is the person dominated by lust for power and constantly employed in trickery and plotting living in a way indicative of perfect liberty?

Ultimately, freedom depends on deepening the inner life. Given a piano, a person can sell it. He can smash it with a hammer. He can produce hideous noise by banging on the keyboard. But these courses of action produce no true value. To make good use of the instrument, he must control himself enough to master the techniques of performing on it. Generating maximum value demands acquiring maximum skill. Self-mastery to make this possible is supreme freedom. Attaining such liberty is manifestation of true human dignity.

The Guides: Intuition and Reason

HUYGHE: Man seems like a ship navigating the ocean and constantly at risk of becoming the plaything of forces that assail him and that he cannot master. He is impotent in the face of the winds, currents, and tempests ready to control his progress. But he has one essential trump card: to defend himself and even to make use of these forces, he can control his own actions in connection with them. Everything depends on the orders he gives the helm. And these orders themselves are functions of the itinerary he has chosen and, therefore, of the final destination he has selected.

Suspended between the part of him that is deterministically controlled and the part that is free, man, armed with reason, steers in the direction of his choice. Everything returns to the problem of command. In the final resort, man must give the command. In such a case, what can he rely on and what personal resources can he apply?

Nature gave animals instincts. Before the appearance of human beings, instincts were used only to fulfill animal necessities and ensure life's prolongation. Under such circumstances, everything is determined. In the case of human beings, however, a margin of liberty has been added to the picture. This freedom permits man, indeed, makes it his duty, to create responses suited to the questions his intelligence enables him to pose. And what is his guide in this operation? His two possible modes of adhering to reality correspond to the division, established at the beginning of the nineteenth century, between the subjective world within us and the objective world around us.

One of the modes arising from the subjective is supported by things manifesting themselves in us as instincts and intuitions and seems to consist of interior revelations rising imperatively from our depths. Through them is established communication with the universe by means of the roots, as it were, of our interior life, our psychical life.

We are an integral part of the universe. The parcel of living energy we represent participates in the global energy constituting it and imparting a forward course to it. We live this energy within ourselves and experience it internally. The experience manifests itself in intuitive form, which is no doubt the purest part of our intelligence, of which reason is actually no more than an organizing method.

This is the first guide that presents itself and sometimes imposes itself on us. Confronting its orders, however, another voice makes itself heard sometimes with enough power to drown that of the first. The second voice comes from the intellect, which, armed with logical reason and nourished by established precepts, strives to bend our behavior to the principles it accepts. Left to its instinctive determinism, the nonhuman animal pays no attention to the duality and the dilemma posed by it. But it is from this duality and dilemma that spring human liberty and the necessity to choose and decide. As a result of this situation, a kind of void for our resolution to fill is created before us. We must confront our instinctive desires and principles ready-made, if at times poorly adapted to reality, with the profound force of initial inspiration propelling and orienting us in the direction of improvement.

At this point, relying on the rational intelligence which it precedes, the intuitive intelligence finds its true role in transforming confused, internal drives and passing thus from the mist of impressions to the lucidity of ideas. It is here that reason, relying on logic, becomes a suitable instrument to guide us in the pursuit of our objectives. Simultaneously, reason makes us see and apprehend the goal of our journey and plots the surest path leading us to it. In this way, it becomes a good and serviceable instrument of liberty, the functioning of which it renders more effective. Reason is, however, no more than this. Ultimately, the fundamental options of our liberty do not depend on reason but rise from the deep, essential intuition that is sometimes called the moral conscience. This alone determines the paths and directions we must follow as we plot a way through the impending desert of the future.

IKEDA: Though it is frequently spoken of as the opposite of instinct, in my opinion, human reason often destroys the harmony that in nonhuman animals is preserved at various stages of mental development. In other words, instead of being their opposite, reason works in conjunction with various instinctive elements and, by causing them to amplify to extremes, in either good or bad directions, disrupts harmony. We must, therefore, concern ourselves not with the distinction between reason and instinct, but with the nature of the force stimulating the amplification of the two in conjunction. The fundamental issue is whether the force is one of insecurity and fear or one of hope and kindness.

People today are confused about choosing something with which to fill the void created before us by human freedom. This choice and reason operate on two different levels. Reason serves only as a guide and proposes no goals of its own. Consequently, reason and the sciences created by its operations are intrinsically neither good nor bad, but always neutral.

Scientists' recollections about their work offer suggestive material on the relation between intuition and reason. It is said that the process whereby scientists arrive at laws begins not with repeated rational analyses and experimentation but with sudden intuitive flashes establishing hypotheses. It is in the subsequent process of hypothesis verification that reason comes into play in analytical and experimental work.

Nihilism, which is currently prevalent, represents a kind of emotional prostration at being unable to find anything to fill the void in front of us. Epicureanism is irritation at the same inability. Both arise from impotence to use the power that is available for attaining goals. People of these bents are like painters who, though masters of the techniques of painting, for want of ideas about what to paint throw down the brush and find relief from tedium in smearing colors on canvas. The canvas is the void left open to us by our liberty. Technical skill represents reason in that it is capable of working out ways to fill up that void. Images to use in filling the canvas are formed by intuition rising from the depths of life. Today, however, many people are losing both richness of intuition and aware-ness of the totality and fullness of the force of life. And this is the fundamental pathological source of our confusion.

To continue the metaphor, whereas, owing to the instinctive-ly determined way they live, nonhuman animals are limited to a single brush and one color for use on a miniscule canvas, human beings have been given a vast canvas and virtually numberless brushes and abundant colors with which to fill it.

Ultimately, reason is the servant of intuition and it is the nature of intuition that matters most. Modern science is vast as is the power latent in the reason behind it. The quality of human intuition determines the direction in which that power is directed. Reason can help build peace or bring about war. But determining whether a pacific or a belligerent path is to be followed is predetermined by intuition. Therefore, although theories for the realization of peace are important, it is far more vital to create a loathing for war deep in the minds of human beings everywhere.

Some scientists interpret reason as the element that enables humanity to rise above the savage beasts. In fact, however, reason is unrelated to the issue and is no more than a means for expressing savagery or development beyond savagery. One of the causes of the confusion prevailing in society today is the blanket acceptance of, and trust in, reason as being intrinsically good. It must never be forgotten that reason is equally capable of constructing theories for the maintenance of peace and evolving theories approving of war.

In conformity with the quality and degree of intuition, reason forms systems. The more ordered the theories in the system, the more absolute and unifying they become. But, created within concepts by reason, such systems are always more or less out of synchronization with the rhythms of life, on which they depend. In realizing this to be true, the rational mind should adopt an attitude of humility before the universal force of life. Loss of such humility is surely a cause of the environmental pollution plaguing the whole world today.

In brief, I believe that true human progress depends not on reason, but on the deepening and qualitative improvement of the intuition controlling reason.

HUYGHE: Unfortunately, modern society is fanatical about reason, which is of course necessary and sufficient in its way. But our society tends to confuse reason with reasoning and is incapable of nourishing it or balancing it with deeper intuitions.

This sets our society apart from all its predecessors. It is possible to compare our society and those of the past on various counts, but the most fundamental difference is the greater proximity between human beings and animals. This closeness was based on an inner understanding combining innate intuitions and acquired experiences. Modern society, however, is willing to admit nothing but objective facts. Ancient societies were primarily concerned about elucidating the subjective experience. By means of myths that are the basis of religions, as well as of evocative, suggestive, and expressive images, they learned and mastered the horde of things possessing them without being logical. Societies codified these things in manners and mores which, little by little, hardened into traditions and codes of law devoid of both rational character and need of explanation since they were often attributed to divine revelation and were, thus, supported by religion.

By contrast, modern society is devoted to affirming its rationalism. This trend has been especially pronounced since the eighteenth century which, to signify passage from a shadowy zone of interior revelations to a lucid zone of logical laws, is called the Century of Enlightenment. Indeed, society is limited to a rational organization of the sensory experiences of the world. With this development, a progressive deformation characterized by increasing utilitarianism has isolated us from all interior contacts with the universe and has substituted for them nothing but sensory contacts ordered by science and logical methods. At the same time, we passed from a civilization of customs and mores to one of administration, which was soon transformed into bureaucracy. This system strove to organize society according to rules ostensibly conceived by reasoning and pure logic and in maximum conformity with scientific methods. The most recent form of society, that of the Marxists, bases its politics on a scientific pretense by now completely out-of-date but persisting nonetheless. Similarly, politics in general turn farther and farther in the direction of sociology of which, in line with the same kind of obsession, people strive to make a new science modeled on the physical sciences.

Current society is compelled to break all true contact with nature because, on top of everything else, it tends to become virtually exclusively urban. And this only precipitates the rupture. A farmer who develops excessively abstract faculties finds natural correctives all around him in his daily life. An urbanite, on the other hand, is almost retired in the segregation of an artificial world. More and more, members of legislative bodies, ministers, and the people who dictate laws are the products of a conventional technocratic society cut off from all experience of nature. Modern man is isolated from his sources, and though he may visit them from time to time, it is only as a distraction. He can be said to go out for a vacation or for a weekend just as he goes out to the theater or to see a film. Nature has been reduced to the role of an exterior spectacle. Tourists looking at the sea for a few hours during their holidays are very much like people seated in a cinema watching the screen.

Moreover, modern civilization grows increasingly mechanical. As we have already said, mechanization is a process of abstracting movement and the normal expression of life. All of this contributes to substituting for the profound, mysterious, diverse, and basically incomprehensible real world an artificial world that has become too perfectly logical and is characterized by the basic flaw of artificiality. Reality is hidden behind a false front fabricated by man with his rational means and limited to reflecting human pretensions.

IKEDA: Although, as an examination from the standpoint of Buddhist philosophy makes all the more apparent, the present crisis is intimately related to their hypertrophy, both reason and desires are essential to the preservation of life. The problem today is that they have been thrown out of balance. Buddhism posits what are known as the Three Poisons—greed, anger, and folly—as sources of all earthly desires and, therefore, essential to the maintenance of life. It can be said in fact that human civilization has been created in the search for ways of adequately and effectively satisfying desires. In aiding and satisfying desires, reason has had a great role to play. From the age of the most primitive tools, civilization has been a product of reason.

Whereas it is true that the angles at which stones were chipped to produce cutting implements and arrowheads reveal acute and rational human observation and creative ingenuity, it must not be presumed that reason was the principal stimulus in their production. Desire always came first, and reason played an advisory part. Civilizations have been created in human efforts to obtain desirable natural products. And, while some have been limited to simple tools whereas others have evolved complex machinery, in all instances desire has taken the lead in the cooperative undertaking of their production and reason has been an assistant.

Modern civilization is powerful enough to threaten the continued existence of the natural order and to satisfy the needs and desires of a broad segment of the general populace.

The driving force behind its achievements has been the pursuit of satisfaction of desires which, however, have proved insatiable since fresh ones invariably arise the moment old ones have been fulfilled. The great technological heights our civilization has attained have only accelerated the pace at which human desires increase.

Buddhism consistently attempts to deal with desires, which, stimulated by the Three Poisons of greed, anger, and folly, are the cause of all human suffering and unhappiness. Primitive Hinayana Buddhism strives to suppress and eliminate desires directly and has devoted much philosophical speculation to working out practical ways of attaining this goal. But, since desire is characteristic of, and essential to, the preservation of life, eliminating it completely inevitably means the elimination of life itself. Desire is a function and aspect of life.

By contrast, instead of trying to suppress or eliminate them, Mahayana Buddhism attempts to cultivate in the mind of each individual the power to control desires and orient them in right directions. Because of the difference in their approaches, the two forms of Buddhism have had different followings. Hinayana discipline is actually possible only for people who have given up the ordinary world for a life devoted to religious practices, in other words for monks. Mahayanists, on the other hand, are mostly of the laity.

Mahayana scriptures offer a variety of ways for establishing mental power to control desire, but all of them are ultimately resolvable to transcending the smaller, nuclear self, attaining unity with all other beings in the greater self, and allowing this greater self to assume control.

All societies have developed either taboos or moral codes to limit human desire. Without denying them, Mahayana Buddhism insists that such restraints alone are insufficient and that the power for self-control must be cultivated from within life itself.

Our own age has seen desire run wild and join forces with science, the product of highly sophisticated reasoning powers, in the creation of a vast material civilization. Concomitant with this, we have watched traditional morals and restrictions, which might control desire and keep it on the right path, grow impotent.

We must not overlook the individualism that lies at the heart of these tendencies. Individualism has played a complementary role in the rejection of institutionalized morality, the liberation of desire, and scientific investigation.

The resurrection of the kind of institutionalized morality that rejects individualism constitutes a rejection of the ideal of human dignity, with which the development of individualism is intimately connected. Although true human dignity does not result from individual isolation, it does require independence as an indispensable condition. In short, we must select the direction leading to both individualism—in the good sense—and correct coexistence with other beings. Devising ways of coordinating individual independence with coexistence must be left to the judgement of each person. Clearly, to enable people to make such judgment we must insist not on the revival of institutionalized morality, but on cultivating the mental power to control desires. This cannot, of course, solve all the issues involved in the current crisis but, unless solutions begin with the way human beings actually live, all efforts will be fruitless.

HUYGHE: I only wonder if human beings can accomplish the task.

The Future for Humanity

IKEDA: Scientists today caution that the contemporary crisis extends beyond any one culture and threatens the continued survival of the entire human race. What is your honest opinion of the chances of our survival?

HUYGHE: Everything depends on the human liberty of which we have been speaking. This liberty is the prerogative of human conscience, which is essential to its manifestation, and is very much limited by the insufficiency of our intellectual means, our sanity, and our control of passion. The determinism of our instincts, too, is a limiting factor. Liberty is very fragile and always under threat, but it exists and is incontestable.

The future of humanity depends on this liberty, and my prognosis is, therefore, very simple: if man gives in passively to the evolution that he has initiated, if he is content to continue like a wheel rolling down a slope, in the direction he is following without attempting to alter course, he will without doubt plunge to destruction. But we have, thank God, a margin of liberty based on sanity. Is not our dialogue an effort to achieve that selfsame, or a greater sanity? We have the basic freedom to make our actions conform to the views of our saneness.

Since moral resistance responding to physical pressures means that the future is only partially determined, we cannot foresee what is to come. Nonetheless, there are possibilities. One is that man will remain blind. If this happens, no measures will remain for resisting the technical means he has initiated and that constantly increase their pressures and expand their amplification. In such a case, it would be possible to envisage the destruction of humanity. I have already mentioned this hypothesis.

But this will not stop the vital drive, the drive of life, that we observe in operation throughout thousands of years of history. It will continue on its course. It incarnates itself in a species as long as that species continues useful to its development. Any species dies the day it loses its usefulness and becomes a hindrance. And life passes outward and onward. Life has already made tentative trials of this kind and has abandoned its materials. For instance, in prehistoric times, the dinosaurs and plesiosaurs disappeared because they proved incapable of, or inefficient in, adapting. Other species have been blocked and have remained stationary. It has been said that human beings are descended from apes. But this is not the case. The ape is merely one branch, an attempt that has stopped where it is. It represents the last branch before the appearance of man, the next branch, or what scientists call a phylum. The ape has been stopped at the point at which it succeeded. Though it could go no farther, instead of disappearing it ceded its place to a new venture.

Man, the new venture, is gifted with means of development unknown to his predecessors. His intelligence is expandable to the heights of the spirit. His failure to profit by that intelligence and his willingness to allow the system he has created to enclose and stifle him like a paralyzing iron corset will in no way obstruct life. Life will simply put out the next branch which we human beings can no more imagine than the apes were able to imagine what the human being would be.

Therefore, the problem is simple. Either man goes on fulfilling his function of serving life in its ceaseless self-improving drive farther along its upward course until, finally, that very drive allows him to overcome obstacles and attain a heretofore unheard-of state of development, or, ignoring the liberty imparted to him and failing to make the required effort, man will prove to lack the intelligence to complete his task. In the latter case, I am convinced, the phenomenon of autodestruction will bring about the disappearance of humanity. But this will not hinder the world from proceeding on its course with other means and other solutions.

Far from contradicting this hypothesis, Buddhist teachings posit a faith that agrees with the thought I have just set forth. For instance, its vision of bounding across successive lives, which progress or regress according to the liberty afforded to make good or ill uses of them, is a concept analogous with the one I take as a guide. Certainly the ability of successive lives to progress ceaselessly as long as freedom of action is well used can be applied to the entire human race.

Perhaps the parallelism I seem to feel between Buddhist thought and my own convictions could be pushed farther still, always with the understanding that the two were formed under historical conditions with different philosophical traditions. At any rate, it is interesting to discover revealing convergences beyond systems in which thought is enclosed by cultural atavism.

It is not absolutely unthinkable that the thrust of life, which conducts its ventures through man (though perhaps it will leave man and go beyond him), could pursue its course somewhere other than on Earth. The farther we go, the more difficult it becomes to believe that life and its enterprises and upward course occur only on this minuscule planet lost in the infinity of interstellar spaces. I believe that a number of eminent scientists think this way, too.

I am fully aware that the French molecular biologist Jacques Monod (1910–76) insisted that the emergence of life is so totally unforeseeable a chance, that it is difficult to conceive the accumulation of circumstances that made its appearance on Earth possible. I disagree entirely. I believe that, unable to free himself of nineteenth-century blinkers, Monod was too firmly attached to an extremely limited scientific view.

Science itself supports my interpretation. Aerolites show traces of the elements constituting life, and the presence of amino acids found in living matter has been perceived in interstellar spaces. Life is not an inevitably miraculous occurrence unique to Earth as the consequence of fabulous chance. It is a power elsewhere as well.

It is by no means impossible, therefore, that the drive of life has had ramifications in other parts of the universe. Conceivably, if, in his aberration, man annuls the part of life occurring on Earth, it will pursue its course elsewhere under other forms and in other conditions. I believe Buddhism envisions the possibility of the reincarnation chain's continuing in extraterrestrial space.

IKEDA: Yes, Buddhism teaches the possibility of being reborn somewhere other than on Earth. The Buddhist scriptures frequently relate instances in which bodhisattvas come from distant worlds—in what in modern terms must be called cosmic space—to attend the gatherings at which Shakyamuni Buddha taught. For instance the Lotus Sutra, which according to the faith to which I adhere is the most important of all Buddhist scriptures, tells of the arrival from the world of Treasure Purity of the Buddha Many Treasures, seated in a Treasure Tower, to hear Shakyamuni teach. In addition, countless other Buddhas from extraterrestrial worlds in cosmic space throughout the ten points of the universe (the four cardinal points of the compass, the four intermediate points, zenith, and nadir) gather to be part of the same congregation.

All of these worlds undergo a repeating cycle of alteration, called the Four Kalpas: Formation, Continuance, Decline, and Disintegration. Life, including individual human lives, exists in an endless cycle determined by the causes and effects of the actions of the given life form. This implies that, when the world in which it has abided is destroyed, life itself moves to another suitable world to resume its operations.

In your comments on biological evolution, you said that when they fail to make full use of their capacities and lose the ability to adapt, certain life forms vanish, ceding their place of primacy to other life forms. This interpretation of the relation between the life form and its environment precisely accords with the Buddhist doctrine called *Eshō Funi* in Japanese. This doctrine explains that the life form and its environment are indivisibly united.

In the Lotus Sutra, bodhisattvas and the Buddha's disciples, especially Shariputra, often ask what the world of the future is like and what its name and the name of its Buddha are. Interestingly, the names of the worlds and their Buddhas always demonstrate close correspondence. For example, the Buddha Many Treasures comes from the world of Treasure Purity. This is another indication of the fundamental belief in close interrelation between the life form and its environment.

Moreover, Buddhism teaches that, according to the good or bad nature of the accumulated actions of the individual, a life that is currently in human form may be reborn in some other form. The nature of the psychological motivations governing the person's actions—greed, malevolence, compassion, and so on—determines the form in which rebirth will occur. For instance, it is said that a person whose life has been controlled by a series of violent hatreds may be reborn as a venomous snake.

Buddhism considers thought and reason characteristics of human life and places great importance on applying reason to control desires for the sake of balanced tranquility. An individual who repeatedly injures others because he cannot control his instincts and impulses becomes an instinct-driven animal lacking the power of reason. By contrast, even should the world be destroyed or become uninhabitable by human beings, people who have consistently made use of and applied their powers of reason will be reborn, in human form, in some other world. But indifference to the fate of the Earth out of assurance of rebirth, in human form, in another world constitutes abandoning the use of reason in a truly worthy form and can, therefore, be grounds for rebirth in a nonhuman form. Consequently, even if for only the sake of our own human rebirth, we must all apply reasoning powers to the full in dealing with the crisis threatening humanity with extinction, and must strive for improvement and the continued existence and increased prosperity of our race.

PART FIVE

Artistic Creativity

HUYGHE: To justify his existence and ensure his future, man must fulfill the one role to which he is suited. Human beings are not only gifted, as are other animals, with instincts making it possible to preserve themselves, to live, and to survive by means of semiautomatic responses to the most ordinary situations. Nor are they endowed only with reason and freedom providing the capacity to adapt to unexpected eventualities by understanding new situations and conceiving the right solutions to them.

Human beings do not limit their task to safeguarding life but embody the ambition to lead life to a higher, still undiscovered qualitative level because, unlike nonhuman animals who simply repeat themselves, human beings command openings to the new, to things that do not exist yet, to progress. Into a world subjected to immutable physical laws, where effects are perpetually repeated in identical manners, man introduces the power to employ creative liberty for the sake of perfecting the world. Like a tested instrument, human reason puts itself at the service of this second propensity, just as it serves the first.

Art exemplifies this power, imparted to man and to man alone. Through art we exercise the capacities that distinguish us from the rest of the known world. A sense of responsibility makes it incumbent on us to apply that power. Actually art is creation and is valuable only in so far as it is creation. It becomes mere illusion or mockery if it imitates, repeats, or limits itself to applying rules and recipes. Art asserts itself only when it adds to what is and even to what is foreseeable. By means of the creative act, art introduces into reality, not a repetition or a consequence, but a new, virgin, contribution, a kind

255

of supplementary richness for which nothing seems to have prepared the way. The artist himself fails to understand its meaning entirely except in achieving it and may himself be surprised at it.

Consequently, art is also liberty—an affirmation and demonstration of our liberty—because its characteristics are valid only when they escape from determinism. Ultimately, art exists only when it introduces into reality a quest for, and achievement of, quality that is completely immeasurable but is inevitably experienced by an active response incited in the spectator by the creator.

1

The Spiritual Value of Art

HUYGHE: Art is one of those activities that transcend the operation of the intelligence (already shared by nonhuman animals) and allows man to attain the domain that he alone is capable of attaining and that must be called the spiritual life. A precise linguistic differentiation ought to be made between the two notions of rational intelligence and spirit, which are too often confused with each other in usage.

Essentially, rational intelligence is the capacity to situate perceptions within a system organized by the understanding. Man uses rational intelligence to isolate, in definite concepts, elements that, confused in reality, he records, whether they exist within or around him. He seizes on some of these elements and articulates them according to the laws of a logic elaborated by himself and dominated by the rules of cause and effect. In addition, he imagines his future actions and the means he will employ to bring them about. First and foremost, intelligence is a means of understanding and clearly managing interior and exterior facts.

By contrast, the spirit is, in the highest sense, a means for transcending these facts and for conceiving ways of imparting to them the impetus to carry them still farther. In this sense, which is confined to confirming the linguistic distinction between the "intellectual" and the "spiritual," the spirit is man's highest path, leading beyond what is and beyond himself in order to accomplish even more of the latent potentialities, the accomplishment of which is the aspiration of the better part of his being.

I am obliged to employ the term better part because, with the spirit, we depart from facts, in which we participate by organizing them, to the better, which we attempt to realize by augmenting value. Innate intuition of value introduces into the universe a novel capacity, the capacity of quality. This capacity is appreciated only because, without it, by means of reason, the intelligence would be unable to understand anything but quantities, things that can be defined and measured. A purely positivist mentality remains closed to the notion of quality, which is unsubstantiated by facts. Grasping it requires an awakening of the spiritual impulse, latent in all human beings. Man must entrust himself to that impulse and demand of it propulsion enabling him to contribute to the progress of the universe.

Spiritual perception of quality opens up new dimensions: aesthetic, ethical, and sacred, the last of which is the source of all religion.

Art is, therefore, one of the most important spiritual activities permitting us to go beyond things that, belonging to the realm of the knowable, depend solely on rational intelligence.

Art, the Third Reality

IKEDA: Each time I look at an outstanding painting, be it a landscape, portrait, or still life, I am deeply impressed by the acute, extraordinary powers of observation possessed by artists. Fine paintings transcend what is visible to the eye. More than by their technical skill I am astounded by artists' power to go beyond a subject's exterior appearance to observe something deeper. Although they are no doubt gifted from birth, artists must refine and develop their abilities through training before they can manifest them fully.

HUYGHE: You are quite right to say that artists go beyond their subjects' external appearances to observe something deeper. It is in this that art assists us in understanding a fundamental fact: there is not only one reality, there are two. Concrete reality, organized in space and constituted by physical matter, is observable by our sensory organs, our bodies. The second, inner, reality depends much less on space than on time, for it is located in no place. It is quite accurate to say that it is in our heads, although we would be hard put to pinpoint its actual location there. It is everywhere and nowhere. Within the precincts of our bodies, it is part of our lives, like which it is nothing but passing time or, as Henri Bergson called it, the interior continuance. In connection with this idea, the notion of space-time as enunciated by physics is useless. In the practice of life, the two experiences are actually irreducible.

The entire problem of human life is the intersection, or interference, of two dimensions: space, in which our bodies are located, and time, which transports and carries away our conscious and subconscious lives. We are of time. We age second by second and are no longer the same. Time can even be called the very substance of our psychical existence.

Our reality is intermediary between these two worlds. It is inscribed in the physical world by our corporal support but unfolds in the continuance as a consequence of the ascent of life toward consciousness. I believe that what is called the present—and is graspable neither in nor around us—is the point of intersection of time and space. When thought sets us outside the present, when we imagine ourselves in the past or the future, we cease to be situated in space. We find ourselves there only at that point of intersection that is called the present.

As we have noted over and over again, the West—the classical West as evolved by the Greco-Roman world—believed man to have grasped the exterior world with his senses and to have organized it within himself by means of logically organized ideas.

But the West has experienced phases other than the classical one, such as, for instance, the Middle Ages, or the nineteenth century, in so far as it showed itself dissatisfied with the world as conceived in Cartesian reason or Newtonian physics. This blossomed into a much wider awareness which has, as we have already said, stirred up the contemporary crisis through efforts to break free of the materialism of modern civilization.

This awareness developed very early in Germany, at the end of the eighteenth century with the forerunners of the Romantic movement. And, again as we have already noted, though the West's discovery of the Orient is not unrelated to this development, there are probably deeper reasons. In the fashion of the peoples of northern Europe, the Germans were predisposed to lay claim to a different explanation of the world and asserted themselves as descendants of nomadic nations and barbarians who had scoured the Eurasian plain and were, therefore, by origin related to the Orient and China. The intermediary peoples, like the Scythes, were the vehicles by means of which sinuous, interlaced decorative motifs were transported from Asia to Europe. Such motifs are to be found as far afield as Scandinavia and even, in the eighth and ninth centuries, in the Christian miniatures of Ireland. The Mediterranean, however, remained more closely locked up in the Greco-Latin world.

The basis created in this way provided the grounds for the discovery of Buddhist philosophy, which explains, among other things, the philosophy of Schopenhauer. The German thinkers were the first to enunciate the opposition of the exterior, essentially spatial, world and the interior, essentially temporal, world. They summarized this opposition in the dualism of objective and subjective or the me and not-me stated by Johann Gottlieb Fichte (1762-1814) in his *Grundlage der gesamten Wissenschaftslehre* (The Basis of all the Sciences of Knowledge).

The objective world is defined by the rule of matter in space. In it, everything obeys permanent laws and can be summarized in statable facts that are identical for everything. The subjective world, however, the dimension of which is duration of time, is made dangerous by the changes of creativity. Though distinct, the two worlds are linked by man. Even the interior man shares his consciousness between the two declivities. Because of his spiritual essence, he belongs to the world of temporal continuance and subjectivity. On the other hand, his corporeality links him to space and objective reality. Thus what can accurately be called his intelligence—his ideas, reason, and logic—are closely adapted to this world.

Between the two worlds dividing him man has created a third: art, which I propose calling the third reality. Art consists of using solid elements like marble, wood, and so on to establish, or inscribe, in the world of matter and space traces and projections of the interior subjective world.

With the advent of art, there is more than habitual cohabitation between the subjective human world, which animates the interior life, and the objective world, in which we are physically located and where we act. All of a sudden, instead of merely cohabiting, the two worlds have fused and been realized and materialized in a work of art. The work of art is then composed precisely of two parts: a physical, material constitution and a content or a kind of interior nature that emanates outward, just as our psychic life emanates in our facial expressions. In other words, the artist endows the materials he fashions with the power to manifest an interior life that they lack but with which the artist impregnates them. This is the miracle of art.

You are correct in pointing out the duality in the artist between innate gift and technical skill. I think the following explanation will make this perfectly clear.

What is innate in the artist is his ebullient inner life, the secret that he possesses and desires to manifest or inscribe in the exterior world. Technical skill is the material medium through which he is able to imbue an object with the expressive power emanating from his interior life.

Consequently, something can exist as a valid work of art only if it originates from the force of the interior life, from the innate. Obviously, this interior life must enrich other human beings by enlarging, expanding, and elevating their ordinary awareness of the world and of themselves.

This is the essential part of genius—derived from Latin *igenium*, and the prefix *in* indicates its interior nature. Genius resides in the interior creative power experienced by an exceptional being who wishes to communicate in order to enrich others. Technical skill—and talent that controls it—is first of all knowledge and mastery of the material media employed: how to cut stone; how to cast bronze; how to apply paint to canvas; and what to mix with pigments (oil, egg white, or water in the case of watercolor and wash drawings).

What is talent? Talent is the ability to utilize technical skill in an effective manner and to provide it with a certain method of inscribing permanently in some material the message the genius wishes to convey.

Essentially subjective by origin, genius nonetheless involves talent, which is the capacity whereby it escapes from itself and translates itself into the exterior world. In addition, technical skill prevents talent from wandering in the void and enables it to attain, effectively and long-lastingly, the goals proposed by genius.

The fundamental goal of art is transition from time to space. In addition, however, it must forearm space against the damage of time. All that we experience in our interior life is condemned to annihilation with the second during which we experience, sense, and even think it. Memory prolongs it but not beyond forgetfulness and, at best, no longer than the individual lifetime. Transition into the world of space—that is, inscription in forms—confers endurance. This is the course that artistic creation follows.

Moreover, in doing this, art introduces quality into space, which is actually the domain of quantity. Science envisions space exclusively as the realm of quantity because it operates on quantities that make mathematics possible. For its part, art emanates from the interior world, the only place where quality can be experienced or created. The moment we enter the realm of the psyche, nothing can be measured. The nineteenth century found it necessary to invent psychophysiology to discover, by means of the detour of physical manifestations—ostensibly equivalent to psychic manifestations—an ersatz measurement that is valuable only in very elementary cases. The enterprise was in vain because it ran afoul of the irreducible opposition between the quantitative, suitable to measure and devolved from the physical world, and the qualitative, obedient to appreciation and belonging to the spiritual world.

Quality cannot be explained in terms of numerically measurable definitions. Depending entirely on interior experience, it cannot be perceived unless one realizes it within oneself, unless one experiences it within oneself in a creative manner. This is why certain beings can never open themselves to quality in, for example, a work of art. Or, if they can open themselves, it is only to the level where their own experience stops. Conceivably genius incorporates in its work quality transcending what admirers can register. Probably, in a work of genius, there is a great deal more than even a gifted person can discover.

At this point, the opposition between the exterior and interior worlds has been passed and we find a new opposition between quantitative and qualitative. And, the moment we evoke the qualitative, assigning a situation in time or a location in space no longer suffices. It is now necessary to add a scale of value gradations; that is, gradations in the augmentation of value. This is an immense innovation.

At this stage, the only thing to be imagined is the progressive ascent leading human beings from the most physical foundations—both sensual and sensorial—to sentiments and thoughts, to ideas and, finally, to spiritual experiences.

Quality is an ascending movement hurling humanity on the ladder of values, the gradations of which move toward a divine infinity. It is the absolute that men embody in God.

Beyond the Visible

IKEDA: You have taken our discussion to a much higher plane by clarifying the essential nature of artistic creation. In considering observation of things beyond their mere physical appearance, the Buddhist concept of the Five Types of Vision—the Eye of Common Mortals, the Divine Eye, the Eye of Wisdom, the Eye of the Law, and the Buddha Eye—is interesting and elucidating. The Physical Eye provides only sensory perception of the actual material, exterior form of the object being viewed. The Eye of Heaven—an idea smacking of the supernatural—goes beyond the purely physical exterior of the object, but perceives no more than is perceptible to the Physical Eye.

The Eye of Wisdom, however, penetrates to the laws operative within and among objects. This is the kind of perception observed among scientists who develop physical laws and among artists with the genius for grasping the true inner nature of things. The Eye of the Law is represented by the perception of the bodhisattva who sees all phenomena in order to save sentient beings from suffering and perplexity. The Eye of the Buddha correctly sees all things and phenomena throughout the universe and throughout the flow of time from the past to the present and into the future. The Eye of Wisdom and the Eye of the Buddha are faculties put to use by Buddhas and bodhisattvas to save human beings from the depths of suffering. In my opinion, as long as they use their work to perform a similar saving role and not merely to satisfy their own creative longings or fulfill themselves spiritually, artists and scientists, too, can be endowed, if not with the Buddha Eye, at least with the Eye of Wisdom. Only a person who completely understands infinity—as a Buddha does—can attain the Buddha Eye.

Without being obsessed by the constantly changing phenomenal world, the true artist directs his gaze to the immutable world within and opens the way toward infinity. It is in this that I sense a deep bond between art and religion.

Since they rely little on exterior forms of objects, though sculptors and painters begin with realistic representation, their versions of their subject matter differ widely according to racial and cultural background. Do you agree that such differences arise less from techniques than from various ways of approaching subject matter?

HUYGHE: Although it may be true that painting and sculpture originated with faithful representation of the visible world, it must be observed that, for a very long time, such representation has been not an end but a means. An artist fixes the appearance of bodies or objects with the aim of using it to evoke the ideas with which it is charged. Specialist studies have shown that representations of animals in prehistoric art embody a whole system of symbols, the key to the deciphering of which still escapes us, by means of which the artists strove to give definite form to the magical or religious beliefs of the society to which they belonged.

Archaeology proves that, for many ages, in already developed societies, art preserved this role. In the first centuries of the Christian Era, the Fathers of the Church reaffirmed this function, the development of which iconographers from Emile Male (1862–1954) to Erwin Panofsky (1892–1968) followed throughout the Middle Ages. All religious art, as has been verified in the Orient as well, employs representation in order to signify something, and the image always embodies an idea.

With this reservation, for the sake of self-perfection, art has ceaselessly developed the realism of its representation. Often, indeed, as in the case of seventeenth-century Dutch painting, realistic representation has been a goal.

Nonetheless, everything teaches us that the role of art is not to re-create exterior reality. The idea of such re-creation became a conviction only with the rise of bourgeois, materialist, and positivist society. Art history has, in fact, shown that the search for exact realism—the trompe-l'oeil style—manifests itself when bourgeois philosophy and aesthetics dominate. The significance of art can only be truly understood as long as we remember that reality has, as we have been saying, two forms. Exterior—or if one prefers, objective—reality is the object of the kind of art called realistic. Subjective reality, which we carry inside us, which we experience, constitutes a psychic complex where instincts, sensibility, thought, and so on come into play. The proper function of art is to create a balance and a bond between objective reality, which brings to the work the materials of its language and the bases of its legibility and communicability, and subjective reality, which introduces into the images of the work (thereafter endowed with symbolic power) all the psychic content it commands.

From this it emerges that, in its role of intermediary, mediator, or third reality, art is suspended between permanent exterior reality, which remains perceptibly the same throughout space and time because it obeys the immutable laws evolved by science, and interior reality, which is diverse, unstable, and changing.

Actually, interior reality differs according to the individual, character, and propensities. In addition, it varies according to the collective to which the individual belongs since, through education and the operation of the environment they constitute, such groupings impress their ideas on each of their members. Various and even contradictory elements influence objective reality, as represented in art, as they bring about an intimate fusion with subjective reality.

It is, therefore, natural and inevitable that not only each society, era, human group, and generation, but also each individual should propose different versions of the same objects. The difference is translated in transcription methods, first of all in the interpretation of the form, because it is in interpreting that the human spirit grasps the spectacle the eyes register in a way permitting it to make itself intelligible. This can even be called the function of art.

IKEDA: In other words, concrete reality projects subjective reality on materials; and art and culture are interpretations of objective reality from the standpoint of subjective reality. Regional cultures then represent distinctive subjective realities created throughout history. And one of the most disturbing trends in current civilization is the devitalization of local cultural traditions in daily life. Many young Japanese find traditional Japanese art and culture more alien than those of the West. They rarely attend performances of the Noh or Kabuki and would never dream of decorating their rooms with ukiyo-e prints or oriental ink paintings. They find Western theater more familiar than traditional Japanese dramatic forms and are most at home with motion pictures and television. And at present people familiar with even Western modern painting are considered classic, and photographs are all the rage.

Of course, uniformity and mass production have something to do with this trend. Eager to have their works mass-produced and accepted by the largest possible audience, some creative workers water down their individuality, their subjective reality. Since what these people produce are works of creative endeavor, subjective reality is not altogether eliminated, but ingenuity is employed to make it inconspicuous.

It may be that people today avoid powerfully subjective art and prefer objective works in which the subjective reality of the artist is suppressed—works that are real and, in a sense, calm and detached—because of their own desire to avoid direct contacts and dialogues. In a modern world in which opportunities to come into contact with objective reality are restricted, artificial products may serve as a substitute. Certainly a photograph of a grassy plain or a forest is a psychological window revealing much more than can be seen from the actual windows of many apartment buildings that face on nothing but the walls of the building next door. Planetariums are a classical example of artificial devices substituting for the real things. I assume they exist in Paris.

HUYGHE: Yes. For instance, the planetarium at the Palais de la Découverte the Sorbonne dates from 1937.

IKEDA: More than twenty years ago, because environmental pollution and electrical advertising obscures the night sky, department stores in Tokyo began operating dome-ceilinged planetariums to provide children with an artificial sky to observe and to educate them in basic astronomy. In many other instances, too, contemporary human beings opt for artificial substitutes like planetariums.

We must be cautious to observe, however, that no matter how such things are disguised as objective, they actually reflect subjectivity. The viewer cannot mistake as objective a work of art that is deliberately subjective in nature. But it is possible to be drawn into believing that ersatz objective reality is true objective reality. In other words, the viewer can come to accept the creative worker's projected thoughts and interpretations as his own and, in this way, accept a fake as the real thing. Brain-washing of this kind is one of the characteristic methods of totalitarianism.

But of course it finds its most nonchalant application in the world of commercial advertising. As long as these methods are used only to stimulate consumers to buy certain products, no great harm is done. They have horrendous results, however, when used in connection with political beliefs or racial preju-dices.

To cultivate the strength to confront the subjective aspects reflected in works of art and in this way to enter into dialogue with artists, it is most important to become familiar with and to understand and master the depth of one's own historically created tradition.

Respect for Art

HUYGHE: Although from the origins of civilization art has fulfilled an essential function in society, human beings have not always been aware of either the true nature or the eminence of that role.

IKEDA: The impression European history has produced on me is that Europeans have always respected art as something connected with the eternal existence. By contrast, in China and Japan individuals in authority have always commanded supreme respect and art has been looked on as lowly and even vulgar. Symbolic of the position art has occupied in Japan for centuries, those Japanese fathers who were not artists them-selves have always been greatly distressed by sons who expressed the wish to devote themselves to art.

HUYGHE: Art itself varies according to race and culture, and is appreciated and ranked in widely diverse ways. Nonetheless, I suspect that Eastern and Western conceptions of art have not been radically different. In the West, too, the artist has not occupied high rank except in antique Greece and again when the idea of the Greek artist was revived by the Renaissance.

The contrast became strikingly apparent, however, in the nineteenth century, when the West came into contact with Japan and China, both of which were suspended in an earlier state of development whereas Western nations had evolved greatly.

The Greek philosophers stopped regarding art as no more than the skillful work of artisans and came to see it as an activity especially noble in itself and almost as one of man's justifiable goals, that is, the search for the beautiful. As they questioned themselves, with all the resources of rational analysis, about phenomena, their nature and reason for existing, these philosophers were struck with the existence of art from time immemorial and by the search for beauty to which art itself bears witness. They meditated on this search and made it one of the great categories, analogous with the good. Though perhaps not the subject of such compelling awareness as that demonstrated by Greek thinkers, art has actually existed as long as humanity. This proves that quality is an irrepressible need that cannot be reduced to the utilitarian, quantitative domain, as modern technical civilization insists it can. The psychical need for quality is as spontaneous as the physical need to eat. I should add that humanity has introduced the novel notion of quality into the world, although attentive observation reveals traces of it among the higher animals. The search for beauty enables man to justify his position at the pinnacle of creation and to set himself apart from the kind of existence that is the lot of elementary beings and thus to transcend mere materiality. It puts him on the path toward a transcendence giving him access to spirituality in quest of the absolute that is the divine.

The search for quality is innate in human beings and has existed since the ancient civilizations and since prehistory. For instance, in making tools, primitive peoples did not content themselves with function alone but created things that bring pleasure through the beauty of line and form—the pleasure that we today call aesthetic. In East and West alike, leaders could not fail to see that an object endowed with quality is more seductive than one curtailed to brute function.

Then religions and governments, priests and kings, came to see how important it was to put this power of attraction to use. In Egypt, Mesopotamia, or India, when priests wanted to represent the great myths of their religions in more striking and appealing ways, they required artists to give them images endowed with this attraction.

This is not to imply that the priests had worked out a theory of art. They observed as clearly as they felt heat or cold that, once endowed with beauty, an object acquires a certain warmth making it more attractive. And they sought out men who were able to convey such power to the images constituting the language whereby the fundamental myths were presented to the eyes of believers. Men capable of doing this were called artists.

Similarly, when a king wished to relate to his contemporaries or to posterity the great events of his reign as support of the glory he coveted, he understood that merely representing a great battle—like the celebrated one waged by the Egyptian king Ramses II at Kadesh—would be insufficient commemoration. The visual representation of the battle had to have the power of radiance. And this is why Ramses II requisitioned the best artists of his reign.

Art had always been a natural human function occupying a necessary place in society. But the artist was only vaguely distinguished from the artisan, or workman. In fact the artist was thought of as no more than a superior kind of workman. Only when the Greeks, the true creators of Western thought, applied to art the same kind of analytical and reasoning faculties that they used in other fields did the artist gain eminent dignity.

Over the centuries, as the memory of Greek philosophy has alternately faded and revived, the West has gone through various phases in which the autonomy and preeminence of art have blurred out or been reaffirmed.

The end of the Roman Empire, marked by barbarian

invasions, and the High Middle Ages coincided with one eclipse in the standing of the artist, whose role became confused. The only distinction possible at this time was among more or less skillful artisans. A striking evidence of this state of affairs is to be found in Flanders in the fifteenth century, when painters were grouped together in the same corporation as mirror makers. This seems to indicate that the technique of putting foil behind glass to produce a faithful image of reality was placed on the same footing as the work of a person who, through the subtlety of his eye, the knowledge of his hand, and the power of his vision, uses paints and brushes to recreate the world and vie with its appearance. People in those times were most strongly impressed by technical success, not by quality. They had forgotten that between the passive reflections of a mirror and the qualitative and creative reflection of a painting is an interval that is precisely the dimension of art.

But, during the same century, in Italy, revival of interest in ancient Greek philosophy, especially that of Plato, who put the beautiful high in his scale of spiritual values, restored awareness of the superiority of the artist. In the Renaissance, artists began signing their own work, a practice unknown until that time. For instance, throughout the flowering of Romanesque and Gothic art, signatures in stone, like that of Gilbertius, are very rare. Hardly a single artist is mentioned at Abu Simbel. In all these instances, artists were considered good workers who knew their jobs and performed the functions assigned them.

Beginning with the Renaissance, however, the artist came to be seen as a person empowered to create the beautiful, a highly prized value, and came to occupy an eminent place in society. To an extent, he became to art what the priest is to religion. Numerous anecdotes bear witness to this. For example, the Holy Roman Emperor Charles V, who never gave way to anyone, is said to have bent to pick up a paintbrush Titian had dropped. Before this period, such a thing would have been unthinkable.

But, in the West, the preeminence of the artist has been sustained only in aristocratic society. The sovereign, or the lord, realized that, in his own domain, the artist is an aristocrat with whom born aristocrats may, with a certain condescension, associate. In the seventeenth century, Rubens behaved like a lord, carried a sword, and possessed both a lordly house at Anvers and a castle at Steen. He enjoyed such high esteem that he was sent as ambassador to Spain and England and hobnobbed with the greats of the world.

It must be noted, however, that as materialism assumes increasing importance with the rise of the bourgeoisie, the qualitative gives place to the quantitative or, more precisely, to the coinable. The bourgeoisie despises the artist for upsetting the scale of values: "What is he good for?" He respects the artist whose works fetch big prices but despises him when he "wastes time" on the mere pleasure of searching and creating.

This attitude gives rise to the phenomenon you mention as observable in Japan. Upon learning that his son was artistically talented, a man of the Renaissance or the seventeenth century, would have entertained great hopes. Giotto was only a simple shepherd but, as soon as his genius was discerned, people pushed him to take advantage of all his possibilities. A materialistic nineteenth-century bourgeois, however, would have despaired and wailed of calamity upon learning that a son was artistically given: "Here is a boy who is going to lose himself in dreams, imaginings, unrealities, and all sorts of negative, unprofitable things!"

True, the bourgeoisie realized very early that its rarity and attraction make a work of art a possible piece of merchandise. With this development, the work of art assumed a growing role in the economic system.

In the twentieth century, works of art have often tended to be more valuable when currency has depreciated. Art has become, in other words, a sure value and an object of frantic speculation, thus greatly augmenting the esteem in which the artist is held.

Another aspect of the situation deserves consideration. Ordinarily, in order to make something that will sell at a high price, it is necessary first to purchase costly materials and, then, to devote considerable time and labor to production. All the materials a painter needs, however, are some paints and brushes and a canvas. Everything else he finds within himself. He is, in short, a person who gives excellent returns on a modest investment. And this is why bourgeois society affords him growing esteem—though for reasons different from the ones accounting for the high rank he held in aristocratic society.

In summary, the situation in the West has varied in a fashion that is complex but I suspect not too far from what has happened in the East. I know less of the situation there than you, but appreciation of the artist there must have been subject to analogous fluctuations. The Chinese emperors knew very well that the poet and the artist, too, are great aristocrats. Occasionally an emperor did not disdain to be a poet or painter himself. In the East, in Japan as well as China, commercial and bourgeois epochs no doubt also depreciated the artist, while aristocratic epochs must have raised him high.

IKEDA: I disagree. I think there has been a fundamental difference between the ways the East and West have evaluated the artist. I can see that, as you say, the passing epochs have worked changes in the situation in Europe and, with the rise of the bourgeois society, the quantitative element of money has replaced the idea of respect for the qualitative nature of art. Changes have certainly occurred in the East, too, and the situation varies from nation to nation and, sometimes, among cultural spheres within the same nation.

As you point out, some Chinese emperors have appreciated art and have even been artists themselves. But instead of lauding them for contributing to a cultural flourishing, their successors, historians, and the general populace have tended to criticize such emperors for departing from the normal way and introducing an element of weakness into the system.

Of course, no emperor was ever considered outstanding merely because he placed little value on art. Fine works of art are produced in times of prosperity and wealth. Emperors are praised, not for loving and cultivating art, but for bringing prosperity and wealth.

In the Orient, the head of the political system, whom I shall refer to as the emperor, is given the paramount position and afforded maximum respect as the spokesman of divinity and the source of national prosperity. In the West, divinity and the head of the political system are separate. The pope or the Church speaks for God. The Caesars were not gods, even though they were often officially deified after death.

In the Orient, divinity has always manifested itself through the head of state—in China called the Son of Heaven—and people who served divinity have been compelled to obey the orders of the ruler through which it makes itself known. In the West, it has been possible for artists to create beauty to the glory of God without reference to the authority of political rulers. In the East, however, the artist, along with everyone else, has consistently been forced to comply with the will of the emperor (the political authority).

There have been a number of epochs in Western history when political power flatly refused to recognize authority in any other party: to cite two, the pre-Christian Roman Empire and the modern period of national states. At other times, gods, the Church, or a universal law have stood side by side with political authority or have even occupied a place higher than political power. Though they may have been of short duration, such periods cannot help having exerted a great influence on human awareness.

In the Orient, the holder of political power has always occupied the very pinnacle of society and has striven to bring prosperity to the nation. In sympathy with this goal, the people too have respected life as lived in the name of prosperity; that is, in your words, the quantitative aspect. Art, which strives for qualitative, not quantitative value has, therefore, been regarded as superfluous and marginal. Only people who were completely content in respect to the quantitative values of life sought the qualitative values.

Authority and Art

HUYGHE: Society frequently misunderstands the true nature

of art. As you point out, sometimes society neglects it or even entertains a certain scorn for it. At other times, society shows too much utilitarian interest in it and enslaves and distorts it through abusive usage. This is usually the case with authoritarian regimes.

IKEDA: The nature of art as a lofty, spiritual, creative act tends to be overlooked too often. The fascist and Marxist regimes encourage some kinds of art and regulate others that political leaders find distasteful. In general, I am opposed to such regulation. Although it is certainly true that degenerate influences are occasionally exerted in the name of art, political authorities must never use force to suppress even these tendencies.

HUYGHE: In this field too, the natural spontaneous play of life must be defended at all costs against rational, authoritarian, and dogmatic influences. The greater the mass of the collective, the more the state, armed with abstract power, applies all its authoritarian weight to become an instrument for coercing the individual. In our day, society wishes to stamp its directives on all forms of human activity, paradoxically, all the more forcefully the more it espouses the ideology of the left, from which we ought to be able to expect an awakening to, or at least a respect for, liberty. This is the meaning of the administrative evil, the technocratic vice. The state quickly demonstrates the temptation to apply the dogmatism of regulatory principles to all forms of intellectual creativity. And this is a disaster because, from the moment this kind of thing is initiated, the natural function of intellectual creativity is withdrawn.

Actually, as we know, the true role of art, in particular, is to make possible a projection of things the artist experiences in his most inward sensibility but cannot perceive clearly. Into the work of art the artist projects things that influence him deep inside, a nebulous original that has not yet taken systematic form. He counts on his work to give these interior things exterior form to make him aware of them. Often, the work of art itself is charged with premonitory undisengaged intuitions. It could be said that the future abides in such intuitions, in which is outlined a reaction offering salvation from a present that blocks the future by being immobilized in abstract fixations.

IKEDA: I agree entirely with you that artists must be free to make public their thoughts, even if they are considered subversive by the existing powers. The vast scale of the modern mass-communications media provides political power with an excuse for interfering in artistic matters. Authorities often claim that artists ought to be prevented from making public ideas that could inspire anti-Establishment and anti-government sentiments.

Freedom of expression as guaranteed in our constitution means that in Japan today there are no restrictions on the expression of such sentiments. Restrictions on explicit sexual material, however, remain comparatively strict. In this respect Japan is frequently criticized for being behind some more liberal Western nations. Many public officials and judges, who refer to themselves as guardians of law and order, are austere and penalize as extremely shocking and shameful things to which ordinary people pay little or no attention. Many people—and I am in sympathy with them—object to judges who, through the management of the law, attempt to make actual social standards of their own personal, subjective ideas. Fundamentally, I cannot condone using authority to coerce powerless ordinary people to bow silently to the judgments of people in power either on political or moral matters.

Since the French Revolution (1789), thanks to the struggles of the people, it has come to be an accepted principle in most of the West for decisions of this kind to be made by the individual. And surely this is an expression of the true spirit of democracy.

Japan, however, has not yet reached this stage. Democracy and various freedoms were conferred on the people of Japan only after World War II as a consequence of pressure from the General Headquarters of the Allied Occupation Forces. Thirty years have gone by since then. Today the generations to whom democracy and freedom were something suddenly granted are in a position of rivalry with younger generations who have enjoyed them from birth. In my view this partly accounts for the instability of society at the present moment. When the younger generations assume a position of overwhelming superiority, greater stability will probably be achieved.

This will not, however, solve all problems, since the extent to which the younger generations will possess the self-awareness to ensure their own independence is by no means certain. Will they have sufficient self-control and the foundations required to make the necessary judgments? Even should leaders be people capable of independent political and moral judgment, they can be expected to make some mistakes as individuals.

I certainly do not imply that we should allow this concern to cause a regression into a situation in which authority to make important decisions is in the hands of an elite minority. Such a development would constitute a major crisis, classically illustrated by the rise of the Nazis from the system established under the Weimar Republic.

The situation is similar to that of a young person attempting to become independent of family. The desire to stand alone is present, though experience is lacking. Trials are certainly in store for people who have not been educated in ways that foster the strength to stand alone. Nonetheless, stand alone they must, even at the cost of repeated trial-and-error attempts.

If I seem to have traveled a little far afield of the topic of authority and art, it is because I consider art to arise from the innermost regions of humanity as a cry of independence and self-affirmation. Religion—especially Buddhism, which seeks the object of maximum respect not in an exterior divinity but in the Buddha nature inherent in each individual—provides a basis for a still more fundamental kind of independence and self-affirmation.

I am not implying a choice between art and religion. On the contrary. Both arise from the depths of humanity. Consequently, both offer strength to resist concentrating decision-making powers in persons of political authority.

To fulfill this lofty function, art must not be confined to displays of virtuoso skill. Nor should it set popularity and fame as its goals. Religions must not be obsessed with ritual and must not ignore the needs of the present in exclusive concern with the past and the future. The religious devotee must be constantly examining his thoughts and actions, while maintaining his self-respect. He must preserve a strong spirit enabling him to deal independently with his own instincts and drives as they manifest themselves in daily life and society. I believe that the artist is subject to a similar schedule of demands because both art and religion share noble, creative characteristics.

HUYGHE: Your conception of art, which approximates that of religion, sometimes escapes the notice of artists themselves. Too often they confine themselves to the application of current ideas, stylish theories, and aesthetic doctrines embraced in compliance with the tastes of the times or the demands of clients—and sometimes out of credulity submissive to intellectual fashions. Under these circumstances, political power is not the sole threat: the artist himself is incapable of finding or asserting himself.

It must be said that modern art has succumbed to the reverse danger by being too aware of its innovative, creative, and subversive functions, which it cultivated for itself, not as an inevitable counter-drive of spontaneous forces, but as a clearly and ingeniously calculated method. A deliberate will to make something "new" took the place of the irrepressible drive that upsets and shocks because its significance is incomprehensible. It therefore became desirable to define this something "new" by means of dogmatic theories revealing far more of a philosophy of art or a recipe for success than of the instinctive creative force of the artist. Everyone believed it would suffice to go still farther, through bold overbidding, along a way already plotted.

It is, however, necessary to maintain a fair limit between artistic liberty, even when it leads to what contemporary opinion might consider aberrations, and perspicacious criticism of the methodical processes whereby certain people authorize themselves to mimic creative activities and the boldness associated with them.

In any case, state authority must never intervene. Such

authority, which is devoted to using laws and rules to maintain a secure organization, an established system, is ill-suited to judging either fecund novelty in a germinal state in a work of art or the valid authenticity of attitudes that might break with current usage, habits, and ideas. Suppressive or encouraging, official intervention must be only regulatory. And regulating art is depriving it of its very function. All that authority can do is to search out and then congeal and neutralize exterior signs of yesterday's sane tradition and today's audacious novelty.

This implies that art cannot be engaged, politically speaking, for to be so leads to the supposition that the artist adopts an already formulated, identifiable system of ideas, perhaps of a party. Such obedience can only obstruct the play of subjective, individual intuition by submitting it to dogmas worked out by a collective. This runs counter to the nature of art, which can only exist by remaining free and equidistant from the authoritarianism of a state and from the temptation to adopt a given doctrine intellectually.

IKEDA: Art can lose its value as art when it has a deliberate nonartistic goal of some kind. This failing is especially apparent when art attempts to transmit preconceived ideas. But works of art lose none of their value when they embody excellent sensibility in the natural expression of actuality in a way that can change despair into hope. Paintings or sculpture deliberately created to glorify people in power may sometimes achieve that end but almost always reveal a flattering, sycophantic attitude on the part of the artist. But portraits and statues of people for whom the artist entertains true respect and affection will reveal those emotions to the unbiased viewer. It is important for us to understand correctly the powerful and intimate relations between the artist and the subject matter of his work.

Creative artists who allow themselves to be carried away by the technical aspects of art forget to examine their own minds with a view to deepening and improving their personalities. This deprives both their art and themselves of dignity and makes the artist ripe for recruitment by the propaganda departments of political authority. Although technical skill and an ability to persuade can conceal the inferiority of such people, the emptiness of their work will be evident to viewers.

I have no technical expertise but am always deeply moved by works of art revealing the richness of the human heart and firmly believe that far more important to a great artist than ability and strong personality are interior human riches and profound affection for all peoples and things.

HUYGHE: You have brought up an issue of major importance: the content and authenticity of a work of art. Having revolted against painting with subject matter, modern art has too often valued nothing but aesthetic pursuits. Once again, we have gone from one excess to another.

Certainly if the pursuit of quality—artistic value—remains primary, there is no reason why a work of art should not have content or subject matter. But the content must be something experienced, and the means employed to convey it must be of the aesthetic order. In no case should the content be a preconceived, formulated idea demanding that art be no more than the supplementary means for its self-manifestation.

With this reservation, it stands to reason that the work of art carries an interior message tending to reveal itself to others through the suggestive, emotive power of images, not by conceptual or conclusive methods. A work of art is thus suited to revealing not only the artist's individual reality (his self), but also his destined participation in the collective reality of his times, of the milieu to which he belongs.

Here we must recall that everything the artist expresses—the primary material drawn from his interior mine—is projected and exploited with nothing but artistic success in view. At this point we enter another domain, that of quality.

This is why art is extremely important and why it constitutes one of the driving elements of spiritual life. In our society, ultimately dominated by the quantitative—matter and its exploitation and the place of preeminence afforded economic affairs—art acts as a reagent. This aspect makes it clear that, in our culture, we ought to allow art to serve as an antidote capable of rectifying some of our current aberrations.

Sigmund Freud contributed a great deal to orienting contemporary culture and to causing it to deviate by making certain partial keys—sexuality, for instance—obsessive. But even Freud happily stressed the complex character of art. He said that images of art, like those of dreams, can be deciphered as projections of interior impulses, hauntings of the secret soul. But he accurately stated that the images of art are unlike others in this respect: the awareness of the artist takes them in hand, deliberately elaborates them, and endows them with aesthetic value. In other words, the artist causes them to pass from the domain of the raw, material fact to the domain of quality. He transforms a quantitative fact into a qualitative fact.

2

Art in the Orient and in the Occident

IKEDA: I should be very interested to hear about the kinds of impressions made on you by Buddhist art that you have seen in Japan or other parts of the Orient. What differences do you find between Buddhist and Christian art, especially painting?

HUYGHE: My experience with Buddhist art has been derived from study, books, exhibitions, museums, and also from travel, especially to Japan.

This experience has only confirmed my belief that two different, sometimes opposed, mental attitudes manifest themselves in occidental and oriental cultures. This is what makes it possible to speak—in a division that is perhaps extremely simplified—of East and West as two distinct entities, each with total and separate characters. But we must allow ourselves ample room for consideration in this matter, for the arts of the Orient are equally as diverse as the arts of the Occident. Nonetheless, the person who is receptive to and penetrated by them cannot fail to perceive that the two arts represent two autonomous mental worlds. Indeed, on various occasions in the course of our dialogue we have underscored this autonomy.

Both arts incorporate representative and narrative intentions. Both have religious arts with firmly established iconographies conforming to dogmas and communicating content by means of images. But there is more. The two arts arise from two approaches to the world and, with numerous readily cited exceptions, relate those approaches with clarity.

The Westerner is attached more to the exterior physical world and its exact appearances—even when he imbues them with spiritual life or delights in translating them in an elliptical fashion. The Easterner, on the other hand, attempts to approach another world, which can be glimpsed only by means of concentration in the self. The lowered eyelids, the relaxed limbs, and the vague smiles of Buddhist statuary seem to me to convey the quintessence of Eastern art.

But it is equally easy to find distinctive traits of two mentalities in the pictorial and graphic writing systems employed in the two parts of the world. Even when concentrated in elliptical signs, in the West script is applied most of all in representing the visible. In the Orient, however, it is more a sign of the interior life and its modulations. The same contrast can, however, be found in scripts themselves, when they are used to translate expressible thoughts.

Art and Writing: the East

IKEDA: Generally, writing is either phonetic or ideographic. In phonetic writing, straight or curved elements are used to represent graphically the sounds of spoken words. Ideograms, on the other hand, present to the eye a graphic representation of the meaning for which the letter stands. Since its significance depends on vocalization, phonetic writing can be said to be one with the vocabulary it represents. The ideogram, however, is strictly speaking distinct from the sound of the vocalized word and is, therefore, a world unto itself. Phonetic writing is to an extent dependent on the pronunciation of the actual living being who writes it. But ideograms, once written, assume a life and controlling importance of their own. This oversimplified view of the differences in these two styles of writing may offer interesting suggestions in connection with the differences between writing and art in East and West.

To further clarify the nature of writing in the Orient, I should like to mention something about the systems used in China and Japan.

Chinese characters—which are used in Japan and Korea as well—were pictographic in origin: three small triangles looking like hills were combined in the character for mountain, and three lines representing flowing water in the character for river. In addition to characters standing for concrete things like mountains and rivers, others representing abstract ideas, indefinite actions, or intangible concepts were necessary. These were produced by combining characters that, when used singly, represent concrete objects.

It is said that the Japanese began importing Chinese characters in the first century of the Christian era. At first, when used phonetically, a single Chinese character was used to write each sound in a Japanese word. This system later proved extremely cumbersome, and in the ninth century two syllabaries, hiragana and katakana, were devised by simplifying Chinese characters for use in writing such things as grammatical particles and inflectional endings. Together with these syllabaries, Chinese characters were employed in their ordinary ideographic function.

Aside from their uses in communication, however, Chinese characters have an extremely arresting and demanding artistic side. They are, as has been said, pictographic and sometimes very complex. Controlling the animal-hair brushes with which they are written in order to produce the required gradations and variations of stroke thickness requires training and skill. In both China and Japan, people have devoted themselves assiduously to mastering the breadth and depth of the calligraphic art; and surviving works of the great masters of the past are treasured today.

Since ancient times, calligraphic ability has been considered a sign of culture and an important element of education. Although with the modernization that began in the latter part of the nineteenth century and the introduction of Western-style writing implements like the pen and then the fountain pen, old-fashioned writing with India ink and brushes lost some of its former daily-life importance, even today signatures on official documents, signboards, and many things for which large written characters are needed are brush-written. Furthermore, calligraphy as a part of general cultivation is widely practiced.

Aside from basic techniques, calligraphy stresses spiritual refinement expressed through the techniques of the brush. Calligraphic training is a means of attaining such refinement. A fairly large number of people interested in preserving past traditions eagerly collect and display in their homes examples of the calligraphy of masters from the past. Not merely decorative, these calligraphic works bring peace and lucidity to the viewer through the combination of the meaning of their written texts and the calligrapher's clear mind as revealed in the manner of writing.

Recently specialists in calligraphy have tended to strive more for pictorial effects that differ from traditional ways of writing. In one sense, this can be regarded as a return to the origins of the essentially pictographic characters. People who do calligraphy of this kind never use models but always strive to express their own emotions and mental images.

Japanese culture has long reflected a belief in the intrinsic powers of the written word and its meaning, as is illustrated in the story "Earless Hoichi," one of the numerous folk tales compiled by Lafcadio Hearn in his efforts to introduce Japanese culture to the West. [Hearn (1850–1904), who was of Irish-Greek parentage, became a Japanese citizen and lectured on English literature at the Tokyo Imperial University.]

In this story, blind Hoichi, who lived at a temple and was a master at singing the famous military romances as he accompanied himself on the lute (*biwa*), became so popular with ghosts from the historical period of which he sang that they wished to drag him from this world to their own. Sensing the danger, a priest at the temple covered Hoichi's body with the written text of a Buddhist sutra, forgetting, however, to write on his earlobes. The power of the written text made Hoichi invisible to the ghosts. But they could see his ears, which were free of writing. And these they wrenched off, leaving him earless.

There is no indication in the story that Hoichi was either a student of, or an ardent believer in, Buddhism. Since he was blind, it was impossible for him to read the text written on his body. But the power of the written word and the sacred nature of the sutra text hid him from the ghosts, thus saving his life. This story indicates the mystical power that the Japanese have traditionally ascribed to the written word itself.

Japanese religious—especially Buddhist—ceremonies often reflect this trust in the power of the word. At funerals and yearly memorials for the dead, wooden plaques (*sotoba*, or stupa) on which priests have written, with brush and India ink, brief passages from Buddhist scriptures are set up in cemeteries. Priests and others participating in the memorial gather in front of these plaques for sutra readings. It is believed that the written text on the plaques has the power, somehow, to ease the suffering of the departed in the other world and bring them happiness.

In transactions among living human beings, the written word, in the form of contracts, is believed to have maximum binding power. Without such tangible evidence, a merely verbal promise is easy to deny at some later time.

At the bottom of all these customary practices is a kind of faith that the written word is more than something that human beings have created and can use. It is a mystical entity divinely created or born and deserves awe because, whereas humankind is ephemeral, the word remains immutable. I imagine that the ideographic and pictographic nature of the characters employed by the Chinese and the Japanese has generated this sentiment of awe. Although pictographic qualities are to be seen in their ancient forms, most characters have lost them in the forms in which they are used in China and Japan today. Nonetheless, I feel certain that it is the notion that the character somehow embodies the life of the thing it stands for that gives the written word a sacrosanct quality in Japanese and Chinese eyes.

HUYGHE: Your observations are profound. There can be no doubt that the soul of a people, like that of an individual human being, reveals itself in customs and behavior and that, among customs, writing and ideas about writing are primordial. Obviously, the converse is equally true; that is, style of writing influences style of thought.

Can it be that writing in the East and West are very different because, embodying two profoundly different spiritual states, they needed to create distinct modes of an almost opposite character to explain themselves? Or is it that the manner in which writing was invented and developed has entailed, or at least accentuated, psychological divergences?

The question is difficult to answer, but there is no doubt that the difference between writing systems is analogous to those between arts and ways of thinking. Well before the beginning of the industrial civilization to which it is suited, the West already had a writing system of an almost mechanical nature. This would seem to indicate a profound tendency made manifest as early as the inception of writing.

The Western spiritual disposition is characterized by an objective will. As we have already said time and time again, the Westerner directs all the forces of his interior life toward efficiency and output mostly in the material world. Above all he strives to arrange and transform that world in order to subdue it more and more to his own appetites. This obviously means that his psychic life is dominated by objectivity. A phenomenon that remains subjective adheres closely to its own proper nature and to the frequently inexplicable differences existing between the interior life of one being and that of others. A person who tends to be objective, on the other hand, seeks to neutralize the variations of the profound life that predispose more to contemplation than to action. Such a person strives to unify identities and ways of thinking in order to facilitate speedier, more practical, common action.

For this reason, the Westerner has afforded the abstract life greater preeminence than the affective life. The affective life adheres closely to subjective differences. The abstract life tends to establish definite ideas available to all minds, which give them all the same meanings, with some similar nuances.

In other words, when a Westerner has an idea, his sole concern is to strip it of the humus of its origins and make it conform as closely as possible to a common type so that, upon hearing or reading it, other people may use it immediately and easily. In this way application, which demands complete neutralization of all perceptible peculiarities, can be better realized.

The Easterner is closer to his interior hearth; that is, to a contemplative attitude directed more toward meditative silence than toward expression and communication. With the Westerner, meditative silence is eliminated by adaptation to the exterior world, a common denominator for all and the projection toward others.

IKEDA: In what way does the different understanding of writing reveal itself in this mental duality?

HUYGHE: The two opposed tendencies of East and West have led to two ways of writing, each perfectly adequate to its goals. The Westerner has organized writing as one assembles the parts of a machine. He has sought practical means to represent different sounds and has used constant signs to notate elements articulating those sounds like interchangeable clockwork parts, which reconstitute desired movements while analyzing them. Immediately, then, interpersonal communication is established on the most objective grounds possible.

Remaining more attached to his subjectivity, however, the Easterner has been led to maintain in writing adherence to a manner of feeling, almost of dreaming, to the ideas he works out. Consequently, for him writing plays a role fairly close to the one that only art can play for the Westerner. This point must now be clarified.

The Westerner must recognize in himself a subjective reality requiring maintenance and development since it is the source of his entire interior life. Nonetheless, in the course of its evolution, this reality must be intellectualized and come into contact with quasi-mechanized abstract ideas. To preserve this source of inspiration, intuition, and everything that is born and surges up within us, the Westerner is provided with another mode of expression. He never confuses linguistic expression, which—consecrated first and foremost to ideas—attempts, by means of writing, to universalize and neutralize itself as much as possible, with artistic expression, which accentuates character and thus tends, inversely, to individualize itself. Throughout the course of its development, the West has been aware of this tendency—perhaps because of its increasingly mechanizing effect—and has needed some kind of compensation.

The West has a natural, initial tendency to direct art toward realism; that is, toward the exact representation of our common possession: the exterior, objective world. But as the Westerner has found himself increasingly influenced by objectivity, he has conferred on art the function of counterweight against neutralization. He has attempted to keep breathing and moving the interior life, which abstract thought and writing—regularized and then mechanized by printing—tend to diminish. Though the fifteenth-century Primitives, mostly in Flanders, wished and believed themselves to be objective realists, later developments forced art to become the personal expression of the individual vision. The nineteenth and, especially, the twentieth centuries have prized artists all the higher for deviating from—even in representing nature—the objectivity that, to the informed, must by definition be identical for all.

Consequently, Western civilization has had to split its culture in two. One side is represented by the literary people, and the other by the scientific people. With exclusive rigor, almost with asceticism, scientists have devoted themselves to objective knowledge and, therefore, have studied neutralized modes of expression devoid of all scope for personal accent. They agree even more readily in mathematical means than they do in abstract ideas. By contrast, the literary people have given themselves the mission of developing the kind of culture that literature and art require. In such a culture, personal transcription can assert itself even to the point of arbitrariness for it must permit others to understand the gap between their way of feeling and perceiving and that of the writer or artist. The French biologist and analyst of literary expression Georges-Louis Leclerc, Comte de Buffon (1707–88) said in a famous formula, "The style is the man."

IKEDA: No doubt the difference between the writer or artist and ordinary people starts to be evident at least as soon as education begins.

HUYGHE: Yes, and the dualism between the literary and the scientific is sanctioned by education in the form of different courses in the two branches with examinations leading ultimately to different careers. Under such circumstances, we have not a culture, but an ambi-culture. Once it was subjected to the influence of the West and of Western science, the East, too, was forced to undergo a similar dichotomy. But it has come later there and contradicts the profound nature of the Orient.

This is why writing is close to art for both the Chinese and the Japanese and speaks not only to abstract knowledge, but also, directly, to the sensibilities. Significance remains partially symbolic and is perceived by the sensibilities, too. The character is not, as it is in the West, a purely conventional sign, like numerals in mathematics. It is not broken down mechanically into limited numbers of primary elements and then recombined in a way already apparent in cuneiform, in which straight lines of equal lengths are combined. A character in Chinese or Japanese is a whole. It is an expressive image charged with symbolic meaning, which conveys itself as readily to the emotions as to the intelligence. Chinese writing conveys an impression even to people who do not understand the language. In the West, however, writing is neutral because it has been evicted from the emotional world and is strictly localized among abstract means.

Graphology, the study of handwriting especially for the purposes of character analysis, attempts to be a psychological science, although some deny it such standing. By definition, printed letters have an absolute identity. When an individual writes letters and words, however, as a consequence of gestures corresponding to his characteristic type, a play of the nervous and muscular systems, and a whole concert of habits, his writing differs not only from printed matter, but also from the writing of all other people. Involuntarily, each individual leaves his own personal stamp on letters that have been totally neutralized by convention. Beginning with the differences existing between model letters and the way each individual writes them and thus conforms them to himself, graphology attempts to delve into the subjective world that personal handwriting reveals. This is the beginning of the kind of transcription the artist performs, although the artist cultivates it deliberately.

It might be said that, in literature, the poet performs a similar role by using abstractly defined words ("tribal words," to quote Mallarmé) in ways that cultivate emotional resonances as a consequence of suggestive grouping. This produces a sensuality of tone just as line and, even more so, color produce sensuality in painting. One could say, then, that on the one hand, the poet uses words in established senses to convey meaning but that, on the other, he creates new significances by intuitive combinations and instinctive paralleling among sounds. For instance, the famous line from Racine, "Pour qui sont ces serpents, qui sifflent sur vos têtes?" evokes the hissing of snakes as much by means of sound as by means of sense. (Is it disrespectful to say that, in addition to complementing the meat, a sauce can be the most important part of a dish?)

In the case of numerals, of which I have just spoken as totally neutral signs, it is possible to observe some peculiar phenomena. Roman numerals—which are Western in origin—are neutral because of the way they are written with repeated combinations and juxtapositions of straight lines, just as cuneiform was written. For instance the sign V, consisting of two straight lines joined at an acute angle, stands for five. X, two intersecting straight lines, stands for ten. It would seem that nothing could be more neutral and aseptic than these straight lines with which it is possible to produce all numerical combinations. Arabic numerals, on the other hand, have an undulating, graphic quality that lends itself much more readily to personal interpretation.

But, when the West replaced the practical Roman numerals with the Arabic system, it subjected these signs, which offered great suppleness, ductility, and an almost emotional quality, to a process of neutralization. Like the letters of the alphabet, they became typographical signs reduced to conventional forms.

You quite justly say that the ideology subtending the ideographic writing system tends to impose itself on the individual. This statement is the corollary of what we have been saying. Oriental writing systems are charged with emotional meaning, as we have seen. It could be said that they speak to the soul as a brush stroke in a painting does. They address themselves to more than the reader's modes of abstract perception because, while evoking an idea, they also evoke an image—an image that is expressive in nature and charged with symbols. Consequently, the reader finds himself more intensely engaged in reading because not merely his abstract thought, but also his entire interior life is led to participate. While comprehending the abstract signs of the text with his intellect, he reads with his sensitivity, which is touched by the graphic quality of the letters and disturbed by the symbols. In this writing system, which is much more difficult and much less practical than Western systems, the reader nonetheless finds a greater human abundance.

I am entirely in agreement with you that dealing with the problem of writing systems is one of the most direct methods of grasping the essential difference between the oriental and occidental worlds, their interior ways of being, and their ways of thinking and of living through thought.

Art and Writing: the West

IKEDA: It seems to me, however, that we cannot make so clear a distinction between the East and the West in this connection. For instance, certain great Western artists, especially in their drawings, have conveyed emotional qualities through nothing more than manually executed lines.

HUYGHE: Actually, if Chinese and Japanese calligraphy is one of the most original contributions of Oriental art, it is not absolutely isolated and without equivalents in Occidental art. But the Orient has been very clearly aware of a resource that, in the Occident, has been used almost unconsciously. Here again, we touch upon one of the fundamental differences between the East and the West.

In contrast to the Oriental, the Occidental is a person who throughout virtually all of his interior life employs reflexive, intellectual methods that give priority to clearly expressed ideas. For his part, the Oriental—and this is his great moral strength—has preserved a greater feeling for things that can be explained spontaneously. He has learned to establish between himself and things or between himself and other beings communications that do not require being passed through the ideological process. For instance, when the Western artist draws according to tradition, he first makes as exact and representative a sketch as possible of all the exterior objects he intends to include. Great artists, who have surpassed the limits of those around them, have asked themselves the same kinds of questions that have been posed in the Orient. It might even be said that Western art has evolved in this sense and has more and more sought expressive possibilities of a kind that it was long ignorant of but that oriental calligraphy has exalted.

To understand this, it is enough to examine the history of Western drawing. The fifteenth-century Primitive was concerned most of all to make a "faithful" drawing. He was taught—and he wanted—to apply observation in grasping the exterior object before him. Then, by intellectual analysis representing contours, he drew lines neatly demarcating the limits between the body of the thing he drew and the surrounding void.

Historically, drawing was first outlines. An old Greek legend traces the origin of drawing to a young girl who noticed how torchlight cast a shadow of the profile of her fiancé on the wall. She knew that the man was about to return to his own home and that the beloved vision before her would disappear. To keep a souvenir of it, she took charcoal from the hearth and traced the outline of the projected shadow of her fiancé's head on the wall. This story shows that the Greeks considered drawing to be the art of using lines to fix, as exactly as possible, the boundaries of forms.

The word *forms* introduces a new exigency. Intellectually, every object may be summed up in a volume; and every volume is expressed by a form. But rationalism and logic tend to analyze forms and to make them more intelligible by returning them to fundamental geometric forms. With this, another new temptation, evident very early in Greek art, comes to light. Instead of being limited to exact drawing—like the girl's passive tracing of the outline of a shadow on the wall—artists made the intellectual effort to disengage the basic geometric form that best expressed the accidental form of a given object. This was done in order that the object might be summed up more clearly for the sake of thought.

For instance, the frontal view of a woman's face is oval. To make drawings more logical and, therefore, more comprehensible, the artist tended to disengage or to assert the oval, which he saw broken by the accidents of flesh and the chances of reality. The artist sensed the oval *under* the appearance and strove to indicate it. Behind the accidents of surface, he asserted a form as intellectually pure as possible, a form approaching geometry.

Work of this kind is apparent in all the great Italian Renaissance artists, who wished simultaneously to be true to their subjects and attain—in a Platonic way—form in its essence. The influence Plato exerted on the Renaissance is well-known. Once such forms have been asserted, the next thing is to establish harmonious relations among them. At this point, the aesthetic sensibility comes into play.

After producing a drawing that would be intelligent, in the sense of referring to fundamental geometric forms, the artist attempted to produce harmony in the drawing in order to reply to the research for quality that is one of the great motivating forces of art. These three elements—exactitude, regularity, and harmony—are the essentials in the flowering of Renaissance drawing. There is nothing in them that resembles calligraphy. Still. . . .

The great artists sensed that there was something else. Let us examine, for example, a set of drawings that Raphael did as preparations for a Madonna. There is the search for the exact form. Raphael makes an effort to make an arm cylindrical and a head ovoid. But in certain other first drawings, we encounter something else. Raphael tries to capture and fix a still-confused image born in his imagination and emanating from his sensibility. He allows his hand to run nervously over the paper in a kind of impulse. By means of this plexus it seems that he wishes to capture the creative influx animating him. A spontaneous drive to grasp the indefinable—something like lightning about to fade—takes the place of exactitude, regularity, and harmony.

Remaining fugitive with Raphael, this new aspect of drawing became increasingly well-established after the Renaissance. In spite of prevailing theories that so-called good drawing must be realistic, well-constructed, and harmoniously rhythmical, artists realized that an immense part of art as they sought it could not be satisfied with such ideas. What is this immense part?

It is a kind of thirst for sensibility. Each being has its own personal manner of being itself and, therefore, of being aware simultaneously of both its own interior world and the exterior world. (The moment it is perceived, the exterior world cannot fail to be influenced by the interior world. No matter how objectively we wish to observe it, we cannot help interpreting it according to the subjective characteristics of our sensibility.)

The intellectualism of classical Western art deprived artists somewhat of the opportunity of expressing those obscure forces that, though within us and requiring discharging, can be neither explained nor rationalized. But why do we need to discharge them? To communicate them to other people? Little by little, artists came to tell themselves that the first gush, the nervous flash that ran over the paper, was a kind of projection or imprint of the emotional peculiarity they sensed deep within themselves. Placed before sheets of paper and asked to draw a single line, no two people in the world would draw identical lines. Graphology, the study of handwriting, shows that this is true. (Treatises dealing with handwriting in Italy date from the seventeenth century.) The artist no more limits himself to copying objects than the writer does to copying model letters.

Artists attempted to develop this new possibility in drawing.

Things moved very fast. With Raphael (1483–1520) we are at the beginning of the sixteenth century. By Rembrandt's time (1606–69), drawing has been totally converted to this different quest. Rembrandt neither attempted to reproduce in drawings the objects he saw nor to disengage rational and artificial geometry from them. He did not seek harmony among forms. Drawing for him was the claw of the lion hovering over its prey. His graphic method is an image of this. It bursts forth like lightning from his nerves and, by their intermission, from his sensibility. As with a blow of a paw, he stamps on the world his personal way of living, experiencing, and even meditating. Rembrandt's deepest vocation comes from the interior life.

And this explains one of his major characteristics: his fascination with light operating in shade, which his work transposed by means of a technique of washes and patches. He introduced into painting darkness riddled with rays of light. Why? All that was necessary was to develop the chiaroscuro initiated by the brilliant initiator Leonardo da Vinci, who was a contemporary of Raphael. Rembrandt worked more than Leonardo to attenuate the objective, realistic aspects of objects, their forms and geometry, which strive equally for a reasoned objectivity. For the sake of such attenuation, the best method was to place objects in shadows and thus to allow the voice of subjectivity—till then too greatly stifled—to be heard.

As a result of shadows, Rembrandt's graphic method is transferred in a single stroke of the brush, whereby the artist makes suggestive accents—like the glittering of a raised area of fabric—leap from the dark. Through methods of this kind, Rembrandt developed a kind of handwriting that asserts his own personality. Furthermore, Rembrandt was fully aware that, by attenuating the materiality of the exterior world and in developing the play of rays and flashes from shadow he was arriving at an expressive equivalent of the spiritual life.

In the first centuries of the Christian era, the neo-Platonic philosophers of the Alexandrian school—especially Plotinus—clearly understood the supernatural power of light. It is lovely, and its beauty resides neither in matter nor in form. It is, therefore, the most elevated of all beauty. In the *Enneads*, Plotinus says that, like light in the night, fire is beautiful in itself; it illuminates and shines; it is on a par with ideas, whereas matter is shade. According to him, we must strive toward a true, absolute, infinite light since, by such dazzling light, inferior things cease to seem beautiful. For Plotinus, this apology for a light that takes the place of matter was linked with a philosophy of rising by successive steps—each of which constituted an effort to attain detachment and elevation—until one achieved ecstasy: that encounter and communion with the divine.

This concept, developed three centuries after Jesus Christ, has analogies in the thought of many great Occidental mystics. And, fourteen centuries later, at the time of Rembrandt it is to be found implied and translated spontaneously by concepts of painting.

In the nineteenth century, Delacroix represents the same line. He paints in flashes from his interior life that blaze like lightning and are inscribed in his method of drawing, in his brushwork, and in the significance he assigns to colors. For him, each harmony of tone, each harmony of color, had to have the same emotional force as the plan of a line. An art like his succeeds in integrating renditions of the outside world, taken as a point of departure, with manual graphic expression, which is dear to Japanese art. At the same time, however, it integrates the communicative ambience of color which, unlike matter and its images, evokes no weight, density, or form and shares in the only visible reality that is totally immaterial: that of light. It is, therefore, closely analogous with the powers of the spirit. The spirit designates those things in us that are the least materially solid and that create the forces of our interior life—perhaps I should say soul, if the meaning of the word had not become unintelligible to the majority of our contemporaries.

IKEDA: The people you have been discussing are certainly exceptional. Do you think their characteristics pertain to the West in general?

HUYGHE: Even though it is distinguished from the East by its sense of concrete reality, the West cannot be said to have been attracted by materialism exclusively. Like the East, the West, too, has been open to spiritual revelations but has arrived at them by a less innate vocation and often as the outcome of reaction against predominant attitudes or as a compensative need to reestablish threatened completeness. Certainly the discoveries of people like Rembrandt and Delacroix remained alien to their refractory contemporaries. It is even striking that Western painting required a continuous effort of several centuries after the Renaissance to transcend the rational, objective standpoint and cultivate freely in drawing and—with more difficulty—in painting the emotional and spiritual strengths of communication that the East had been practicing since time immemorial.

It should be noted that Rembrandt was interested in Oriental art and even made pen copies of some Persian miniatures. Moreover, Leonardo da Vinci cannot have been ignorant of the Orient; and I am not the first person to point out a similarity between the smile of the Mona Lisa and that of the Buddha.

Scholars have often asked whether Leonardo could not have had some knowledge of the Far East. Certain of them, like Charles Sterling, have advanced, with considerable probability, the idea that, since the time of Marco Polo, it has been possible for travelers to bring Chinese scroll paintings back to the West with them. This could explain some strange parallels that have been notable since the fifteenth century.

It must be added, however, that artists involved in these parallels could have been curious about the Orient because they perceived in themselves something that the West had not yet explained and that for which they felt a need.

Today, certain people become Buddhists and become deeply involved in Buddhism, which they feel has discovered and brought to full flower spiritual truths that the West has barely extricated. This does not, however, hinder them from remaining within the Western tradition. Leaving it was not their reason for becoming Buddhists.

IKEDA: Perhaps through the genius of their own intuition, a

few Western artists have approached the kind of enlightenment embodied in the Chinese and Japanese writing systems. I would not go so far as to say that the Chinese and Japanese systems are as rational and systematized as Western alphabets. But, unlike Western alphabets, Chinese and Japanese characters appeal intuitively to the minds even of people of other cultural traditions. In other words, the form of the character conveys something of its nature and mode to people who cannot read it.

I certainly do not imply that all the world should adopt these ideographic systems. Nonetheless, knowledge of established conventions of writing (spelling, etymology, grammar, and so on) is not always necessary to comprehend the meaning of characters.

The existence of meaning within the character's very form helps explain why the Chinese and Japanese have made calligraphy an art with a long tradition of great masters of undying fame. Though I am not an experienced calligrapher, I frequently take up the brush to write the few characters needed for such Japanese poetic forms as *waka* and *haiku* and find the very motions of employing it can convey the writer's mental attitude.

HUYGHE: This discussion of Chinese and Japanese calligraphy leads us to a better understanding of a fundamental duality in communications that is applicable to both painting and writing. In the case of writing, as you aptly point out, it is a double power.

First, letters have the power of grouping themselves into syllables and words to evoke meaning. In this connection, they are bound to the intellectual and rational realm. To say that they have sense is to say that, by virtue of the system of accepted conventions constituting a language, they can express ideas.

But, as you observe, through the suggestive power of the graphic, written letters are endowed with another sense, which, without passing through the organizing filter of rational thought, is an act of communication and direct expression coming from the interior life of the writer and going to that of the person who beholds what is written. The Orient has developed this second aptitude to an extreme degree.

But, traveling different paths, the Western painter has arrived at analogous results. Endowed with a tradition that has raised realism to the highest degree, he knows how to represent an object exactly so that others can recognize and understand it. His images are first of all intelligible. Moreover, in order to extend his capacity to the representation of the realm of ideas, he uses allegory. A complex of conventions permits him to establish a customary correspondence between an image and the abstract idea it is supposed to represent. Custom, reinforced by iconography, makes it obvious to everyone that a flying figure crowned with a laurel wreath and blowing a trumpet stands for Glory. Thus, in the fashion of the word, the image becomes a translator of an image.

But, as we shall see, an image can communicate something felt with force by means of the nature of that force as imprinted on the means of execution. It even has the secret power of evoking by means of obscure associations that it provokes and employs to disturb our life of sensitivities. It is charged with a symbolism of which the author is not truly aware.

Allegory consists of representing a personage or thing endowed with distinctive conventional characteristics that confer a preestablished sense. The meaning of this sense can be deciphered by reference to a book on iconography, just as the meaning of a word can be looked up in a dictionary.

A symbol, on the other hand, intuitively employs certain images to communicate a certain state of the spirit. The artist explains it neither to himself nor to anyone else.

A remarkable psychologist named Max Pulver observed that the empty space on a page or canvas on which a person is about to write or draw something has potential significance (what he says holds equally for art and writing). A line or composition extending from the lower left upward and rightward communicates a sentiment of a triumphant thrust toward the future. A diagonal rising from the lower right to the upper left, on the other hand, suggests something much less victorious and almost nostalgic. Psychoanalysis has said that the right is the correct side for the father and the left the correct side for the mother. A composition of descending diagonals—leftward or rightward—creates a feeling of depression, defeat, melancholy, and so on.

What is true of space is even truer of the entire subject. As I have often said, we should have made a considerable expansion of iconography, which ought not to be limited to connections revealed by facts—events or texts—but ought to be reinforced by an iconography of those obscure communications that awaken our emotional life, often by the intervention of a shock to the subconscious.

Please try to imagine a figure strongly inscribed in the soil. Little by little it disengages itself and assumes a vertical position. It draws itself out. The addition of wings accentuates the impression of uprooting. It seems to rise in the air with its arms extended on high toward the light. Such an emblem can be experienced and perceived by anyone without explanation. The impression it produces is that of struggle: against matter bound to weight, in order to escape; to find liberation in the immaterial that is the air, light, and altitude; and to rise toward spirituality.

When Delacroix painted a combat between the sun god Phoebus (or Apollo) and the Python on the ceiling of the Galerie d'Apollon at the Louvre, he was employing an old myth, an allegory referring to a known subject that historians of Western culture can easily locate in Greek mythology. But, by means of a flash that strikes the spectator, Delacroix is actually using this myth to communicate the effort exerted by humanity to deliver itself from instinctive bestiality, represented by the monster rolling in filth among cadavers. The rushing forth of Phoebus in his chariot drawn by four white horses (from ancient times, the horse has been considered a noble animal associated with a symbol of the soul) becomes the aspiration of the human being to conquer himself in order to be delivered up to his profound destiny and his duty to ascend. Delacroix projects into us something quite different from the superficial mythological subject: he makes us participate in an essential drama of the interior combat about which he spoke often in his own writings and as a consequence of which the superior part of each being must master the inferior part.

Thus, with means proper to Western painting, he has managed to express a message. And that message is conveyed equally as well by the nervous flashings of his drawings as by the intonations of his colors: muddy, heavy, greenish shadows for the monster but rising in association with the variegations of the rainbow toward the light and its solar fire. He employs the gamut of colors the way a pianist makes use of the full extent of the vibrations of his keyboard. With this keyboard he communicates the kinds of things that Japanese calligraphy communicates through signs and brushwork.

In addition, it must be said that, in the course of the upsets that have marked the evolution of Western art in the modern period, neither drawing nor painting has felt constrained to reproduce objects as they stand in front of the artist. The lack of such constraint initiated the adventure of abstract art. Side by side with the art based on geometry and represented by the work of Kasimir Malevich and Piet Mondrian is another that the American expressively call action painting. Represented by Jackson Pollock in the United States and by Georges Mathieu (1921–) or Hans Hartung (1904–) in France, this approach conceived of an art founded on the pure graphics of the brush registering the force of the hand. Many artists of this kind were interested in Japanese calligraphy. For example, Mark Tobey spent an extended period in the Orient.

It is important to notice that tendencies of this kind appeared in the West only well after knowledge of Far Eastern art had been acquired at the end of the nineteenth century, most notably through Japanese prints.

IKEDA: Yes, those were wood-block prints known as ukiyo-e or genre prints of a kind that was part of the culture of the townspeople, as opposed to samurai, during the Edo period (1603–1867). With intensifying Westernization during the succeeding Meiji period (1867–1912), this culture was over-shadowed; and many Japanese forgot all about the formerly very popular ukiyo-e. It was, therefore, a great shock for many of them to learn later that these prints had exerted a great influence on modern Western, and especially French, painters. What was the nature of this influence?

Japan and the West

HUYGHE: The contact that took place at the end of the nineteenth century between Japanese and Western art is actually an extremely important phenomenon deserving to be registered in the general historical development.

As early as the eighteenth century, commercial contacts had been established between the Far East and the West, though the two worlds remained alien to each other and made no attempt to interpenetrate. In France, chinoiserie was all the rage; and, in keeping with the development of the rococo style, picturesque fantasies and exotic details were borrowed for use in the production of startling and exciting—because new—effects. But these trends never went beyond the realm of superficial attraction and reflected neither comprehension nor agreement.

A real awareness of distant Eastern lands was wanting. And it was begun by the study of Indian philosophy, and in particular by investigations into Buddhism. In the nineteenth century, the Collège de France, to which I belong, played a pioneer role in these undertakings. True to its policy of establishing positions for research and instruction in new cultural fields, as of 1832, it devoted a chair to the study of Buddhism and awarded it to the famous scholar M. E. Burnouf.

German philosophy was demonstrating similar curiosity at the same time. Indeed, long open to the Euro-Asian plain and to invasions from it, Northern Europe was readily accessible to Oriental thought. To escape from the excessive rationalism and intellectualism of the French eighteenth-century Enlightenment, or *Aufklarung,* German romanticism was compelled to turn eastward. After having ousted France from India in the eighteenth century, England installed herself there for more than a century and found herself drawn into an intellectual and artistic confrontation sanctioned by the creation of museums and institutions.

In other nations, notably France, following the example mainly of the Germans, the Romantics instigated a movement against the desiccation caused by overemphasis on Reason because they were disturbed to see the impetus the physical sciences afforded to the development of an increasingly objective, abstract, and mechanical civilization. They believed they could find in the Orient vast resources for their struggle to preserve the vital springs of the interior life and of sensibility and imagination. They approached the undertaking with a methodical progression that can be traced in painting.

Delacroix, followed by Dehodencq and Fromentin, revealed the Arab world. The generation of Gustave Moreau turned to India, where they found suggestions of mysterious dreams of architecture and overburdened decoration. The third stage arrived at the discovery of China and, all the more important, Japan, just at the moment of emergence of the Impressionists and their followers. This history has been fully studied by specialists.*

I will, therefore, limit myself to a single example. Van Gogh's letters clearly say that, shortly after his arrival in Paris from the north, he wanted to move on to the South of France. It would be reasonable to assume that he intended to discover the Mediterranean. The truth is nothing of the sort: he says he wanted to approach the Land of the Rising Sun. Artists of the time were so preoccupied with the opposite pole represented by Japan as the antipodes that they looked upon the South of

---

* In 1948, at the École du Louvre, Yvonne Thirion defended a thesis—unfortunately still unpublished—on the influence of the Japanese print on French painting in the second half of the nineteenth century *(L'Influence d l'estampe japonaise sur la peinture française dans la second moitié du XIXe siècle)*. Agnés Monneret did a more general study on Japanism in France between 1860 and 1920 *(Japonisme en France de 1860 á 1920)*. In a collective work directed by M. Dorival and entitled *Dialogue in Art, Japan and the West,* it has been published in Tokyo.

France as a stage in drawing closer to it. Some of Van Gogh's paintings do more than indicate the influence of Japanese art: they are actually transpositions of Japanese wood-block prints.

Soon the merchant Samuel Bing (1838–1905) became the great intermediary between France and the Japanese taste, which had a lively influence on the modern style.

But, at this point, I should like to introduce a personal recollection. Forty odd years ago, a very old painter I met in Dieppe told me how, during his childhood, at the time of the Second Empire, he had wandered about the piers exploring the packs of crushed paper sailors from the Far East used as ballast and tossed out on the docks as they unloaded their merchandise. (The very weight of these packs was known.) The boy and his pals threw themselves on bundles stuffed with wood-block prints that the Japanese sailors valued no more than old newspaper. The children were engrossed by these brilliantly colored, fascinating, but commercially worthless images. Perhaps it was from these prints that the boy heard the call to be an artist. They were the kind of prints that later conquered the literary and social worlds.

But painters had sensed the trend even sooner. For instance, I discovered allusions to Japanese prints in original, unpublished correspondence between Théodor Rousseau and Jean François Millet from the middle of the nineteenth century. Rousseau, who was an acute observer of landscape, represented the naturalist phase. He entertained no more than curiosity about the Japanese prints and sympathy for a study breaking with the Western tradition, of which, however, as a disciple of the Dutch seventeenth century, he was an embodiment.

But it did not take long for the influence of Japanese prints to make itself felt by causing a deviation from traditional Western continuity and indicating a new aesthetic direction. In about 1880, incited by the young artist Emile Bernard, Paul Gauguin and his friends of the Pont-Aven group were, as has often been mentioned, converted to a way of painting that renounced the Western models that produced trompe-l'oeil effects and had been practiced for centuries. Instead of these methods, they applied flat colors to their canvases and bounded them with supple and undulating lines. They had grasped the principles and aesthetic meaning of ukiyo-e. By transplanting these principles to the West, they unleashed a revolution that developed in the twentieth century, leading modern painting not only to rid itself of visual verity, but also to turn its back resolutely on nature and to deal instead with abstract art, which the Greco-Latin tradition has always overlooked.

But the connection between the two arts was sometimes more distant, as was the case with Claude Monet. He was an Impressionist. An Impressionist considers himself a hyper-realist in that he penetrates to optical veracity, which is the most demanding of all veracities and the one most closely conforming to scientific discoveries. Principles of this kind are apparently part of the positive materialist line from the nineteenth century and would seem to be opposed to Oriental thought. But such was not the case with Monet.

I recall visiting his house in Giverny shortly after his death and seeing a room entirely decorated—I might say papered—with frames containing only Japanese prints, and oddly enough only blue Japanese prints.

Monet believed himself to be and wanted to be a realist. Nonetheless he was introducing a new vision of the world, a vision that his contemporaries found so distant from their own customs that it created a memorable scandal. Some people felt like condemning his works and those of his friends as nothing but folly. What was the essential novelty of a version of the world that upset the public to the verge of revulsion? In brief, it was the practice of not representing the world in material aspects.

Impressionists, and especially Monet, were dematerializing reality by eliminating the forms of which objects consist. They were making of reality a pure phenomenon of energy translated by variations of light. A few years later, modern physics discovered that what had till then be called matter is, in reality, energy. So-called solid matter consists in a cohesion, or an especially strong and fixed adherence, among energy molecules.

To suggest the magnitude of the evolution that took place in this connection, I might cite two books. First is Paul Janet's *Leçons d'électricité,* used by students between the two world wars. It says, "The world in which we live is composed of two distinct worlds: one is the world of matter and the other the world of energy. Matter and energy may assume a great number of diverse forms without matter's being able to transform itself into energy or energy's being able to transform itself into matter." But, as early as 1905, in his *Evolution de la matiére,* a precursor that was, in fact, a record of current discoveries, Dr. Gustave Lebon could say, "Form and matter are two diverse forms of the same thing. Matter represents a relatively stable form of intra-atomic energy. Heat, light, electricity, and so on represent unstable forms of the same energy . . . Disassociating atoms or, in other words, *dematerializing matter*: simply transforming the stable, condensed form of energy known as matter into unstable forms known under such names as electricity, light, heat, and so on. . . .

Einstein, too, in the first part of the twentieth century demonstrated this assertion theoretically; and some years later, the explosion of the atomic bomb over Hiroshima provided irrefutable, dramatic proof of it.

In passing, I should like to say that the Impressionists intuitively foresaw what science was to discover. By perceiving nothing but moving, dynamic phenomena and seeking the most representative aspects of reality in fluids, water, reflections, and luminous irradiations, they exorcised the superstition of the solid and concrete, the basis of the cult of matter.

In the end, Monet saw the world as a mirage and painted apparitions of trees and phantoms of architecture like the *Houses of Parliament á Londres* or the *Palais de Venise,* which barely condense themselves in the midst of luminous colored mists.

Similarly, Monet discovered that things have so little objective identity that they change with time and that the appearance of the most stable objects modifies with varying lighting at different hours of the day. In this connection, he conceived the extraordinary idea of painting series of landscapes with haystacks or of the facade of a building, like the cathedral of

Rouen. In a series of canvases, he painted his subject at five in the morning, eleven in the morning, two in the afternoon, and five in the afternoon. Each day he worked in the same order so that each canvas corresponds to a fixed hour. He saw, and makes us see, the haystacks and cathedrals changing color, aspect, and almost form to such an extent as to be scarcely recognizable. Reality is returned to a play of light, shade, and atmospheric glistenings. It becomes optical and supplants objective, concrete, material reality, which is reduced to the role of a substrate. The eye is detoured and no longer recovers the abstract identity that thought imposes on it and that thought wishes to recognize. By renouncing the shrinkage imposed on it by objectivity, reinforced by the discipline of the physical sciences, the eye approaches an Oriental conception.

Near the end of his life, Monet purchased the property at Giverny, to which I have just alluded. There he was fascinated by a branch of the river Epte, which deviates to cross his land and form small ponds covered with water lilies. The bridges he erected there, in imitation of similar structures in Japanese gardens, are indicative in themselves.

He would hang over the ponds' watery mirrors, contemplating them till he became dizzy and everything became a confused medley. Being nothing but a reflection, the water appeared to be the sky. Monet would follow with his eyes the weeds undulating in the depths of the water and the cloud floating across the sky, yet reflected below. Here and there the water lilies served as guiding marks, though they were at the same time paradoxes confirming the horizontal plane of the water surface, which one would "know" abstractly but which one would not actually see, since it is nothing but transparency and reflection.

In this final phase of his long life, Monet executed landscapes as luminous mists in which it is impossible to distinguish horizons, shorelines, or anything else material. Nothing can be seen but colored flashes that are difficult to identify, floating colored outlines, and hazes of light. The positive elements he sometimes introduces only emphasize the mirage. Water lily pads and flowers seem to float in the void.

I think it would be interesting to place these Monets side by side with some Chinese paintings—perhaps those from the eighth or ninth century. I believe doing this would make it clear that, following a process of evolution leading to curiosity about the Orient, Monet, the pure Occidental, finally came to the point of inventing a world vision that agrees with that of the most traditional Chinese painting.

Undeniably the two civilizations are different, but there is no sense in being hypnotized by the obvious differences, which are made all the stronger by distance. Since man is always the same and always man, it is normal to be able to find, behind deviations established by cultures and civilizations, a substratum in the depths of which he confesses his identity. Because of this identity, a painting by Monet, who, on the threshold of the twentieth century, represented the supreme flowering of Western evolution, unites suddenly with painting that China, according to its own ideals, evolved a thousand years ago.

Similarly I do not consider the curiosity our own time demonstrates for the Far Eastern world, its art, philosophy and religion—Buddhism in particular—a historical accident. Under pressure from the physical sciences, the West has specialized too exclusively in a kind of representation that is both abstract and objective and thus, in connection with revelation from the sensitivities, is deliberately neutral. In doing this, it has come to experience a need for a spontaneous reaction against this excess. This became apparent first in literature and art with the Romantic movement. Later it developed and opened windows to fresh air from the East, which appeared as a compensating element reestablishing equilibrium.

Growing knowledge of texts, thought, and works of art accelerated this evolution, which may permit the West to enlarge itself sufficiently to discover a total humanity. This is an ideal that ought to be proposed, not merely to the West, but to the entire world.

IKEDA: Your comments, based on your extensive knowledge, clearly show that Japanese ukiyo-e prints aroused more than superficial curiosity or exoticism in Western painters. I am moved to learn both of the keenness and depth with which such artists as Monet pursued their search and of the apparently inevitable attainment of spiritual union between the East and the West in this field.

Art in the modern period in Japan has been unable to make a clean distinction between the Eastern and the Western and has striven to discover and express universal humanity. Some painters have rejected Western methods while clinging to venerable Japanese traditions. Others have launched frontal attacks on tradition while absorbing the art of the West. In the least admirable instances, such people have been content to do no more than copy Western models.

Nonetheless, some Japanese artists have attempted to integrate their own traditions and Western realism in the pioneering of new realms. Taikan Yokoyama, a painter for whom I have great respect, incorporates and learns from Western methods while vigorously expressing the Japanese spirit. Kai Higashiyama, too, integrates Eastern and Western methods, though his expression is more tranquil and lucid than the extremely forceful and decidedly Japanese work of Yokoyama.

The traditional feeling in Japan and China, whether in painting or sculpture, is that works of truly outstanding artists have lives of their own. For instance, an old story has it that when a painter added the eye to a painting of a dragon he was completing, the dragon leapt from the picture and flew into the sky. This story has given rise to a familiar expression, "The eye in the dragon picture," which means seeing a piece of work to a conclusion in such a way as to give it life.

Indicative of Chinese and Japanese feelings about ideals in art, one or two such stories have been circulated about virtually every famous painter or sculpture. Although they are all totally fictitious, people have handed them down as if they were the truth.

Eastern artists are thought to play the midwife in a process whereby the work of art is a remanifestation or rebirth of the life of the object depicted. In order to perform this role, they must acquire the farsighted vision to penetrate to the life deep within individual objects and all of nature. In addition to innate talents, acquiring this vision requires extraordinary diligence, not merely to acquire the requisite level of technical skill, but also to refine oneself profoundly in the spiritual realm.

In the Orient, the artist accomplishes the creative process by abnegating himself: the life that is reborn in the work of art is not his own but that of his subject. This aim seems different from that of the Western artist, who strives to regenerate his own life and endowments even as he faithfully renders the subject before him. Perhaps the most symbolic illustration of this attitude is the prevalence in the West of the self-portrait, for which the artist observes his countenance objectively while producing a likeness of his subjective self.

As you say, deep beneath these differences between the East and West, there is a fundamental similarity: in representing something, the artist affects a union and assimilation with himself through observation and thought. The finished work of art may be forceful self-expression or self-abnegation. In either case, it will constitute unification of the object and human nature. Your example of Claude Monet is an especially striking example of identity between East and West established on a profound level transcending superficial differences.

PART SIX

The Religious Surge

1

Transcendency

HUYGHE: Many of the uninitiated think that art is only homage paid by realism to the world of appearances. Actually, however, it is a means of transcending the physical world and of revealing, sometimes through that world itself and sometimes through the creation of signs existing outside the opaque world surrounding and enclosing us, an invisible, purely spiritual dimension. Art is an immense effort in the name of transcending our visible environment, charging it with a meaning and importance it lacks, and giving it the perceptible appearance of which, by definition, it is deprived. Art is created to add to the visible something that reveals the invisible and inexpressible.

Paul Klee pregnantly said that the intention of his own painting was to make the invisible visible. André Malraux said that the artist has the power of suggesting, through his creations, things that inevitably escape the eyes of the living. The artist is then an intermediary between the known, which can be experienced collectively and is the object of science, and the unknown, which is accessible solely through the exceptional interior experience of the isolated individual. He can intercede between the banal and what Baudelaire called the surreal and others the sacred. In this way, the artist seems analogous to the magician, the shaman, or the priest.

Art and Religion

HUYGHE: Art leads us thus to the verge of religion, the other primordial activity of the soul that human beings try assiduously to bring to their own level by means of rites and dogmas that, if not symbols, demarcate the limits of the technical and rational. The menace in this case is analogous to the one that realism imposes on the artist. Art and religion travel the same path leading human beings outside themselves toward a reality that, while unknown, is pre-sensed and that reveals itself only to those who live it personally.

IKEDA: In the East and West alike, religion has exerted an immeasurable influence on art. For instance, practically all branches of traditional Japanese art are connected with religious ceremonies or have religious significance. The Noh drama and traditional dancing were originally performed for the gods. Ink painting is closely connected with Zen Buddhism, the teachings of which explain its styles and spirit.

Of course there have been periods in Japanese history when art and religion have shared little direct connection. For example, the famous scroll paintings of the Heian period (794–1185) reflect the splendor and elegance of the imperial court with little religious content. And the art of the townspeople in the Edo period (1603–1867) is basically secular. Both of these periods saw great cultural flowerings with little relation to religion.

Nonetheless, religion has played a role in artistic endeavor in most other periods of Japanese history, whether of cultural flourishing or cultural stagnation. The connections between the two have tended to be more apparent in times of less conspicuous development, just as the trunk and branches of a tree are more visible in autumn after the leaves have fallen.

Art and religion have been connected in a similar way in the West, too. The Christian church's need for painting and sculpture to decorate walls and ceilings and music to praise God stimulated artistic endeavor in medieval Europe. Of course, these branches of art predate Christianity; but the church has done much to develop them to their present levels.

Expression of the religious emotion has been a source of art. Today, however, I am afraid mercenary interests all too often take its place. Consequently, original works of art are generally priced out of the reach of ordinary people, who satisfy themselves with the reproductions that modern printing techniques make abundantly available. Because of my respect for art, I have founded a modest museum in which a number of paintings are displayed in the hope of providing more people with the indescribable joy of contemplating art in the original state.

I always attempt to include art museums in my schedule when I visit Europe. At the Louvre, I have been made profoundly aware of the ineffable happiness of experiencing directly such great treasures of human culture as the Mona Lisa, the Venus de Milo, and the Winged Victory of Samothrace. No mere superficial reproduction can move the mind as profoundly as an original. The difference is as great as that between looking at a photograph and meeting the person photographed face to face.

The original has warmth and breath and a life that make dialogue possible. Life of this kind is the essence of true works of art. Furthermore life that converses with and moves the mind of man is the common ground between religion and art. It is in this sense that I see the religious emotion in art. They are not, however, the same since they exert different influences on the human spirit.

HUYGHE: Art and religion are founded on the exaltation of quality in humanity. This is their common ground. In attempting to accomplish this, art makes use of a range of means from visible, physical elements to entirely spiritual inspiration, which is accurately expressed as lifting us above ourselves.

Art and religion are united in this exaltation of quality, but, because art is bound to such physical realities as matter, form, line, and color, art is on a more encumbered level. Nonetheless, art insists that these elements play a part in the creation of beauty, the highest quality. In arranging colors, forms, and lines, the artist has more in mind than merely cooking up something pleasing and harmonious. He attempts to make images the instruments of revelation. He senses within himself a confused ensemble of sentiments aspiring to assume form and aspect, to manifest themselves in a legible form, and to express themselves. He realizes that this does not exist as it is in the exterior reality of his senses and that it is differentiated from such reality by the desire to increase the kind of quality that concrete reality fails to offer. Ultimately, the striving for quality desires to communicate itself to others. Surely such quality consists already of the altruistic desire to allow others to benefit from interior pressure and the hope it arouses. The work of art employs the attraction of lines and colors to draw attention to the interior message.

IKEDA: Art is, of course, the classical example of the need for cooperative abilities in both the concrete and the spiritual. Actually, however, for the sake of true fulfillment and reliable wisdom, all aspects of human life require balanced attention to both the interior world and the exterior world. Knowledge of the exterior world is gained through the five senses, which, as I have said, Buddhism teaches as the Five Consciousnesses (visual, aural, olfactory, gustatory, tactile). As is explained in the Lotus Sutra, Buddhas are endowed with what is called the Wisdom of the Three Worlds (of desire, matter, and spirit) and, therefore, understand all exterior phenomena with perfect accuracy. An important incident in the life of Nichiren Daishonin shows that he had such wisdom and, therefore, proves that he was a Buddha.

At a time when the Hojo clan held political power in Japan (latter half of the thirteenth century), Nichiren Daishonin remonstrated with the Hojo regent on the danger of invasion by outsiders. Eight years later, a Mongol envoy arrived demanding that Japan recognize Khublai Khan's superior authority and threatening to attack in the event of refusal. Thereafter, on an almost yearly basis, numerous similar menacing communications arrived. Japan continued to refuse the

Khan's demands and, finally, fourteen years after Nichiren Daishonin's initial remonstrance, a great Mongol army was dispatched to attack the archipelago. Since Buddhism considers the ability to predict the future a sign of Buddhahood, the accuracy of Nichiren Daishonin's prediction of the Mongol attack proves that he was a Buddha.

Further, correct knowledge of both interior and exterior worlds is essential to true wisdom, and the teachings of Buddhism are in accordance with such wisdom.

HUYGHE: The artist, too, attempts to unite experience of the exterior and interior worlds, but manages to do more. He tries to lead these experiences in an unceasing progression. When he finishes one work, he abandons it in the hope of surpassing it with another. He always intends to go farther in a constant pursuit of increasingly higher quality. The completed work is dead and past. The ceaseless quest, which he concentrates in a work as long as he is engaged in its creation, must continue. As long as he lives, he furiously creates, one after another, new works that lead him farther and higher.

In a manner of speaking, art rides on the great ascending current of perpetual effort to surpass. This ascent indicates the spiritual function of the human being and the current finds no better expression than in religion—so long as it does not bog down in the kind of cult rituals and dogmatic theology to which people incapable of pure spirituality limit themselves.

IKEDA: Ritual and dogma are important to people who are still in a state of spiritual underdevelopment. Those who are farther along, however, must advance from precepts governing behavior to a mystical drive. The method of teaching employed by Tiantai the Great (538–97), the founder of Chinese Tiantai Buddhism, embodies the proper kind of evolutional process. For beginners and people of limited intellectual capacity, he taught a system of simple religious practices like intoning the name of a Buddha. For more able or advanced people, he taught deepening of doctrinal understanding through the study of such scriptures as the Lotus Sutra. And, for the still farther advanced, he prescribed meditation and effort to comprehend the truth of life as expounded in the Buddhist scriptures. Enlightenment through meditation as taught by Tiantai corresponds to what you call the mystical drive.

In his own all-inclusive system of discipline and training, Nichiren Daishonin, who had immense respect for Tiantai, established a system whereby any person is equally capable of carrying out the practice and attaining enlightenment. The person burdened with great material desire, the person striving for great wisdom, and the person aiming to perfect his personality can all attain their goals by abiding by the method established by Nichiren Daishonin.

The system consists in believing in the Mandala of Supreme Enlightenment and reciting the Daimoku *(Namu-myōhō-renge-kyō)*. In these ways, striving for the satisfaction of material desires is sublimated into lofty wisdom. Although, in comparison with the ultimate teachings of Buddhism, they are lowly indeed, even such desires can provide driving force for the spiritual surge leading to the final goal. It is for this reason that I insist desires must not be subjected to control from without. Instead, the individual must be allowed to shed his desires naturally and allow them to serve as causes for sublimation along the path toward growth to a nobler human being.

HUYGHE: Religion and art rejoin but only when they are valid; that is, when they do not imprison themselves in the mechanism of routine but require the most profound and most authentic motivation.

Johannes (known as Meister) Eckhart (c.1260–c.1328), one of the noblest mystics of the Middle Ages, wrote that between art and religion there exists not a relation, but an identity. I should like to add that, in his book *The Transformation of Nature and Art,* Ananda Coomaraswamy, an outstanding Indian philosopher, devotes a chapter to Eckhart and says that his *Sermons* should be considered the *Upanishads* of Europe. Another sign of contact between the East and the West.

Religion and art bear witness to the existence, beyond what we are and can perceive, of an attracting force, like that of an enormous magnet, orienting all evolution on Earth toward the relative success represented by humanity and continuing, after humanity, through those beings permitted to advance always farther.

IKEDA: I agree entirely. Human beings are not swayed by the happiness resulting from the satisfaction of minor desires once they know the joy of giving themselves to the attainment of a definite goal. The search for such higher joy is innate in human nature. In reinforcement of my belief in the doctrine of the Ten States, which I have already mentioned, Buddhism teaches that aspects of the life of an individual human being strive for different kinds of happiness: that derived from the satisfaction of material desires; that arising from enlightenment to loftier truths; and that born of service to others.

If these characteristics are innate in all human beings, so is the possibility of self-enlightenment. The problem is how to bring about such enlightenment. This is the central role of education, the raison d'être of which is the awakening of the highest human spirituality.

As you insist, art provides a nobler joy enabling us to overcome material desires. But so do altruistic practices and the philosophical search for truth. The teacher who experiences such joys himself and enthusiastically communicates them is certain to awaken the spirits of his students.

The Ceaseless Ascent

HUYGHE: The profound human vocation, which instigates and justifies behavior and becomes art, philosophic thought, love of others, or religion, is nothing but the extreme and clarified thrust of the progress of all Creation as it perfects itself and, so to speak, corrects its trajectory during evolution.

As clear and intuitive a brain as that of the French philologist and historian Joseph Earnest Renan (1823–92) understood this more than a century ago, even at a time when materialistic determinism was triumphant. Nothing more vividly reveals this than his correspondence with his friend Berthelot, who was totally attached to the positivist ideas that some scholars felt ought to reign exclusively. I should like to quote what Renan wrote, in about 1863, to demonstrate how new and penetrating his viewpoint was: "Two elements—time and the propensity for progress—explain the universe. A kind of innermost spring drives life always toward an increasingly developed state. This is the necessary hypothesis. We must admit in the universe something that is to be remarked in plants and animals: an innermost force inducing the germ to fill a frame outlined in advance".

This innermost spring or force that impels life toward progress is what I perceive in evolution, the uninterrupted trajectory of which we have traced from time immemorial, passing from matter to life, from life to consciousness, and throughout all the other advancing stages of development that it has been capable of attaining. All we know of the history of creation is included in this ascent which, until now, nothing has stopped and of which, thanks to his ability to bring his intelligence to the point of spirituality, man currently represents the most accomplished degree.

From this known curve we should be able to extrapolate, as mathematicians say, and deduce its extension and destination. Therein lies the secret of the meaning to which Creation directs itself and in which human beings play a role, to use my metaphor, like that of a rocket's homing device.

Victor Hugo perceived these stages with astonishing clarity more sharply and earlier than Renan. His meditations of a seer, in the April 17, 1852, edition of *Journal de l'Exil*, written while he lived in isolation on the islands of Normandy, contain this passage: "Mineral life passes into organic and vegetable life; vegetable life becomes animal life, of which the highest specimen is the ape. Above the ape begins intellectual life. Man occupies the lowest rung of the intellectual ladder, which is invisible and infinite and by means of which each spirit rises to eternity, the summit of which is God."

Hugo had a presentiment to the effect that the spirit must attempt to escape by dashing against the black bolted door of humanity and that art and religion are the two ways open to it. The connections linking the two are not, therefore, surprising. You have most justly pointed out the inestimable influence religion has had on art and you have explained this influence by saying that art is originally a way of expressing the religious emotion. We have also noted how, largely owing to reasons of social efficiency, art has been constantly associated with religion. In its sanctuaries and holy places, religion has made use of the special attractive power of art.

But an infinitely more profound connection is the movement of the soul toward God. This movement begets religion, and is aligned in the same direction as the movement inciting human beings to create art. This is where we must readdress the problem more deeply.

There are diverse levels of reality in the complex nature of man. Through the body, he belongs to matter. But the body also belongs to life which, even if chemical analysis is taken to the ultimate, cannot be totally reduced to matter. Nor is life limited to cells since it presents another irreducible phenomenon called consciousness. Consciousness in human beings differs from consciousness in other mammals, in the case of which, although it confers the gift of perception, it is subject to the automatisms of instinct or conditioned reflexes.

Thus man has cleared a rung, but there is yet another, one that distinguishes humanity from the rest of Creation. Actually, human consciousness is empowered to go beyond intelligence, of which at any rate there are traces in the superior nonhuman animals. Human consciousness has access to a new order that can only be called spiritual.

At this level, everything is subject to the perception of values based on quality. The qualitative aspect is conceived of by thought but perceived through the sensibilities. At this level, the freedom to choose and make decisions, the arbitrary freedom, takes the place of the determinism reigning in the domain of matter and instincts.

Whether we like it or not, here more than in the development of intelligence is to be found the essential distinguishing feature, the capital contribution, of humanity. We must remember that quality is neither defined nor demonstrated. It is only experienced, and this must be by means of an interior effort for the sake of amelioration and perfection. Thought is the sole valid basis of morality and aesthetics, both supreme creations peculiar to humanity. It must be experienced at its own basis by a sensitive perception as obvious as that of instinct, to which it is not, however, reducible. Instead of requiring passivity, thought demands effort on the part of the whole being.

Perhaps the question of the destination of this effort is the greatest mystery of humanity. What is its direction? If the faculty of choice is revealed only to the most developed beings, and singularly with human beings, why and how did it come about?

Let us return to the ascent we have outlined in the course of evolution and attempt to clarify it and determine the incentives behind it. Matter reigned first, registering primordial energy in space and assuming form and consistence. But clearly matter does not conform to time. It obeys constant, permanent laws defined by the physical sciences and subject to no modification with the passage of time, to which it reacts only negatively through phenomena of attrition and entropy leading to destruction. In the womb of life, its sudden appearance seems to have been a response to some kind of correction in the effort for perfection. Certain biologists have been unafraid to apply to their subject the notion of negentropy, which you brought up in connection with Schrödinger. As we have said, whether in effective reality or appearance, life indicates a change of position. Animated by life, matter which has been inert until this animation, enters the adventure of time and participates intimately because of its efforts to endure, adapt, increase, and reproduce.

Animate matter encounters perpetual, renewing, and diverse dangers threatening destruction and death. To respond better than is possible by means of simple mechanisms or to adapt these mechanisms to risks and the unforeseen, life found it necessary to mount another step by attaining consciousness and thus enabling the organism to perceive obstacles in its way, gauge them, identify their connections with itself, and adapt reactions to the results of this inquest. In addition, it was necessary to perceive necessary nutritive resources and manners of attaining them.

At this stage, consciousness was oriented toward a new faculty, that of choice. In the kind of finality or, if one prefers, in order to avoid philosophical implications, striving for perfection that appeared together with life, consciousness seems to have been provoked by the need for option, without which life would, again, find itself insufficient to deal with the unexpected introduced by time. When means were evolved, the most ancient nonhuman animals were empowered by their primitive consciousnesses to do no better than control automatic responses that arose exclusively from innate or acquired instincts. In dictating behavior adequate in a given situation, instincts imposed choice on them. When flight was essential, a creature likely to drown would hesitate to hurl itself into the water. Similarly, such creatures would not take flight into fire that would burn them. Thus automatically a dry, normal, less dangerous terrain would be chosen as a route of escape.

As the chain of animal life develops, the element of choice becomes more complicated, richer in nuances, and more deliberate. Intelligence develops, making it possible to think and to weigh eventualities and consequences in all their diversity. Before the human level has been reached, the moment arrives at which quality intervenes in, and completely modifies, its importance. Anyone who has kept animals knows that, among such higher mammals as dogs and cats, quality is sensed, especially in connection with food. It becomes an adjunct to the need to eat. I know very well that if I offer a piece of dry toast to my dog he will spit it out. If I butter it lightly, however, when he is hungry, he will accept it. A cookie, on the other hand, he will snap up under any circumstances and, whining, sit up and beg for more. Clearly, in such instances, choice has ceased to by purely utilitarian and has become qualitative.

At the risk of contradiction, I would even say that superior animals make qualitative auditory and visual choices. Cats demonstrate preferences for certain kinds of music. The most refined cats—and dogs as well—like to sleep on fabrics that harmonize with their coats.*

My own red setter is fond of blue cushions. To skeptics I offer an argument based on an experimentally established fact: if colors are not endowed with seductive powers, why has nature seen fit to increase their sexual attraction by giving a number of male animals—especially among the birds—striking and harmonious colorations? Does not this power imply in the partner a perception that could be called aesthetic?

This perception arises from a qualitative appraisal, no matter how confused and elementary. It would be fascinating to attempt to discover the first germ before the emergence of consciousness—perhaps in flowers—where it is possible to determine the aesthetic quality connected with the power of attraction associated with the reproductive function. Of course, flowers do not perceive. . . .

Man is the end and culmination of both the intellectual faculties and the perception of quality arising from faculties of sensitivity, which are traceable in superior animals. And in both of these domains the capacity to exceed the utilitarian indicates man's superiority. The highest intelligence does not limit itself to practical questions, but confronts philosophical problems as well. The loftiest sensitivity does not limit itself to documenting things that exist or actual interior or exterior states, but draws us into the exigencies of quality. In both cases it commands openings to things without concrete existence. It involves a new drive: aspiration to cross the bounds of what is given in order to gain access to a superior world that, even though not at our immediate disposal, can be attained at our own ultimate extreme and farther beyond.

This is what distinguishes man, humanity, from the other animals and gives him a sense of advancing toward the future. More than an actual goal toward which one travels, this future

* It is true that a dog's eyes do not perceive color as do human eyes since, lacking cones, they apparently cannot see, as we do, long light waves like those of the color red.

demands the convergence of all our efforts and exerts over us an attraction in which it is perhaps possible to perceive the raison d'étre of the entire universe. This unlocatable, indefinable pole draws us always farther and higher.

Still, as he marches toward it, the human being sees the horizon constantly receding. The horizon is only the threshold of the infinite. And, in my view, the "still more infinite" represents the very idea of God.

Certainly the divine is made incarnate and assumes aspect as it is represented by the artist's creativity. Just as an artist's inspiration is manifest in a painting, so the notion of the divine is translated by various gods according to the civilization in question. Churches are grafted on gods as schools are on art. They transform the qualitative flow that the artist attempts to materialize in his work into teachings and dogmas repeated by students. But the students never reach the level of the master because they make definite formulas of something that was pure impulse, pure aspiration. What do religions do with gods? They submit to being shut up in ritual.

I do not limit myself to any school of art because I am attracted by art itself. I survey all religions in order to draw from them nothing but their convergence toward the Absolute, toward the point that is beyond our reach.

Undeniably, for many people such cult ritual as, for example, prayer can be a means of reestablishing connection with the movement of ascent. For other people, prayer is something that can be neither enclosed in words nor defined in phrases, since it is solely upward movement toward something outside our means of comprehension and representation and toward which creation strives for its own completion.

It is in this sense that I find art and the search for God on the same trajectory. God is the supreme goal, on which everything converges, including the irrepressible ascent initiating the need for quality.

IKEDA: Certainly constant, unbroken forward movement is the only progress. From the standpoint of actual Buddhist training, the enlightenment clearly established by Nichiren Daishonin is final only in the sense that continual forward motion is its true ultimate. To think that one has attained the goal and thus to stop going forward are to lose one of the most important elements in the drive for perfection.

The Buddhist teaching of the simultaneity of cause and effect means that perfection (the effect) can only exist if it is simultaneous with the cause producing it (that is, religious practice or the striving for perfection). If the cause is not present, the effect ceases to be. Although we human beings are incapable of perfection, as long as we realize our imperfection and make ceaseless efforts to attain the ultimate goal, we are manifesting a perfect image of humanity. To be truly vital, a religion must inspire continuous striving for perfection in its believers. A religion whose believers have stopped trying to improve and content themselves with ritual and dogmatic debate must be called dead.

HUYGHE: The effort for perfection can only be living if it is free. The progression, the ascent of which we have been tracing, clearly extends from the fatal determinism of matter to the adventure of life. From there it continues to choice, which makes self-direction possible and which necessitates freedom if it is to be exercised fully. In addition, however, it requires perception of quality if it is to become engaged in the scale of values. At the present time, then, the qualitative is the most highly developed point attained by Creation in this progression.

It is only with the qualitative that we escape the fatalities of the quantitative, which controls the physical world implacably and imposes finiteness on it. In the realm of the quantitative, choice is always limited to fixed alternatives. It is pre-fixed and implies no progression in time. It is always identical with itself. Just as, under identical conditions, water always freezes at zero degrees, so a certain appetite will always be satisfied by the same quantity of the same food. This is the same for the past and the future. A sense of quality makes it possible to prefer dietary restraint, but as a matter of choice. The question of moral quality can incite a person to deny himself food in order to feed someone less fortunate than himself or to undertake a fatal voluntary fast in the defense of a noble cause.

Only the human being has the option of spiritual quality enabling him to free himself of vital instincts like hunger and sexuality, which in nonhuman animals dictate conduct. Man can replace these instincts with spiritual ends even to the extent of infringing on the basic law of life par excellence: self-preservation. The human being is capable of sacrificing himself and of dying deliberately for an ideal. Only man has been able to establish a scale of values immeasurable in the strict meaning and perceptible only to the person who sharpens his own sense of quality. Man can prefer spiritual progress over the technical and material progress, the cult of which enslaves and makes degenerate our civilization. This is human might and the justification denoting man's place in world history.

This, too, is the location of the key to the close relationship and collaboration existing naturally between religion and art. But art and religion have different means of acting. Art employs means found at the level of life to exalt the sense of quality in man. Religion, on the other hand, searches outside of life. It is on the same route but its projection toward the supreme goal is more directly aimed at the target. All the same, certainly art at the level of high genius is much farther along the way to God than is the faith of a mediocre believer in even one of the best religions. Once again, everything depends on the quality brought either to art—in the case of an artist—or to religion—in the case of a believer.

Values of Life According to Buddhism

IKEDA: Returning to your scheme of the development of life—inert matter, living matter, consciousness, and spirit—I am reminded of the theory of values advocated by Tsunesaburo Makiguchi, the first president of Soka Gakkai. President Makiguchi proposed these three values: Profit *(Ri)*, Beauty *(Bi)*, and Goodness *(Zen)*. By Profit he meant the material conditions necessary for supporting life. This corresponds to what you would call the pursuit of the existence of life. His Beauty includes not merely things that are pleasing visually, but also all those other things that appeal to the senses and the emotions. This seems to me to correspond to what you term values pursued at the stage at which the consciousness orienting life manifests itself. By Goodness, President Makiguchi meant all those acts that contribute to general happiness by offering profit and beauty to others and to society. Acts that have the opposite effect are evil. This corresponds to your pursuit of the spirit that orients and gives meaning to consciousness. What is your reaction to this system of values?

HUYGHE: I should like to begin by attempting to understand precisely the meanings of the words President Makiguchi used. If Goodness and Beauty in this context mean what they mean in the West, the word Profit invites misunderstanding and would surprise French people desiring to understand Buddhism. I propose replacing it with a word like increase, which actually implies an extension of what life, which cannot be limited to conservation, demands; that is, life requires developing itself. In addition, this word avoids the suggestions of gain and material cupidity aroused by the word Profit, which, in French, is most often used in connection with money.

With this reservation, we should return to President Makiguchi's three values. The first is a basic necessity for the operations of life. It is a point of departure instead of an aim. And, in my view, it is not, strictly speaking, a value because in itself it does not include the search for quality. It is, however, allied with it in order to give life its full meaning and corresponds to what Western thought calls the desire for self-preservation. Each living being has the irresistible, biological impulse to preserve itself and everything associated with its existence in the exterior world that ensures such preservation, even if it is no more than the air it breathes and the food it consumes.

Increase, however, implies more. To this must be added the idea of extension, similarly inseparable from the operation of life, which obeys the instinct not only to extend its existence in time, but also to make progress. This impulse can be added to the list of values in the sense that it concerns both our physical being and our mental, sensitive, and intellectual faculties. I must say again, that, from my viewpoint, increase is not, strictly speaking, a value. But it does guarantee a natural point of departure for the pursuit of true values. It prepares the way for, but does not constitute, a value. Nonetheless, it is indispensable to a program of human progress.

Though increase ensures the operations of being, it is valuable only when put to the service of the other two deeper values: Beauty and Goodness, which cause us to cross the essential threshold beyond which begins the spiritual life, surpassing the quantitative in order to attain the qualitative and its search.

The human being who wishes to make the fullest of his life realizes he cannot limit himself to survival or physical increase. We hear a pressing call to go farther, to surpass ourselves. Each individual has a scale of values to which to devote his existence. Although he may mistakenly define or choose them, he is subject to the impulse to refer to them. This is why a guilty person, even a criminal, attempts to justify himself in his own eyes, even if by means of a system of false values. Such a person treats himself to arguments. Self-justification of this kind proves that, to give in to instincts, such people are obliged to stifle a certain voice rising within them and demanding that action be founded on reasons that are themselves based on a scale of values.

Ascent up the scale of values may be accomplished by two paths: Goodness and Beauty. Goodness is concerned with acts and conduct conforming to intuition about quality. Won through effort, quality demands constant amelioration. Though it is deeply rooted in Western languages, I should like to replace the word Good with the words The Better. A morality that holds to obtained results will, for that very reason be sterile since it limits itself to the abstract application of a rule. Effort and progress are essential.

Beauty represents a pursuit of quality, not through acts, but through works. It is the transition from ethics to aesthetics.

When a writer writes, a philosopher thinks, or an artist builds, sculpts, paints, or composes, it is in order to transfer into his work the things he finds most valuable in himself. Furthermore he wishes not merely to give real expression to, but also to perfect, those valuable things. The artist is not content with inspiration—the reference to what he has inside himself. Instead he wishes to use inspiration in order to transcend himself.

Once again, we must recall that these three ideas—Increase, Beauty, and Goodness—must be explained as a response to an impulse rising from the depths of the human being, from the very law of life. At the pinnacle of Creation's ascent from matter to the spirit, only man has arrived at a consciousness of transcendency, at the thrust that justifies time which, if no more than a repetition of what exists, is irksomely useless.

Though more than the opposite of the ugly, the Beautiful is connected with ideas of pleasure and displeasure, agreeableness and disagreeableness. It is possible, therefore, to consider the Beautiful the value that searches for "consciousness giving direction to life," as you suggest.

As you say, "Goodness is offering Profit and Beauty to others and to society. Acts that have the opposite effect are evil." I agree that what you call the thing that seeks the spirituality giving direction and meaning to consciousness is indeed the Good.

IKEDA: Let me begin by saying that your translation of the Japanese word ri as increase *(accroissement)* instead of profit comes closer to President Makiguchi's true idea and is an extremely helpful reference for me. Thank you for making it.

Your interpretation of increase as a starting point and not a value probably arises from a difference in our definitions of value.

Buddhism teaches—or, better said, clearly points out as a truth inherent in the depths of animal instinct and human consciousness—that life is more worthy of respect than anything else. This attitude is reflected in some famous Buddhist sayings: "A day of life is more valuable than all the treasure in the universe" or "Offering one little finger to the Buddha is more precious than offering a universe of treasure."

This viewpoint sees value in maintaining and ensuring the growth of life. It does not contain your element of quality, which only comes into play when care is taken to make food appetizing and visually appealing. A tiger has no thought of quality when it devours its prey. But this is no reason to discriminate against such animal behavior as completely different from human behavior. The tiger has the right to feed itself, and its efforts to preserve life deserve respect. By the same token, the infant feeding at its mother's breast has no idea of quality, yet mother's milk is more valuable to it than anything else.

The value is not to be found merely in maintaining life and its growth, but in the effort enabling life to carry out its various pursuits. If as you say the first of the three—increase or growth in support of life's operations—becomes a value only when life pursues goodness and beauty, life itself can be regarded as no more than a means. Under such circumstances I am afraid it would be making light of efforts for living to deny this value, and a negation of the dignity of life, since, as Kant says, life is supremely important and irreplaceable.

It must not be assumed, however, that merely preserving one's life, possibly at the expense of others, is in itself valuable. No one of these three values—Increase, Goodness, and Beauty—should be pursued in isolation from the other two. They must all be sought together. As you say, Goodness and Beauty are lofty spiritual products involving value. Although it may be permissible to sacrifice beauty for the sake of doing good, doing evil in the name of the creation of beauty must never be condoned.

The high value of acts done to support and advance life becomes all the more apparent when such acts are altruistic. Goodness is offering the benefits of increase and Beauty to others. Depriving others of life and happiness is evil. According to Buddhist teachings, altruistic acts are a cause producing the effect of a better state of future life for their perpetrator. In this light, it might be possible to view elevated altruistic acts as selfishly oriented. But I prefer to see this teaching as a wise way of sublimating low human selfish instincts into lofty actions.

Wanting and working to bring about the happiness of others are a manifestation of the best that is in human nature, expressed in Christian doctrines as love and in Buddhist teachings as compassion. Instead of the self-interested desire to reap material rewards in a future life for altruistic acts in this one, such love or compassion is a reflection of current spiritual magnanimity.

The great significance of President Makiguchi's system of values lies not in establishing utility in the value system, but in the elucidation of the nature of goodness and the provision of principles for the elevation and spiritual fulfillment of humanity. Goodness as a value enables human beings to manifest the best that is within them and, therefore, cannot be stressed too much in these selfish times. Today we are in need of a human revolution that will turn selfishness into altruism and that will stand firm on the side of love and compassion.

HUYGHE: As always in philosophy, the difficulty arises from the terms employed and the exact meanings assigned to them. These meanings are increasingly fluid and subject to interpretation the farther the discussion goes from concrete realities that can be designated objectively and, therefore, give rise to no ambiguity. For example, the word value can mean something as concrete as the calculable price of an article but can also designate worthiness of appreciation. All good, material and moral, therefore, represents a value more or less great. It is consequently completely natural to speak of the "value" of life as being great.

But, as you yourself justly observe, this does not contain the element of quality. It is actually the idea of quality that introduces the scale of values. I attach immense importance to this scale, which elevates the human being and permits him to fulfill himself because, to judgment of facts, it adds judgement of quality, thus suddenly opening an infinite perspective beyond material reality—a perspective perceptible only to the human being, to whom it opens the way to self-perfection.

No one denies that life is in itself a prime value. Nonetheless it is only the point of departure in the scale of values that permits all life to elevate itself and increasingly amplify its worth. This capacity seems to me to explain the role and primordial task of the human being. This is the point at which Goodness and Beauty appear as two primary directions permitting each life—of which, its raw value, if I may use the term, is fundamental—to become more valuable and better in quality. In short, this endows life, which is a known quantity, with increasing merit.

In sum, I would say that life, a value given to each of us, is, as Kant says, irreplaceable. But it is so precisely because it alone possesses the capacity, the gift, of pursuing increasing value. I am convinced that this is its raison d'être.

The Scale of Transcendency according to Buddhism

IKEDA: The Buddhist teaching of the Nine Consciousnesses, of which I have already spoken and shall here only sketch by way of a résumé, explains how life evolves and, through its own capacity of increasing its value, arrives at self-cognizance. The first five consciousnesses depend on the organs of sense (eyes, ears, nose, tongue, and tactile receptors). The sixth sense controls these five and, operating through the brain, corresponds to ordinary consciousness.

The seventh (called *mana* in Sanskrit) is the seat of operations on the self and, in contrast to the sixth, which is awareness of the self, is actually cognizance of the self.

At a still deeper level is the eighth consciousness called the storehouse (*alaya*) in Sanskrit because, as the repository of all past karma, it provides the materials from which the self is formed. Because it thus extends backward in time, this consciousness perceives the deeper levels of the self.

Deeper still is the ninth (*amara*) consciousness, which perceives the deepest part of the self since it is in union with the life of the universe. The word *amara* means pure and in this case indicates that the ninth consciousness is unsullied by karma. In this system, cognizance of the self, usually taken as the support of mankind's most outstanding characteristics, is only seventh out of a total of nine. In other words, Buddhist teachings insist that we must delve further to two additional consciousnesses.

HUYGHE: This theory of nine consciousnesses corresponds to modern psychological ideas but goes farther than they do by opening ways towards the spiritual life. I should like to try translating it into Western concepts—or at least into terms familiar to my own thought.

First come the senses, the organs of information. The Buddhist designations indicate the eyes for sight, the ears for sound, the nose for odor, the tongue for taste, and the body for, in a more limited sense, the sense of touch.

Mentioning a sixth sense—or consciousness of the self—to control all these is important. This probably could be equated with the organic self-consciousness referred to by modern psychology as coenesthesia, a word derived from the Greek *koinos* (common) and indicating a general sense communicating to us awareness of our physical existence.

The seventh consciousness—the reflective consciousness— is also self-awareness, but on the psychic plane, where our language can distinguish sentiments by name. At this level we realize the existence of "Me" in all its emotional complexity.

With the aid of memory, the eighth consciousness adds the dimension of the past to continuity in time. For Buddhism, karma, or destiny followed throughout previous and future existences, ensures such continuity. And consciousness considers itself not merely in the present, but also in connection with its responsibilities.

Beyond the memories of personal lives, consciousness is attached to a duration from which it issues and of which it assumes the burden. Western science uses heredity, verified by genetic transmission, to bind our selves to a past with which we are united and which imposes on us certain kinds of behavior and even defects that are consequences of our ancestors' actions. But if the past restricts us, we must remember that we reciprocally restrict the future. Karma not only defines us as being and having been, but also reminds us that we are to be accomplished and completed in the future. This implies a direction that our present life will either deviate from or approach. Once again, our personal, ephemeral life must be bound to a duration transcending it.

The ninth consciousness goes farther—to the junction of "Me" and the infinity of the universe. At this point, it extends to our limit, our basis. This corresponds with my own conviction—often repeated in the course of our discussion—that in this way our perceptions—physical and psychological, current and remembered—of ourselves ultimately at our greatest depths attain the fabric of total, universal existence from which we branch outward. In biology, the branch is attached to the trunk (which could represent heredity); and the trunk sinks roots into the earth for the sap that keeps it alive.

We are both participants and detached beings. Since we are detached, we enjoy all the thinking and sensing forms of our self-awareness. But, because we are bound to the universe in its totality, we have access to a destiny transcending our own, a destiny that guides us and in which we are only atoms. This obscure consciousness—this presence within us of a world that is no longer before us, as our senses perceive it—makes us feel like participants in a much more general undertaking. There, beyond our own person destinies, we draw on a sense of evolution with which we are one and in which we, no doubt, discover our basic meaning.

As you point out, it is essential that human beings prevent themselves from, as is their custom, stopping at what I call the empirical consciousness, or passive cognizance that imposes itself on them. They must strive to traverse the individual atmosphere gravitating around the "Me" as a center. If they do traverse it, they will arrive at the ninth consciousness, which goes beyond them and is connected with the totality of which they are only participating, temporary particles.

The ninth consciousness is closely connected with the eighth because both encompass time. But, whereas the eighth consciousness is oriented toward the past, the ninth unites us solidly with the creative action of the future, toward which the universe advances and which is, ultimately, the increase of quality that we must pursue through time.

IKEDA: You very accurately interpret the Buddhist ninth consciousness, especially in pointing out how the eighth consciousness is directed toward the past while the ninth, which connects us with creative activity, is oriented toward the future, the goal of the universe. The ninth consciousness is the source of all activity, physical and psychological. In addition, it is the origin of creativity.

Our present has been formed as the outcome of past acts. Some physical characteristics apparent at the present result from and reflect the activities we have undertaken since our birth into this world. Clearly, however, some are determined before birth.

Generally, inherited characteristics are thought to be passed on by parents according to biological laws of genetics. Certainly physical and psychological resemblances between generations can be explained in terms of fertilization and birth. But some elements resist such explanation. For instance, children from the same parents usually differ in one respect or another. And, although the differences can be accounted for genetically, there is no explaining why one child receives one set of genes while another set goes to his sibling.

The Buddhist explanation is that each individual has had past existences, the accumulated karma—results of actions—of which determines individual differences in innate characteristics. In such a case, the genetic mechanism provides the material whereby karma-determined characteristics find physical manifestation.

This holds true for psychological as well as for physical characteristics. Physically and psychologically, then, we are the product of karmic results of both past existences and actions that we have perpetrated since birth. In some instances, what we have done in this life is the cause producing results encountered at a later stage during this same life. Sometimes, however, they are the results of acts from former existences.

Ignoring a traffic signal can be the immediate cause of an accident. But even people who carefully observe signals are sometimes involved in accidents. In other words, the effect is apparent but not the cause. This is not to say that the effect is causeless. The cause occurred in a previous existence.

The eighth consciousness, which is the repository for all these accumulated karmic causes, is the source of all the operations forming the self. It establishes the program the individual life follows. Included in this program is the possibility of extensive individual freedom of action.

Employing this freedom, human beings may struggle with apparently determined fate, resist its control, and in this way strive to be still freer. In this they resemble people who win greater political liberty by employing freedom of speech and expression against a despotic regime. Restriction to an established system severely limits scope of freedom. Jean Jacques Rousseau interpreted the ideal society on the basis of a reversion to primitive natural conditions. In a similar fashion, the ninth consciousness breaks from the bonds of the eighth consciousness and its infinite complex of causes and effects to point the way to a fundamental revolution founded on the true nature of primordial life.

HUYGHE: As you forcefully point out, Buddhism makes a distinction between what is given us with life and what we extract from it as a consequence of our own responsible actions. This explanation involves two parts. First is a succession in time dependent on causes that are exterior to us and that are part of our fate. Second is another extent in time, that involves our own responsibility and depends on our margin of liberty.

IKEDA: I should like to take this chance to refer to still another Buddhist theory related to time and the stages of human development: the teaching of the Ten Worlds, or States of Existence, which is connected to the teaching of the Nine Consciousnesses.

The Ten Worlds refer to a categorization of human life into

ten categories: Hell, Hunger, Animality, Anger, Humanity, Heaven, Learning, Realization, Bodhisattva, and Buddhahoood. The Buddhahood state manifests the ninth consciousness. Though not having attained the ninth, the Bodhisattva state represents the eighth consciousness. The states of Learning and Realization are operative in the seventh consciousness. The state of Heaven and all below it are mostly operative in the first six consciousnesses and occasionally, though very rarely, manifest the seventh consciousness. In other words, these states relate only to the pursuit of the satisfaction of instinctive desires.

The states from Hell to Anger entail the suffering of instinctive desires remaining unsatisfied. In Hell, all desires, including that for existence, are suppressed and the life entity is bound. The state of Hunger, too, is one of torment caused by frustrated desire. Animality is the state in which the self gradually causes its own suffering by being obsessed with the desire of the instant. Anger is the state of obsession with the desire for self-display. The temporary moments of happiness experienced by life in that state are immediately converted into suffering by the appearance of another better or happier individual. Humanity and Heaven are states in which instinctive desires are satisfied; the former is characterized by tranquility, and the latter by joy. But such satisfaction is transient and fragile. Consequently, the life in all of the inconstant states from Heaven to Hell is constantly shifting from suffering to happiness.

The four final states—from Learning to Buddhahood—are free of obsession with the pursuit for satisfaction of emotional and instinctive desires and entail the search for the constant joy of enlightenment to eternal truth. The state called Learning in English is called *Shravaka* in Sanskrit and means a person who attains enlightenment and its associated joy by listening to the teachings of an enlightened being, or a Buddha. The one called Realization, is termed *Pratyekabuddha* and means a person who finds enlightenment and its happiness through his own efforts while residing in, and conversing with, all things in the world of nature. Bodhisattva means both a being or state of life, in which the eternal truth is recognized as abiding in compassionate affection for other people and life entities and in manifesting this truth in one's own life through compassionate acts. Finally, as I have already said, the Buddha state is one in which the individual has attained the profoundest self-cognizance and has established the eternal truth within himself.

HUYGHE: Thank you for having clearly explained the theory of the Ten Worlds, which complements that of the theory of the Nine Consciousnesses. The gradation it expresses in its own language and characteristic designations suggests a general line corresponding to my own convictions. I believe that elevation is the necessary journey to which humanity has been called. Man starts with what you designate as the most elementary bases, where he is in rapport with his physical nature and where he obeys his instincts and attempts to satisfy his appetites and his sensuality. There he attains the fullness of his inner consciousness, brought to fruition through meditation. Thus he completes something very important by means of a transport toward something other than himself, something founded in love.

We must not, as is too often done in the West, limit our interpretation of knowledge to intelligence about things. Intelligence must be lined with love. Perhaps, when it ceases addressing itself only to the things around us and elevates itself to something beyond us, love becomes the highway to transcendency. Supreme knowledge binds us to the innermost and total law of the universe. This is the state that the mystics in all developed religions have attempted to reach in order to fuse with God. Your state of Buddhahood is a way of explaining this ultimate reality. In a specific form through a precise doctrine you expound a very profound truth.

A teaching of this kind strikes me as one of the most valid ways of leading man to his own fullness by elevating him ceaselessly from an inferior to a superior state of consciousness. Few religions in history have stripped the issue to essentials as completely as this.

2

Religion in History

Stages of Religion

IKEDA: At the start of these dialogues, we said that civilization has passed through three stages: prehistory and the hunting-and-gathering phase, an agricultural phase, and an industrial phase. I believe that religions, too, can be divided into three large categories. First are the primitive religions in which things and phenomena in the natural world are worshiped as gods or spirits in the hope of gaining their good graces. Next come the ancient religions that, as extensions or variations of primitive religions, worship either collective human might or intensified authority.

Third are the higher religions, that reject the idea of deifying natural or socio-collective phenomena and teach the worship of something transcendent and absolute. In contrast to Christianity, which conceives of an anthropomorphic God, Buddhism teaches an absolute Law. A Buddha is a person enlightened to that Law.

This classification is extremely important from the viewpoint of the origins of civilization, since all cultural activities are ultimately rooted in religion. Of course, developments in civilization and advances in natural sciences have reduced the authority, and in some cases have brought about the rejection, of some religions. It is important, however, to attempt to discover which of the many religions have been invalidated by scientific advances. Failing to make such an investigation could cost us the brilliance and riches of a spiritual heritage intuitively grasped and elucidated by the mind of man. This would be like discarding an old house without saving the gems and gold it contains.

To illustrate of the way in which primitive religions turn their eyes toward natural phenomena I might mention the principal deity in the indigenous Japanese religion of Shinto. The name of this goddess, Amaterasu, means Illuminator of the Sky, a clear indication of association with the sun. Because of the importance of the light and heat of the sun to all things and especially to the physical and mental well-being of humanity, the ancient Japanese personified the sun as a way of propitiating it.

Speaking to the personified deity in prayer was considered an effective way of gaining good graces. But there were other ways of cajoling her, as a famous legend reveals. On one occasion, for some reason, she was in so bad a mood that she hid in a cave, refusing to come out. This, of course deprived the world of light and warmth. Desiring to remedy the situation, the other gods assembled in front of her cave and set up a hullabaloo of singing and dancing that seemed so interesting that Amaterasu, unable to resist temptation, put her head out. At this, an especially strong god seized her by the hand and pulled her the rest of the way, thus restoring light and warmth to the world. Although the story is probably based on a natural phenomenon like a solar eclipse, it reveals how gods in some religions are endowed with such very human traits as emotional moods, curiosity, and so on.

Primitive Japanese religions have had no connection with developments in the natural sciences. But because of its concern with astrology, the religion of the Babylonians resulted in careful observations of the heavens, thus providing knowledge that was important to astronomy.

The personification and symbolization of natural phenomena played an important role in the evolution of drama, literature, and art. On the other hand, people who turned their interest to mathematical treatment of the mystical powers of nature, as revealed in positional relations and cycles, prepared the way for the emergence of the natural sciences. With developments in these sciences, people came to investigate nature rationally and to evolve techniques to apply what they learned from such investigations. This endowed them with considerable freedom in the use of great natural forces and laid the foundations for the emergence of modern scientific-technological civilization.

Both technology and civilization based on natural sciences and primitive religions turned their attention toward natural phenomena. And inevitably, as the field of science expanded, that of primitive religion shrank. This is the reason why advances in science and the dissemination of the scientific way of thinking greatly reduced the scope of primitive religions.

The ancient religions inherited the gods of the primitive religions but with altered meanings. In the case of Japan, long ago the emperor was considered a descendant of the sun goddess Amaterasu and, as such, was himself deified. This had the effect of making his authority absolute and of generating a system of control around him as the central element toward whom religious submission was due.

Centuries ago, the Japanese imported the Chinese legalistic system, which they employed in structuring a nationalist state. Nonetheless, underlying this system was the idea of religious submission to the divinely connected emperor. This has proved a powerful bond in reinforcing the collective unity of the Japanese people.

Intervention of the divine on behalf of a nation is not an unusual phenomenon. For instance, Jeanne d'Arc heard celestial voices telling her how to drive the English from France and, in so doing, prepare the foundations for the French national state. To a greater or lesser extent, the practice of claiming religious origins or the special favor of a divinity in order to ensure the submission and fidelity of subjects is common throughout the world.

HUYGHE: Here again, modern civilization has turned everything upside down, most of all by applying science.

IKEDA: The rational and scientific ways of thinking that are essential means in managing the extreme complexity of the modern nation state have generated social sciences, which have rationally analyzed the meanings of old mythological symbols, thus stripping away their veils of mysticism. Just as in the field of natural phenomena, development of the natural sciences deprived primitive religions of most of their vital faith, so in the field of group and personal relations the social sciences have mercilessly caused the failure of the ancient religions.

Of course scientific advances have not completely invalidated the strengths of primitive and ancient religions. Because both natural and social phenomena are too broad to be exhaustively dealt with in rational thought, such religions remain deeply rooted in the minds of their adherents, in whom they continue to inspire a sense of stability.

For instance we find it impossible to regard the death of another human being as no more than a matter of official records. Nor is it sufficient merely to cremate or inter the remains. We feel the need for some kind of religious ceremony on such occasions, even if it is merely a substitute for rejected traditional religions. Because we cannot deal with death in a strictly rational fashion we require the kind of mental calm that only a religious observation affords.

Nonetheless, with natural- and socio-scientific development in the modern period, the primitive and ancient religions have lost their field of action for the following reason.

In terms of concrete explanation and metaphor, Buddhism and Christianity, which belong to the third category of religions, adopt ways of thinking and accepted kinds of knowledge from primitive and ancient religions. But the aims of these two higher religions are on an entirely different plane. Consequently, the fact that science has proved some of their borrowed elements unjustifiable has had no effect on the fundamentals of Buddhism and Christianity. For instance, though science discredits the Christian tradition that God fashioned human beings on the sixth day of Creation, this does nothing to discredit the basic Christian teaching of the importance of emphasizing the dignity of humanity. Buddhism includes an ancient Indian tradition to the effect that the world is like a heap of cakes on a tray, but this has nothing to do with the goals of Buddhist teachings, which are the law of cause and effect in human life, the need to live better in this life for the sake of better conditions in a future life, and guidance along the path leading to ultimate human perfection.

As I have already pointed out, in contrast to the anthropomorphic deity inherited from primitive and ancient religions and recognized—even if only symbolically—by Christianity, Buddhism defines the object we must follow for the sake of self-perfection as a Law. Of course, the foundation for the Buddhist belief in the Law was already laid in the philosophy of the *Upanishads.* By requiring submission to its anthropomorphic God, Christianity restricts the dignity of the individual human being. With its assertion that Law is the ultimate entity, however, Buddhism makes possible perfection of human dignity. Since the Law is equally present in all things and all persons, it makes possible equal dignity for all people.

Religion and the Position of Humanity

HUYGHE: Religion always poses the problem of relations between the individual and society. It would be interesting to hear your views on the roles imparted by man to religion throughout the successive stages of its development.

IKEDA: In the prehistoric period, for the sake of good hunting and sufficiency in life, human beings depended virtually completely on the good graces of nature. They consequently regarded nature and natural phenomena as either benevolent or sternly punishing divinities.

After the development of agriculture, various technical skills and modes of organization became the principle conditions for well-being and stability. Of course, dependence on nature could not be overlooked, but it was no longer the sole support of life as it is for people who live by hunting and gathering. As you point out, practically all developments in agriculture are accompanied by the emergence of great empires. No doubt this was because of a need for unified governmental bodies to deal with irrigation and riparian works essential to agriculture and because surpluses of agricultural products and other material wealth permitted the emergence of specially privileged classes.

To sustain their very existence, large governing bodies needed to employ the authority of deities deeply rooted in the minds of their subjects. For example, in Japan the imperial family was said to be direct descendants of the sun goddess Amaterasu, while during the upsurge of modern nationalism, the emperor was declared a god. With allowances for discrepancies resulting from different epochs, similar examples of rulers' attempting to endow themselves with absolute authority are to be observed all over the world. Furthermore, this phenomenon can be interpreted as indicating a stage in the development of the universal human spirit.

But authoritarian religions inevitably suppress the individual human being. The emergence of Buddhism and Christianity from subjugated peoples on the fringes of great empires suggests that this is the case. Both Buddhism and Christianity, and probably Islam, attempt to elevate the dignity of the individual by relating him directly to the ultimate entity they posit. In other words, in contrast to the second-category religions of the agricultural phase, which made the collective and the authority controlling it sacred, Buddhism and Christianity set their goal at the sacredness of the individual. But throughout later history, attributions of sanctity have, time and again, been imparted to the collective; and, almost without exception, the higher religions have served as the means in this process.

Certainly today, as always, the power of an organized collective is essential to human life. But the sanctification of the collective body always has been, and probably always will remain, dangerous. Our epoch knows better than any other how fearsome such group power can be from the standpoint of the individual. This is probably why, although some people turned to extreme individualism, generally ours is a time in which, while the necessity of the collective is generally recognized, we strive to give recognition to the search for philosophies and religions permitting the affirmation of the individual's inner life.

One of the causes of the current crisis is traceable to relations between the individual and the collective. Though stability has been preserved heretofore because of the overwhelming superiority of the might of the collective, increasing respect for the dignity of the individual has put these two elements almost on a par, thus producing a kind of instability. Essentially, in itself, this constitutes no crisis. In fact it is desirable. But wholesome guidance is required if spiritual balance is to be maintained and if equilibrium is to be preserved so that neither the individual nor the collective takes overwhelming precedence. Dissemination of the higher religions, which affirm the sanctity of the individual, can play a big role in making this possible. But it must be not distorted dissemination of the kind that has occurred in the past, but a dissemination true to the essential spirit of the religion.

HUYGHE: In the West, Christianity once played this role and asserted the equilibrium that must exist between the individual and the collective. But since then the diminution of its influences has upset the balance. The nineteenth century tended to regard the cult of the individual, sometimes exacerbated, as the supreme law, as such terms as *égotisme* or the *"Culte de moi,"* as used by the French writer Maurice Barrés (1862–1923) demonstrate. By contrast, the twentieth century has tended to crush the individual under collective discipline incarnated in dictatorship, technocracy, or political regimes allied to communism. But evolution modifies the position of man not only in relation to the collective, but also in relation to the world and its enigmas.

The primitive religions correspond to a state in which man has succeeded in mastering neither his means of defense nor his exploitation of the exterior world. Under such circumstances, he feels threatened and realizes that he depends on both his own resources and willpower and on forces transcending and surrounding him. Quite naturally, he assigns to those forces an impenetrable and mysterious character. He responds to these forces by attempting to evoke others from beyond physical possibility. This is the beginning of magic. By means of it man creates a whole ritual enabling him to associate and even, he thinks, control, powers that transcend him. Religions of this nature have survived in later religions to represent an empirical attitude toward the unknowable and impenetrable. They are the most obscure of all.

You are correct to say that the ancient religions mark the attainment of a new stage, represented by the Greeks and their Pantheon. At this point, seeing his powers increase, man began, to an extent, to consider himself equal to the gods. By this I mean that he gave his gods physically and morally human characters, although they are amplified and superior to humanity. They are superhumans endowed with eternity and great powers but, because they are analogous to human beings, apparently feel, think, and live as humans do. Their mysterious, impenetrable character has been dissipated. A similar stage is reached when, in evolving agriculture, a civilization becomes increasingly aware of the capacities of nature and, by associating with nature, learns the means of extracting primary resources from it. This is apparently an intermediary stage.

But I am convinced that only religions that turn, not toward the phenomenal, but, as you say, toward the absolute and transcendental completely fulfill their functions. The new stage they represent corresponds to awareness of the transcendency that humanity must accomplish. By adding heretofore nonexisting responsibility, this stage reveals to man his most essential vocation: to collaborate in the progress of the universe. Man then feels himself at the summit of the enormous effort running throughout Creation and progressively perfecting it by leading it from matter to the spirit.

Once again, we encounter Buddhism and Christianity. Before

making some comparisons, I should explain my own religious position. I belong to neither one nor the other faith. Although my family is Christian, my own thoughts do not obey Christian dogmas. My childhood education was not religious. Consequently everything in me that responds to the feeling of the sacred or, if you prefer, to the religious emotion, is mingled with the sentiment of spirituality. This is the result of study and personal experience including passionate reading of mystics like Ruysbroeck l'Admirable and Saint John of the Cross but which entails the observance of no doctrine. Therefore, although I come of Catholic stock and am acquainted, through marriage, with Protestantism, I am unqualified to speak for Christianity.

My philosophic interests have taken me close to Buddhism. I first came into contact with it through attentive explorations in commentaries by a certain Vivekananda and Sri Aurobindo, which I read more than forty years ago. What I have to offer is a personal position. My viewpoint is that of a witness even if it is no doubt deeply influenced by Christian thought.

It is necessary to state clearly a few points about Christianity and its concept of a personalized God. Religions employ symbols that should be interpreted on different levels of meaning: the literal and the more profound. By distinguishing the Holy Spirit from God the Father and introducing the Son as mediator between the Father and humanity, Christianity indicates the existence—to varying degrees—of something impenetrable to the human spirit in the reality of God the Father. The descent of the Son who assumes a place midway between man and God indicates awareness of an absolute beyond our grasp.

Of course there is another meaning. The Son's coming to Earth and suffering human suffering out of love for humanity and His winning the love of humanity for God constitute a call to our emotional resources. Love is disinterestedness. It is preferring something that is not ourselves to our own egoism and to our own selves. Love is the driving element essential to leading man toward transcending himself, his appetites, and his self-attachment. Consequently it is a symbol. It is unnecessary to reduce Christianity to a personalized form. Personalization has a profound meaning.

Transcending Humanity

HUYGHE: The Buddhist position is more clear-cut. In establishing contact with and clarifying an impersonal Law, it makes a very direct appeal to the Infinite by progressively transcending and abolishing whatever not only attaches the human being to the ephemeral aspects of things, but also confines him within the limits of his own capacities. It becomes necessary to pass beyond intelligence and even beyond sentiments.

We must notice, however, that herein lies an element characteristic of the most elevated manifestations of mysticism and that such elements can be found in many religions. They can best be described as the mystical drive. It can be demonstrated, for instance, that when Saint John of the Cross, whom I have already mentioned, declared that, in order to attain the light of God we must escape from our own light (the light of evidence), he means that it is necessary to transcend the world of appearances and material realities. But, when he says that we must enter Night, he means that we must abolish our own means of perceiving. It seems to me that this indicates that we must create within ourselves a Night of the Intelligence and a Night of the Emotions. Consequently, in this mystical drive—which certainly is within the reach of only the most select, developed few—Saint John approaches the kind of abolition that can be seen in Buddhism.

Elsewhere, Saint John says that ultimately we must pass through that Night, which must be understood as the negation of our means and ourselves. After having passed through the Night that follows our rejection of the too facile lights at our disposal, we arrive at another, new light—a light not made for human eyes. And this puts us in touch with the revelation of divinity.

All of the beliefs current in various parts of the world admit at their pinnacles a level attainable only by mystics. At this level, differences among religions practically vanish to give place to a sense of the ineffable. A Christian mystic can find himself very close to an Islamic mystic. I have seen evidence of this kind of thing among the Carmelites, the most mystical monastic order in the West. A Carmelite who has played a very important role in his order related to me the things he finds he has in common with mystics from the Islamic world or with the most elevated Buddhist thought. Outside the barriers of dogma and ritual, it is possible to find a comforting convergence among spirits oriented toward God.

During the forty years that have passed since I began taking an interest in it, Buddhism in its purest form—especially in reference to the Lotus Sutra, as it is in your case—has seemed to me to open a road, both demanding and essential, to transcending human nature.

IKEDA: Religions of the third stage open ways of this kind to human beings and will survive the vicissitudes of historical period and culture as long as they are not deliberately destroyed. They pose eternal topics and goals that will endure as long as human beings remain human. People today, however, attempt to avert their eyes from such things.

Representatives of persisting primitive and ancient religions as well as societies supporting their residues must have been fully aware of the novelty posed by higher religions even in their formative phases. This, no doubt, accounts for the fierce persecutions higher religions have encountered in their attempts to reach wider audiences. Today we live in an age far removed from violent oppositions between old and new religions. Indeed, many people have lost religious faith to the extent that they regard clinging to differences in religion as peculiar. Some people would even dismiss such an attitude as evidence of barbarian cultural backwardness.

Paradoxically, however, in their ignorance, such modern people entrust themselves to ways of thinking reminiscent of primitive and ancient religions. Of course they do not engage in ritual worship of natural phenomena. They do, however, consider the key to happiness to lie in scientific systems and the technologies that have developed through their application. And, since science has resulted from observation of natural phenomena, such people can be said to have faith in a variation of a primitive religion.

Still clearer is the way in which modern humanity has revived reverence for collective might, which is a characteristic of ancient religions. As Arnold J. Toynbee once pointed out, modern nationalism is an extreme example of this. Human beings form collectives at various levels and endow each with symbolic meaning to inspire allegiance. This was done in the ancient past and will no doubt continue after the demise of modern nationalism. Nonetheless, nationalism certainly represents the most advanced kind of faith in the collective might that has yet emerged.

Primitive and ancient religions inevitably arise from human instincts and from the actual conditions in which human life is lived. No matter how much civilizations develop, relations between human beings and nature, which are the essential premise for primitive religions, remain. Civilization can be considered a cushion between the two, but not even the thickest and largest cushions can prevent the power of nature from influencing human life. Indeed the forces of nature are capable of destroying both human beings and the cushioning civilizations by means of which they surround themselves.

Furthermore, the most advanced science is incapable of completely understanding and elucidating the complexities and subtleties of the operations of nature. As Sir Isaac Newton once said, in the face of the great sea of truth, human wisdom is like a child standing on the shore examining a sea shell. To be sure, science has made considerable strides since Newton's time. But, even so, how much have we come to understand as a consequence?

To continue Newton's simile, we might say that humankind has now succeeded in building a boat that can sail from the shore of the sea of truth out into the offing. At its present state of development, science has shown that the farther into the offing we proceed, the vaster the ocean is and the unimaginably richer it is in various forms of life. Moreover, its current is incomparably stronger than what we were able to judge on the basis of waves rolling to the shore.

It is natural, essential, and noble for human beings to regard nature with a religious humility that is something entirely unlike the magical practices of primitive religions or the rationalism of the natural sciences, which constitute a variation of primitive religion in the name of unlimited control of natural forces.

In all historical ages, the collective has been capable of manifesting immensely greater power than the individual. Furthermore, the power of the collective is essential to the preservation of life, the generation of civilization, and the creation of circumstances under which lofty spiritual functions can be developed. Prizing and protecting the collective are necessary to the preservation of life, the realization of human dignity, and the insurance of human happiness. But the respect for, and trust in, the collective must always be for the sake of protecting, revering, and enlarging human life. We must never put so much faith and trust in the collective that we allow the rights and dignity of the individual to be sacrificed to it.

If the philosophies reflected in primitive and ancient religions are inherent in and vital to humanity, they must always be used in ways that protect, not suppress or harm, human nature. In this connection, the individual human being must confront himself and search for ways to manifest himself correctly.

The higher religions strive to bring about self-confrontation and self-enlightenment. At their emergence great strife arises between higher religions on one side and primitive and ancient religions on the other side. The causes of the discord are lack of concern on the part of lower religions in self-manifestation and self-improvement—or their treating them as matters of mere secondary concern—and the use of such religions as tools by ambitious people monopolizing authority and power.

Even higher religions lose their essential roles of individual self-manifestation and improvement when they become involved in the power systems of actual society. It is precisely because of perversions arising from this phenomenon that many people today distrust religion.

I believe that the anthropomorphic God of Christianity is, in contrast to the Law taught by Buddhism, essentially symbolic in nature. The majority of practicing Christians, however, believe in a personified God. This belief has given rise to discrimination between people loved and favored by God and people outside his favor.

Although the Lotus Sutra teaches that the Law is the fundamental basis of faith, other scriptures revered by various sects teach faith in a personified Buddha in whose name various ceremonies are performed. In Asian nations, this way of thinking has resulted in discrimination, just as Christian teachings have in Europe.

The Lotus Sutra teaches that the ultimate entity is a Law that is called the Mystic Law, because it is too profound and wonderful to be understood by ordinary human intelligence. In discussions we conducted, Arnold J. Toynbee said he believed there is an entity beyond human comprehension behind all phenomena. The Christian and Islamic mystics you mention must, to some extent, perceive this same incomprehensible entity. Making connection with the ultimate Law provides great power to transcend and gain control over the desires and selfishness that bind us in the phenomenal world. By directing their attention toward truly essential things, the higher religions can build the foundation for an eternal, inexhaustible spirituality. This is why I have resolved to devote my life to the mission of carrying Buddhist teachings to the peoples of the world.

The West and Christianity

IKEDA: After having discussed these stages in the development of religion, we should now compare the East and the West and attempt to discover the characteristic conditions and profiles of religion in each.

HUYGHE: One can see the Western position taking form at

the time when primitive religions—religions that attribute a divine character to nature—held sway. It is easy to understand why. These religions correspond to a phase in human evolution, a time when, leaving prehistory, man had to defend himself, albeit clumsily, against aggression from the exterior world. He had entered a somewhat more developed phase when a modus vivendi (called agriculture) with nature had been worked out to take the place of the formerly predominant pure defense against external forces. Nature ceased being merely a reserve of forces to conciliate and render harmless. Instead, it had become an immense reservoir of produce that it was essential to bring to fruition in order to make consumable and useful. It is, therefore, only normal that religions should, perhaps roughly, correspond to this phase in human development. These pagan—and we must not forget that the word *pagan* derives from Latin *paganus*, meaning a person who lives in the country and is, therefore, related to the French word *paysan* or peasant—religions expressed wonder, respect, and love mixed with a certain fear for nature. These emotions still persist. Human beings must collaborate with the powers of nature in the form of gods in order to stay in their favor. In Homer, for instance, anthropomorphic gods are all-powerful but may be sensible to cult, ritual, or offerings and may be softened into becoming partners in understandings. As is only normal, such primitive religions do no more than reflect current stages of civilization.

But suddenly in the West a new position emerged: a position that can be summarized in the term Judeo-Christian. Even though historically it can be shown that Christianity emerged from Judaism, essentially their viewpoints are profoundly different. Judaism, the older of the two, always embodies a reverent fear before a divinity representing the forces confronting humanity. God is a god of anger, a terrifying god, of exactly the kind that is to be found in the first stage of agricultural development when the peasant, with his primitive methods and tools, is confronted by natural forces that he must conciliate.

Christianity represents a much more advanced stage than that of the Old Testament, since it effects a transition to love.

Humanity is no longer face to face with angry menacing powers like those of the classical pantheon or the God of Israel, who must be calmed and made propitious through human means. Christianity establishes a relationship of love, and that love is reciprocal, because God, the lord of the universe, demonstrates his love for humanity to the point of wishing to share its worst sorrows through the intervention of His Son. Human beings must respond essentially by means of love.

This can be seen up to the eve of the Renaissance, when aesthetics attempts to intellectualize itself by extolling the Platonic idea of the Beautiful. Saint Francis of Assisi (1182–1226) condensed human love into a flame. He exalted nature through love. Since nature is God's creation, in loving nature one addresses God. One loves God through nature. In his admirable poems the *Fioretti*, Saint Francis invokes "Sister Moon and Brother Sun." He inclined himself wholeheartedly to the birds and fishes even to the point of preaching sermons to them on the glory of God.

One episode in his life is filled with symbolic value. A town named Gubbio was making preparations to defend itself against a wolf that had been menacing it. This beast can be interpreted as an incarnation of the forces of nature confronting and opposing humanity. Saint Francis intervened by means of love.

Advancing toward the animal, just as he had done with birds and fishes, he addressed the wolf, not with a systematic discourse of words and ideas, but with the warmth of his heart revealed in his voice. By speaking to it, he calmed and pacified the animal. When it had become gentle, the saint and the wolf returned to the town together. Love had established faith and had exercised its power of uniting.

Domination of nature, which we have observed as having developed in the West, is properly speaking a fact not of Christianity, but of the Greco-Latin culture that became associated and integrated with Christianity. Greece introduced mastery of human rational faculties and gradually replaced empiricism, its rituals and incantations, and the sacrifices of the ancient religions with a dispassionate, rational rapport between nature and man. This was achieved with some difficulty because philosophy dispelled the ancient religion. And it was precisely for this reason that the traditional Greek city-state condemned Socrates to death. The city-state saw that the atavistic beliefs, for which Socrates substituted rational thought, were threatened with elimination. And, indeed, with Socrates and then Plato and Aristotle, rational thought received irreversible impetus.

With abundant nuances and great suppleness and sensibility, Greece laid the main foundation for Western culture but then was compelled to pass the baton to her Roman successor. Although the student of Greece and Grecian rationalism, the Roman was of a far more utilitarian disposition. He was greedy and combative. The Roman gradually built an immense empire that had nothing in common with Greek republics, which, for better or worse, coexisted in the midst of rivalries and battles. For the Romans, one city was to dominate the world to the boundaries of the East. One Roman power attacked both Parthians and Scythes. And where Roman armies did not go, Roman commerce penetrated (traces of it are to be found as far as the Indies).

The heir to the highly intellectual Greek culture, the Roman spirit attempted instinctively to extract a practical instrument from it. No doubt, the Western attempt to use reason and its resources to subject the world to human will must be dated from the Roman era. As Descartes was to state much later, by means of reason and its resources humanity wished to make itself master and owner of nature.

Rome was first to assign prime importance to the engineer. For the Greeks, science was a disinterested instrument of knowledge in quest of truth and understanding of nature and its principles. They held the engineer in certain disdain for applying discoveries of scholars to the attainment of exclusively utilitarian, pragmatic aims. By contrast, Rome demonstrated the liveliest interest in the engineer and especially in the military engineer and his machines of war. By orienting the Greek rational spirit toward practical applications, the Romans mark a sharp transition. As we have already seen, reason, which was essentially a faculty for adapting to the world of matter in space, was by Roman times, already moving toward science.

In keeping with the process of rotation that life inevitably evokes, however, the Christian religion intervened as a safety valve and a compensating reaction. Aside from bringing reflections of the Orient, Christianity wished to oppose its spirit of love against the material greed and growing aridity of Roman civilization, already facing the problem of the exploitation of the lowly and weak in the name of economic cupidity. Coming to the aid of the downtrodden, in the name of love, Christianity attempted to propagate goodness and justice.

It is true that, at a later time, the Church was unable to prevent itself from making alliances with controlling powers in order to assure its own might. Nonetheless, many returns to the evangelical vocation occurred.

In the Middle Ages, in the thirteenth century, perhaps to offset the dogmatism of theologians, who turned now to Plato, now to Aristotle, a spirit of tenderness developed. On the civil side it resulted in the so-called Courts of Love that formed around such women as Eleanor of Aquitaine (c. 1122–1204) to form cultivated societies to discuss the affairs of the heart. On the religious side, it found expression in the Franciscan movement, which opposed the effusions of the soul overwhelmed with love of God, other creatures, and nature to the intellectualism of the Dominicans.

The West has committed the error of allowing one of its component elements—the rational spirit applied to practical, utilitarian greed—to triumph; and, if modern civilization is the excessive fruit of the tendency to make such a mistake, we must not forget that the same West has preserved its powers of sensitivity, love, and communion with nature. Such powers are especially apparent in France, where they nourish both literature and art. A quasi-Franciscan painter like Corot (1796–1875), in the middle of the nineteenth century, was imbued with a dazzling tenderness, constituting the most convincing kind of response to the spirit of greed and aridity developed by bourgeois society.

With the few reservations I have made in the name of a more equitable understanding of the West, I consider your position just. One of the things that I admire most about Buddhism is its struggle in the name of balanced development of the interior human life and a relation of interdependence and unity between humanity and nature. Buddhism battles against the spirit of greed, profit, and domination that has weighed too heavily on the West. This is certainly one of its principal attractions. The awakening of curiosity about Buddhism in the nineteenth century reflected the desire of the most vividly aware people to react against the domination of the utilitarian and the actual that science, industry, and technology were amplifying dangerously and that, in the twentieth century, menace the future of humanity.

IKEDA: Undeniably, Christianity has been an important source of Western civilization. How would you describe the positive and negative effects that Christianity has had on that civilization and the ways of thinking of Western peoples?

HUYGHE: The major role of Christianity was to reveal a religion of the highest spirituality to a world exceptionally devoted to rationalism. Western civilization was headed in this direction established by the Greeks and pursued still further under the weight of Roman materialism. By the time the Roman world had reached its end, the West was already in a state of crisis analogous to the one confronting us today.

Even before the advent of Christianity, a muffled call for it could be heard. At the end of the Roman world—as is happening today—many people became aware of being increasingly stifled. As is well known, fascination with Oriental religions grew during the last centuries of the Roman Empire. The Orient appeared already as a complementary source of the spiritual life in opposition to Roman rationalism and materialism. As scholars, especially Jérome Carcopino of the University of Paris, have pointed out, various new cults were introduced into Rome. Some of them revived the cult of Orpheus, by means of which the Hellenistic world had been able to preserve the dualism, which, already in mythology, opposed Pan to Phoebus-Apollo. Others—for example the cult of Isis—arrived from Egypt. Responding to the same call to which these other cults addressed themselves, Christianity developed at a stunning rate enabling it in a few generations to annex the whole of the Western world; that is, first the Empire and then the barbarian frontier zones.

Once again, we observe the natural movement whereby life—both physical and psychic—ceaselessly strives to reestablish equilibrium by balancing opposites. As soon as he finds himself transported by a unilateral tendency, man is irresistibly driven to apply counterweights in order to restore the totality of his potentialities. It is impossible not to imagine that our current situation offers numerous analogies with the one encountered and responded to at the time of the emergence of Christianity.

IKEDA: I agree entirely with you that the desire to move from materialism and rationalism in the direction of spirituality accounts for the acceptance of Christianity in the Roman world. No doubt, in addition to this, the love that Christianity teaches aroused sympathetic responses in personal relations.

HUYGHE: Perhaps this is because, although reason ignores it and materialism reduces it to physical desire, love is the very foundation of life.

IKEDA: The striving for connection between the self and a profound, ultimate entity causes us to correct materialist and rationalist tendencies and to move in the direction of the spiritual and mystical. This can, however, inspire people to live as hermits isolated from the rest of society. The more seekers strive to achieve the ultimate entity, the more they are likely to take a sternly critical view of ordinary individuals who find breaking with material desires impossible. While showing people how to break free of the ordinary world by striving to reach the ultimate reality, Christianity teaches that people should return to their fellow members of society in a spirit of love. This is why Christianity was widely accepted as one of the world's guiding religions.

Later, however, with the formation of the Church and the authoritarianism and formalism accompanying it, Christianity lost its original elan in the red tape of administration. Ugly lust for power has often meant that the Church actually did society harm. This can, of course, be interpreted as a revival of control by materialism and rationalism. But it seems to me that authoritarianism deprived the Church of the love it should have shown to the ordinary people and especially to the poor and that this has caused many people to turn away from Christianity.

Protestantism relied on reason in its opposition to the ritual and superstition of the Church of Rome but failed to restore the love that was the foundation of early Christianity. For this reason, its struggle ended with the battle with authoritarianism. Martin Luther's denouncing and supporting the ruthless suppression of the Peasants' War (1524–26) indicate the limitations of his religious reforms.

HUYGHE: Nonetheless we must not forget that Protestantism has always emphasized texts by Saint Paul and Saint John that profess that God is love.

We must remember, too, that problems among sects usually concern churches and not profound faith. Historical occurrences never arise from profound faith but more often from human political behavior; that is, opportunism in the face of an event. The contribution of Protestantism should no more be confused with occurrences in the historical order than that of the Catholic Church should be confused with the Inquisition.

IKEDA: Love and religion must be intimately related. In my opinion, religion is the sole source of the spirit of the love, or compassion, that can guarantee the rights of the weak and protect them from victimization at the hands of the powerful. People require religion—and will respect it only if it fulfills this requirement—to keep this spirit constantly in the public awareness so as to inspire acts of love and compassion.

The relation between religion and the ultimate entity is reflected in actual society in the love and compassion of its adherents. In the case of Buddhism, these are reflected in the Bodhisattva and Buddha states of the Ten Worlds that I explained earlier.

As a person dedicated to spreading the teachings of Nichiren Daishonin, I consider the manifestation of Buddhist compassion in the acts of individuals and in the principles of our movement to be of maximum importance. Part of my work in this connection is visiting the U.N. headquarters and meeting with leaders in such nations as the United States, the Soviet Union and China, and holding discussions of the kind we are conducting now in the hope of providing some reference material on the way the world and humanity of the future ought to be.

HUYGHE: You asked me what harm I thought Christianity has done. In all honesty, I do not think we can lay any blame at its door, for it is the Church that must be examined in this connection. A striking passage in Dostoevsky's work describes Christ who, having returned to Earth, is the object of hostility from His own Church which, in fact, has condemned Him.

It is always to be feared that, in a large institutionalized and organized Church, fundamental revelations will be replaced and virtually stifled by intellectual commentary, the establishment of dogma, an orthodoxy, and a punctilious judicatory. The initial surge—the contribution that I like to call progressive—gives way to a regulating administration and, as is to be expected, politics and a taste for power. Rites become minute and, if he does not resist the propensity, the believer is led to substitute detailed cult writings, which too often depend on superstition, for essential revelations. Obviously lighting a candle on the altar before a statue of Saint Anthony of Padua in the hope of regaining a lost purse has very little to do with the fundamental essence of Christianity. But such dangers always lie in wait for churches.

It is important to follow the history of the Church in order to discover how, faced with the necessity of expanding, it organized itself as a civil and financial power and how it became endowed with dignitaries to the point where a palpable risk was felt of stifling the profound sentiment, of which the Church ought to be the bearer. This took place in the fifteenth century and resulted in the Reformation and the dawning of Protestantism. To oppose what can be called rituals and superstitions, Protestantism relied on rationalism, which regained its impetus at the end of the Middle Ages. In wishing to purify the Church and return it to its original path, Protestantism rocked it with schism. But, above all, it prepared, though involuntarily, the way for the gradual descent that, by proscribing all emotional apparatus, returned to naked ideas and enthroned the intellectual rigor that, associated with the rise of science, inevitably led to the materialistic and positivistic spirit.

Obliged to look to official power for support, especially when schism had produced two rival branches, the Church more and more allied itself with the authority of the moment. Having opted unconditionally to side with the bourgeoisie in the nineteenth century and having flattered in that class a desire to be sanctified by tradition, today the Church is increasingly seduced by whatever ideas triumph at the moment, even those, like Marxism, that most radically negate its very essence. Open to pressure from the spirit prevailing in its environment, the Church is now undergoing the same crisis that upsets the whole West and for which, by its very nature, the Church ought to provide a remedy. Sometimes by turning from profound revelations of faith and regarding the Church as no more than a social and socializing organization, priests bear witness to the deep degeneration of its role. Obviously the Church must be the natural protector of the weak and poor against the powerful of the world. But this cannot be done by becoming so bound up in material affairs that the proper mission of saving misguided people by returning them to the way of spiritual transcendency and love is forgotten.

I especially admire the dualism in your religion. On the one hand, Nichiren Shoshu preserves the doctrine and the faith and confides them to priests. On the other hand, Soka Gakkai, the lay organization of which you are honorary president, has charge of propagating and establishing the doctrine effectively not only in Japan, but also throughout the world. This duality seems a good way of avoiding the confusion of the spiritual and the secular and the consequent contamination that are a major danger for a religion.

Christianity and the East

IKEDA: As you just commented, Christianity introduced into the Roman world a characteristic trait from the East. It would seem that, in their fundamental essence, the Christian concept of love and its attitude toward God have something in common with Buddhist compassion and the Law that is the source of Buddhism. Since it is older than Christianity and was no doubt at one time propagated in the Middle East, Buddhism may have had an influence on Christianity in its formative stage. What is your opinion of this possibility?

HUYGHE: You pose an extremely interesting and essential problem: that of connections between the East and the West—in spite of their fundamental duality. This duality, which is very real, puts these two groups of civilizations in the relation of opposite, not antagonistic, but complementary poles. Once again, in this relationship, I observe the action of that play of tension between opposites that is apparently inherent in life and that is also essential to the interior life.

Upon assuming a constitution, an organism tends to define and formulate itself and to specialize in its own major characteristic. As a consequence, it places excessive importance on that characteristic and in this way disrupts total harmony.

The West has put all of its weight on the positive, material, and technical aspects of life, whereas the East has attempted to give priority to spiritual preoccupations. This is why, in the history of world thought, connections between East and West occupy a decisive position. I mention this in order to demonstrate my interest in this problem, which I have made the subject of a course pursued for many years at the Collège de France.

The geographic origin of Christianity has a definite importance. It was born on the eastern shore of the Mediterranean world where it came into contact with those lines of transportation, like the Silk Road, laid out across the Asiatic plain to satisfy the needs of commerce.

IKEDA: Certainly since it came into being on the east coast of the Mediterranean near the terminus of the Silk Road it is entirely likely that Christianity came under Oriental influence.

At about the time of the birth of Christianity, Mahayana Buddhism flourished in Central Asia just above Northern India at the midway point of the Silk Road. The old Persian empire was located to the West of this region. In other words, the cultural, political, and economic void between the Mediterranean and the region in which Mahayana Buddhism flourished was probably not as great as is sometimes thought today, especially since a dense transportation network was maintained by the Persian empire.

Of course the deserts were, as is made clear by the campaign records of Alexander the Great, difficult to traverse. Nonetheless, routes through the Persian empire connecting the zone in the east, where Mahayana Buddhism flourished, and the zone in the west, where Christianity originated, were probably not as difficult as is imagined now.

People familiar with both religions are sometimes surprised at certain startling similarities between the two religions. For instance, Christ was born in a stable. The mother of Siddhartha Gautama, who became the Buddha, was walking in a garden when her time came and entered a stable to give birth to her child. The Bible relates how Christ was threatened and tempted by Satan on a mountaintop. Similarly, according to tradition, evil forces threatened and attempted to seduce Shakyamuni just as he was about to achieve enlightenment.

But similarities in such minor episodes have very little significance. The important point is the resemblance between Buddhist compassion and Christian love. Buddhist scriptures contain the following story about compassion. Once a disciple asked the Buddha why, although he ought to demonstrate love and compassion equally to all sentient beings, he was especially compassionate toward people who suffered. The Buddha replied, "Imagine a father with seven children. He loves them all equally but, if one falls ill, he is takes special care of the sick child." In a sense, this story resembles the famous Christian parable of the Prodigal Son.

Without specifically referring to Buddhism, you mention Oriental influences on Christianity as a result of the location of its origin. We ought to remember, however, that Oriental tradition, too, contains many materialistic and rationalistic elements. In very ancient times, for example, the Indians and the Chinese achieved things that can be considered distant sources of later Western scientific technology. On the other hand, of course, Oriental tradition includes much that is extremely spiritual, usually other-worldly, pessimistic, and highly mystical in nature. Since they reject actuality, philosophies of this kind are, by their nature, unsuited to fostering compassion and love for the people of everyday society.

Even in the East, religions that teach both union with the ultimate entity and compassion for the members of actual society are extremely limited. The most representative is Buddhism; within Buddhism, Mahayana teachings; and among those teachings, the Lotus Sutra. Furthermore, since at the time of the inception of Christianity only Mahayana Buddhism fostered a missionary spirit, it is only natural to assume that whatever influence was exerted on the West was Mahayanist.

Of course, I neither insist that such influence existed nor attach much value for the present in things that happened two thousand years ago. But, in the light of the needs of contemporary society, I hope that, by recalling a wide-scale historical spiritual drama that occurred between the East and the West two millennia ago, I can contribute to a speedy and correctly oriented revival of our modern world.

HUYGHE: It must be recalled that Christianity constituted an effective reaction against positivistic Roman thought because it allowed itself to be suspected of bonds with the opposite pole, namely, the East. After Alexander's dream of reaching India, Rome opposed Iran by way of the eastern Mediterranean. But, even as early as the fifth century B.C., Plato's philosophy seemed sometimes to echo the thought of the East. This was even clearer eight centuries later with Neo-Platonism. It is well known that Plotinus followed armies campaigning against the peoples of Persia in the hope of coming into contact with Oriental thought, which was already then decked with mysterious attraction.

I have alluded elsewhere to the incursions of mystic cults into a decadent Rome. They, too, represent a reflection of the Oriental world acting as an antidote. Doubtless, during the course of the Western Middle Ages, too, a vast quantity of elements that have become characteristic of our civilization were introduced, as one learns more and more, as a consequence of contacts established by the Crusades with an East in which Islam had, by this time, already expanded as far as Persia and India.

In modern times an analogous, though reverse, transfer resulting from an undertow movement, has thrown the West toward the East and, after the colonial era, has caused the extraordinary expansion of the industrial-technical civilization that now contaminates all the regions of the globe with the disturbing effects we have already discussed.

The very extraordinarily materialist power of the West now makes us hope for a reaction, continuing the effects of the law of alternation, that adds interest to your efforts to evoke a therapeutic wave from an old source.

3

Humanity Facing the Unknown

Reason and Faith

IKEDA: The modern materialistic world came into being as a consequence of the development of reason. The introduction of the rational spirit into the philosophy of primitive religions, which concentrated on the world of natural phenomena, gave birth to the natural sciences. The ancient religions revered the power of the human collective. The application of scientific methods in relation to methods of controlling the human collective resulted in the evolution of the social sciences. The outcome of these developments was loss of faith in the primitive religions to the natural sciences and diminution of the religiosity of the ancient religions owing to social sciences.

Increasing insistence on the importance of the dignity of the individual has eaten away the foundations of those higher religions that posit an anthropomorphic or personified deity diminishing the dignity of the individual. Religions that interpret the ultimate entity to be Law, on the other hand, agree with the modern requirement for individual dignity. Since the Law can abide equally in the minds of all, each human being has as much dignity as any other.

HUYGHE: I propose the following version of the evolution of

religion and its consequences. In primitive societies, religions make tangible and accessible to man the mystery of the world surrounding and pressing in on him from all sides. It offers him the aid of myths, which are symbols of things felt in a deep, if unintelligible, fashion. The myth makes it possible to be aware of such things by making them exterior and concrete and converting them into images and shows. Mythological stories function in such a fashion as to romanticize—if that is the correct term—things that human beings perceive obscurely. In relation to myths, human beings are able to react as they would before exterior, tangible truth.

Similarly, the members of an audience at a play or motion picture see in the performers their own secret thoughts. And suddenly, through the performers, they become aware of things dwelling within themselves. Modern psychiatrists employ this power of transposition in what is called psychodrama. They allow the mental patient himself to project imaginarily and, in this way, make available and perceptible the phantasms producing his internal confusion.

Thus primitive religions showed human beings those things that wandered obscurely and barrenly at the bottom of their thoughts. They animated these things and made then perceptible or intelligible. Under the guise of myths, they regulated and instructed them.

It could be said indeed that this was the normal state of human thought until the appearance of philosophy in the sixth and fifth centuries B.C. in Greece. Myths gave way to a rational ordering of the confused problems of the soul. This ordering was achieved with the aid of abstract ideas. In a manner of speaking, thinkers poured them into a palpable mold of coherent ideas mutually bound together with the universal bonds of a logic striving for mathematical certainty. When this happened, the West entered a new era, the Age of Reason.

Brought to the forefront and applied to the study of the surrounding and essentially physical world, reason had no recourse but to eliminate radically the image-power of the myth. It cut the roots binding it to the most obscure kind of sensibility and based its own undertakings on things that can be expressed logically and explained in "*notions claires et distinctes*," to borrow an expression from Descartes.

The narrowing process was very gradual. Greek reason, for example, is charged with poetry. Plato did not hesitate to invent images and myths. Aristotle, however, narrowed the field further. He had no wish to deal with anything but empirical perception ordered by reason and codified by logic. The Western mechanism of abstract desiccation was already in operation.

The religious resurgence evoked by Christianity counterbalanced this trend. Though quickly penetrated by Greek rationalism, which nourished Scholastic theology, Christianity brought about a radical return to the sources of the interior life, of its transports, fervor, and ecstasy.

But the irrepressible march of rationalism brought about an eclipse of religion. From the seventeenth century, following a series of great thinkers initiated by Francis Bacon and including Descartes, Spinoza and, later, Newton, rationality took exclusive possession of mental life. Such a life could only advance science and the rigorous establishment of scientific methods. It remained intransigent in the face of everything that was not based on physical, logically controlled experimentation. Methodically the mystery of the world was replaced by a network of general laws rejecting everything falling outside its meshes.

The result of this situation was a dangerous partiality of the human spirit: religions were condemned for attempting to understand all those things in the world and in man that exceed the grasp of rationality. Nonetheless, the idea of the mystery, which was later to become unintelligible, remained alive in the seventeenth century, when the French prelate and historian Jacques Benigne Bossuet (1627–1704) was able to say that, in the face of one of these mysteries, we are like a man who holds one end of a long coil of rope in the right hand and the other in the left hand and, observing the rope to disappear from view in opposite directions, refuses to admit that the two meet, though only at infinity. Later than Descartes, Bossuet was a great spirit and, although a man of the Church, held that some things transcend reason, the frontiers of which probably correspond with those of physical experience.

Soon belief in a god who created and controls the universe weakened. And, in the West, as organized science took form, atheism became increasingly widespread.

The pride of modern man has been exalted by the expansion of the physical sciences, the certainty of their discoveries, the fecundity of their application, and the new capacity science confers of dealing with the forces of the universe and, understanding their physical origin, of mastering, reproducing, and utilizing them. As a consequence of this pride, man is disinclined to bow before the personalized God, who replaced antique myths. Modern man feels completely self-sufficient in relation to an exclusively physical world that he can explain with the aid of laws, namely, the relationship between physical effects and causes. In place of the infallible intelligence of a moving Spirit, admired for centuries, modern man limits himself to demonstrating a mechanism of rules and laws intelligible to reason. To human dignity, which you frequently evoke, we must add human pride.

It may be, indeed, that at the present time, a religion like Buddhism, that replaces the idea of a personal god with that of a Law, has a better chance of remounting the stream of rational materialism. Still, the meaning of the Law might seem obscure to a Westerner. For my part, I interpret it by returning to what I have repeatedly said: it is necessary to take each human being beyond the phenomena constituting appearances and enable him to understand—most of all through introspection extending to the very sources of his being—that, in the profoundest part of each of us, there lies the possibility of understanding a more universal reality.

Although we have already referred to it, the metaphor of the ocean is extremely expressive. Each individual human being is no more than a wave, and waves are superficial, episodic phenomena that do not explain the ocean. The ocean resides in the depths where it establishes its totality and unity. The human being must go beyond superficial perceptions, beyond the "Me," and descend toward the self. In addition, he must become capable of approaching the profound perception that is the very meaning of the universe and its ultimate. Toward what is the universe moving? What is the goal of the continual thrust guiding and modifying the universe according to perceptible evolution?

Awareness of that thrust is how I define awareness of the Law that, beyond the phenomenal world, directs and orients that impulse.

IKEDA: I consider excessive faith in reason, undeniably one of the causes of the unjust lowering of the position of religion in the minds of people today, harmful to contemporary civilization. Reason should be applied in determining whether the object of faith is suitable or right. It is an error, however, to make reason itself an object of faith or to use reason to deny faith. What are your thoughts on the relation between reason and faith?

HUYGHE: With your important observations, we have reached the nucleus of the problem. Your remarks are valid for humanity at all times but are especially acute in the crisis we undergo at present.

I should like, however, to begin by explaining the meaning of the term faith, which you contrast with reason. It is unnecessary to accept the word faith in the pejorative sense sometimes given it by making it a synonym of passive and absolute credulity in a revelation or a way of thinking imposed from without. The word faith actually means profound intuition as opposed to reason. We should remember that we human beings possess two modes of understanding reality. One arises from basic sensations and results from their being ordered in a clearly coordinated way by reason. The other is by means of contact with—a kind of injection into—the mystery of things. This is followed by a jet from the depth toward the light, much as water from an artesian well bounds from the earth. We state the fundamental duality by confronting these two modes of knowing—the rational mode, which holds to the benefits of objectivity, and the intuitive mode which, though more uncertain, penetrates farther.

In modern times, the rivalry that, to some extent, has always existed between these two modes of knowing has been exacerbated by the growing claim of reason to monopolize and resolve everything. In older times, when it became blind, faith played an inverse, dominating, and harmful role. We are always faced with the problem of establishing understanding and equilibrium between the two, often adverse, powers at our disposal and of allowing them to enrich each other.

IKEDA: The word faith means absolute trust in something or someone. At the present time, people mistrust putting faith in individual human beings because, making a specific person absolute in this way invites the subjugation of many other people. And, should such faith become widespread and blind, it could run counter to the dignity that belongs equally to all human beings and could threaten democracy. There is currently a strong tendency to despise putting faith in and following not only a living individual, but a person's teachings, since this seems to signify abandonment of rational investigation. It is true that some people put faith in and abide by their own premonitions and intuitions. But, since these are often erroneous, it is both foolish and sometimes dangerous to follow them.

It would be wrong to reject these misgivings and mistrusts of faith because they derive from important historical lessons. On the other hand, reason is not always deserving of extensive trust. As a matter of fact, the idea that everything can be rationally investigated and judged flies in the face of reality.

In brief, we human beings invariably make one kind of error or another. Realizing this from the outset is the way to minimize mistakes and reduce the harm they do. Since reason is an extremely effective means to prevent mistakes, it should be used extensively to that end and should be developed and refined in order to function correctly.

But, no matter how polished, refined, and strengthened,

reason properly operates only in situations like the one mentioned above; and, as human beings, we must constantly enter   domains that are inaccessible to reason: the future toward which the present life is always striving.

Of course, the relatively constant laws operative in various phenomena make possible a certain amount of forecasting on the basis of rational investigation into the past. Since it is impossible for an individual to have rational understanding of all phenomena, however, it is sometimes necessary to attempt to cope with the future by believing in elucidations made by other people. People who are ignorant or untutored in teachings from the past must use their own premonitions and intuition as guides to the future. Under such circumstances, we must put faith in our premonitions and intuition just as in daily life we must put faith in information received from our eyes and ears.

From this viewpoint, it becomes evident that faith and reason do not necessarily fight for territory on the same plane. We incorporate many things into ourselves through faith, and reason, too, can be an object of faith. Since reason is used in investigations to evaluate objects of faith, reason itself often escapes investigation. This must not be, especially since reason has the wisdom and clarity to make possible clear investigating. People wishing to transcend themselves and go farther and deeper require faith. People today must come to understand that, although reason must be employed to the limits of its capability, faith is essential in those lofty spiritual regions into which reason cannot penetrate. The object of faith can be found in the teachings of great figures of the past like the Buddha and in intuitions formed at the deepest level of individual life.

HUYGHE: As you very justly point out, blind faith in reason is a paradox. Reason creates nothing and reveals nothing. It is valid only to the extent that it makes possible clear, constant control of those things that nourish it and are subject to it. A priori, it cannot be a negation of faith. It must be lucid and intelligent enough to realize that our knowledge is not limited to those objects and mechanisms called rational. Its roots should be deep enough to penetrate beyond the ability to understand a logical system.

The weakness of faith is to have no process of objective control at its disposal. It can fraudulently lead to credulity or mental weakness that submit themselves blindly to authoritarian pronouncements. To be valid, faith must arise from a great internal effort. Of course, reason must involve the same kind of effort because, as is too often forgotten, it can find rational justifications and demonstrations for any kind of statement at all—as the Greek Sophists proved.

The important thing is the great, sincere, profound, and intuitive effort that brings us face to face with certain revelations and that is the source of the great discoveries of science. Reason intervenes only to control and employ these things. The problem is having access to the evident.

IKEDA: People today believe in another truth. They seem to think that satisfying desires constitutes both human liberty and human dignity. The general tendency to approve satisfaction of desire accounts, in part, for the current social malaise. Nonetheless, control of desire must always be carried out on the basis of individual will and conscience. Sometimes, of course, desires cannot be satisfied because of misery or poverty. But all attempts on the part of exterior authority to control desire violate human freedom. Thoroughly considered religious faith can be the source of power enabling each individual to cultivate willpower and conscience within himself.

HUYGHE: Humanity is directed toward the satisfaction of desires as an inevitable consequence of the materialism on which modern civilization is built. Essentially, desire is a greed connection between the human being and something outside him. When that other thing is material, desire takes its most concrete, its lowest, form. This is a fault that must be remedied.

And the only possible remedy is reeducation and endowing the human being with desires other than those pertaining to the material world. Here again we return to the problem that

we have encountered several times and that we can now envisage together: it is essential to teach the search for quality as a
fundamental. We have already sketched a direction that could
be imposed on education and that, without limiting it to the
study of concrete, material facts, could modify it by associating
with it the development of the sense of quality, which could
later admit all kinds of extensions. As we have said, the practice of art could serve as a good starting point.

This kind of education should lead to the renascence of a
religious spirit in the broadest sense of the word. We have
already said that the significance of religions must not reside in
dogmas and rites. Religion must awaken in us enthusiasm for
something including but transcending us, something that is
usually summed up in the word God. I should prefer, however,
to use the word the Infinite, which suggests the limitless that
liberates from the finite world of the physical and material.
Infinite is a word indicating that the goal is not something to be
attained as an object that can be seized in the hand. It is only a
direction that, while positive, is always farther away. The thing
beyond human beings, which we sometimes call the divine and
to which philosophy refers as Being-In-Itself and The Absolute,
is not within the command of the means of our intellectual
understanding, which can grasp only limited things. Our aspiration to attain Being suggests an endless effort to fulfill its need
to transcend farther the more it progresses.

Beyond its first impulse, which is always beneficial, a religion can be efficacious only if it avoids becoming rigidly fixed
in restrictive formalisms like decrees, established dogmas, and
intangible rituals. Religions are more valuable when they admit
a spiritual drive than when they entail limitations and accepted
organization. Without any doubt, Buddhism—and especially in
the form in which you accept and explain it—seems very free
of the restraints that constitute obstacles. Most of all, it strives
to respond to the essential driving force that elevates the
human being and opens an endless road to him.

The following conception of the human being might be
drawn up as a resumé. First come the fundamental necessities
of life. The human being must ensure his continued existence

through the satisfaction of certain material needs inherent in his makeup and essential to the preservation of life: nourishment, sexuality, and so on. Indeed life has the duty of preserving itself in order to attain ultimate perfection. This demands a constantly awake conscience supported by a robust willpower, because contentment with no more than the vital and necessary hampers human beings on the journey they must make.

The journey must not, however, be undertaken without caution. It must be conducted on the basis of an exact knowledge of life and its conditions. And this is where intelligence must intervene. Intelligence is necessary to enable us to understand exactly the situation into which existence has cast us. This understanding must include both the exterior world, with which we must ensure the continuance of life, and the interior world which, once life has been ensured, furnishes it with action and a raison d'être. We can attain lucidity through intelligence.

Thus we arrive at the third stage of the journey. Now ensured by knowledge, the journey must be oriented in the right direction. To do this, the human being must foresee and perceive the natural direction of all Creation, of the life inscribed in it, and of the individual life that is a constituent element of it. Such perception of our ultimate raison d'être allows us to reach the immense field of the spirit.

First, however, we require the material element to guarantee subsistence. Then we need the intellectual element to serve as a basis for lucid comprehension of the actions we perform in relation to our environment and ourselves. And, finally, we require the spiritual element to allow us to glimpse our own raison d'être and that of life. It is in this realm that religion can play an essential role.

But, clearly, religion must adapt to the diversity of human means. Addressing people whose stage of development is not advanced requires a variety of dogmas and ceremonies. In the case of people demonstrating greater development, rites, dogmas, and precepts give way before the mystical drive presented to human beings as their essential vocation.

It must be said, however, that at a still higher level certain beings can—and, as a superior duty, must—try, on their own initiative and through the exclusive effort of their own personalities, to continue the forward journey and attempt to reveal the point on the horizon toward which it is directed. The journey is actually an ascent. And, as in the mountains, whereas less-experienced climbers must be attached to guiding ropes, the one lone climber responsible for his own actions is all the more praiseworthy for remaining alone.

Each individual must have the ambition to travel far and the prudence not to make excessive demands on himself. Within the full range of possibilities, the human being must find the level most efficacious for his own full flowering.

Human Responsibility and Eternal Life

IKEDA: People of the past were taught that the meaning of religion was connected largely with a life beyond the grave. Buddhism, too, taught that the moral and religious good or bad of actions in this life could be the causes resulting in the perpetrators' going to either hell or what is called the Pure Land after death. Christianity treats the issue of human responsibility with the doctrines of Heaven and Hell. What are your opinions of these ideas of postmortem states? How should they be restructured so as to be meaningful in these modern times?

HUYGHE: Actually almost all religions propose a future life that is a ratification of ordinary life. The aim of this view is to create a sense of responsibility in human beings. Similarly, child education must be a blend of threats of punishment and promises of reward. In Christianity, the dogmas of the Catholic Church include the doctrine of a future life promising Paradise or Hell, determined at the Last Judgment, representations of which portray a symbolic pair of scales with suspended pans for Good and Evil. Buddhism arrives at a similar result through the dogma of reincarnation: successive lives, each of which ratifies its predecessor by representing either an improvement or a regression.

In exclusively materialistic modern civilization, the idea of the human being's end and his responsibility for his life is doomed to disappear. The current and the present are given priority. To this is added only a vague belief in technological and social progress, which attempt to project a better "present" into the future. But the human being remains alone with his desires and greed.

Progress only attempts to assure each individual of the satisfaction of both his needs and his desires. In other words, the human being has been reduced to the immediate, which deprives him of an awareness of a meaning or reason for being and robs him of motivation. This, in turn, engenders the moral emptiness and bitterness that leave our less-than-enlightened contemporaries in despair.

We can only wonder how human beings will fill the great vacancy left if religions continue to decline. Malraux was thinking of this when he pointed to art as a substitute for the sacred. In a materialistic civilization, culture, in the broadest sense of the word, is the only thing that can reintroduce the notion of quality. We have sufficiently frequently indicated that literature and art imply the idea of a scale of values and demand ambition to climb always higher. We know perfectly well that the tendency to self-perfection has no end, but persists into infinity. Modern materialistic societies have come to understand that the only counterweight to the sterilization threatening them is culture, which they have virtually sanctified as the French Revolution sanctified reason. These societies are willing to devote governmental ministries to culture but immediately recover their natural inclination by tending to confuse culture with diversion—the so-called leisure pastimes—and by reducing culture to a function of amusement.

We have already considered the role education ought to play if it is to counterbalance the vacuity and prejudices of the contemporary world. But, instead of taking this road, education only seems to try to emulate currently popular ideas.

IKEDA: It is impossible for us to know anything about the postmortem world during this life. Buddhist doctrines of transmigration teach that one life follows another in an infinite series. This means that each life has experienced the postmortem world, although all memory of it is lost—according to one theory, because of the suffering endured at the moments of fertilization and passage through the pelvic channel.

Most religions, no matter whether they hold, as Buddhism does, that the birth-death cycle repeats itself infinitely, or, as Christianity does, that life once lived is a unique, nonrepeating affair, teach that the self continues after death and good and bad deeds of the present life affect that self. I agree with you that one reason for such doctrines is to cultivate a sense of responsibility for one's actions. We will strive to live this life better if we will be better off in a future existence for doing so. Feeling responsible for one's own future is important from the viewpoint of human dignity. It would be difficult to stimulate effort to live this life as well as possible if postmortem existence were to be completely denied or if it were to be assumed that such an existence is unrelated to the way we live and is, instead, determined arbitrarily by divine power. The current tendency to live solely in pursuit of the satisfaction of desires and to have no awareness of the meaning of, or reason for, living reflects modern humanity's lack of interest in the postmortem state.

Creative art stimulates the will to leave something behind to bear witness to one's having existed, even if life is a unique, nonrepeating, one-time affair. But this avenue is open only to people with talent and self-confidence in their talent. For most people, leaving testimony of themselves in the form of creative art or other cultural creativity is out of the question because of lack of talent or lack of suitable conditions. Moreover, of how much significance is it to the dead artist that his outstanding work remains and that his name is remembered in the world? Our contemporaries regard their postmortem selves as void, not on the basis of certain proof but because, lacking the ability to make a judgment, they prefer not to think about the topic.

It is characteristic of modern people who regard only scientific thought as accurate to devote consideration solely to those things about which it is possible to make judgment on the basis of objective cognition. But people who have mastered scientific thought and have contributed to the development of science usually refrain from denying the existence of things outside the possibilities of objective cognition. Indeed, they have realized that their own fields are only parts of a complicated, diverse whole and have assumed a modest posture in relation to things outside their departments.

People who neither understand it well nor understand its position in the whole world sometimes apply scientific thought with blind faith and reject the existence of things that do not conform to its methods. I believe, however, that accurate mastery of scientific thought and its proper position can open the eyes of such people to many things, including religious ways of thought.

The religious way of thinking entails a qualitative interpretation of one's life and entity. Instead of striving to devise ways to make the present life as long and pleasant as possible, it finds its fulcrum outside this life and beyond the self and evaluates both. The fulcrum of religions—including Buddhism—in the past has been the postmortem future. Their teachings have included narrative explanations of the pleasures and pains of that state. But people today put no credence in the imaginary pictorial versions of heaven and hell that were once widely used as concrete representations. They can, however, understand that human life may be qualitatively high or low, superior or inferior. I believe that this is the nature of the things that religions have tried to teach.

Whereas Buddhism deals with this problem by means of the concept of the eternal nature of life, Christianity rejects the infinite past and future of the individual life. From the Judeo-Christian standpoint, it is impossible to go farther back in time than the moment at which God the Creator created everything in the universe. Am I correct in assuming that, under this system, the individual life, which is created by God, cannot have an infinite past?

As I have said, the Buddhist philosophy is that all life has both an infinite past and an infinite future and that the birth-death cycle recurs over and over an infinite number of times. Within this continuing current of life, a chain of cause-and-effect relations comes into being. In other words, the effects one experiences in the present life were not created by God but have come about because of one's own causal activities (whether at an earlier point in this life or in a previous existence). I consider this doctrine important because it clarifies one's own responsibility in relation to one's faith and because it establishes human dignity.

HUYGHE: From my viewpoint, like that of infinity, the problem of eternity exceeds the human spirit's capacities to investigate and understand. We are capable of understanding in time, as in space, only the finite and defined. All limits raise the question of what is beyond them. We are, therefore, led to move limits ahead and then to repeat the process to the point of vertigo. This vertigo is what is called infinity in the case of space and eternity in the case of time. But a certain negligence always keeps the solution more and more at arm's length and confines itself to negating things we cannot understand. In this I see the negligence of our mental means, which, while capable of understanding the real environment, in the case of most brains cannot, alas, be called omniscient.

Doubtless, a living being finds it difficult to conceive that something existing will cease to exist in the future and that it could not have existed in the past. Considering themselves to be something "revealed," religions have felt it their duty to resolve and answer this problem, which philosophy limited itself to posing. Moreover, wishing to establish moral conduct among human beings, religions were led to declare the eternal life of humanity in order to make us responsible after the present life for acts performed.

The Christian solution involves a future life that is, in a sense, definitive. This approach arises from the Western taste for the fixed, for arriving at the absolute and immutable. It should be stated clearly, however, that Christianity started with sacred texts (like Saint John's Apocalypse, for instance) that are far from affirmative and ended up by decreeing that, after death, there will be a judgment, the Last Judgment (the term is significant), at which human beings will be expected to give an account of the good or ill uses they made of their God-given lives. On the basis of this, as a consequence of their responsibility, their eternal destinies, reward or punishment, are determined. The need to represent this theme in holy images gave it a much more concrete accuracy than it originally had.

The Buddhist position is located in the logic of the Oriental spirit, which, unlike the Occidental spirit, seeks less to establish things in definitions than to follow them in continuity. The Westerner prefers to think in the changelessness of logic, just as we construct a definite form in space once and for all. His thought is a rational construction. The Easterner prefers to abandon himself to a feeling of time and its flowing, moving rhythm. (I fully understand that excessively general definitions of this kind are precisely Western and categorical and must be represented in facts with a variety of nuances. Nonetheless, they offer valid bases.) Christianity envisages an event that is the conclusion of a life—or of all lives—and that imposes on each its status in eternity. In contrast to this, Buddhism conceives of an involvement in time, in which life continues to be responsible. The individual resides in the continuity of his responsibility, which is operative through successive existences representing gradations of good and bad, descent or ascent. Complete success implies an exit from this unrolling and from the personal "Me" and absorption into the absolute, which is outside space and time and which, I believe, you call satori.

May I add that I opt for neither of these solution. I understand that they are well-founded and have a lively interest in them. But, in my philosophical position, I think that the human brain lacks the capacity either to solve or to understand the content of the problem. Religion replies that it offers revelation. But revelation implies faith. And, personally, I have no faith that would permit me to adhere to one or the other of these two revelations.

I believe it is possible to extract from the primordial, the unknowable Being, the material trinomial—matter, space, and time—that constitute our universe and the narrow implications of which modern physics has demonstrated.

This might be called Creation. But, aside from mental conceptions precisely modeled by the universe, who is to say that Time might have existed before this? "In the beginning was the Word." Perhaps the secret lies in the depths of this one phrase. The Word can be the primordial, from which matter, space and time have been forthcoming. This could imply that they do not exist in the depths of the unknowable.

Since thought reaches its limits at this point, what other support, what resources, are we to look for? Reason cannot transcend actuality. Only the spirit permits us to go farther and to think beyond ourselves and, at the limit, to glimpse the inconceivable. Armed with, and founded solely on, the qualitative experience, the spirit glimpses through the future the progression of humanity toward the point in infinity—the point that exercises an allure and an attraction for all creation. Human responsibility—that of each individual participant in the responsibility of all humanity—flows toward that point.

The knowledge of this responsibility must be sufficient unto itself without reinforcement by the ideas of reward or punishment that religions have justly introduced in the name of social effectiveness. I can easily imagine that my passage into existence in individual form should be provisional and that my personality was extracted from nothingness by my birth and asserted during my infancy, a kind of apprenticeship making it aware of its responsibilities.

But this convergence and association of diverse energies—physical, biological, psychic, and spiritual—the fascicle of which is located in the fundamental part of my being, will disassociate and return to the mysterious source on the day of my death, like a spark struck from a flint that fades into the night. As we witness in others and may experience ourselves, aging often represents the start of disassociation. Some elements persist in ossified form; others fail. First the memory goes, and the sense of responsibility sometimes grows confused. And there are no longer means to replenish them. Certainly this prelude is indicative.

I have no revelation permitting me to go further. What need is there of future ratification? It is more noble for the individual to envision his moral responsibility within himself, for its own sake. Surely it is normal to act, in this instance, as in the case of Beauty, which offers no recompense but itself. Will we never come to measure ourselves according to Kant's criterion?

Moral quality may be the sole valid reason for living. Consequently, if we live, it is to accomplish life. Their nature as plenary forces for that accomplishment is necessary and sufficient reason for us to strive to attain moral quality and spiritual quality. This is probably why we are here. We ought then to do what we were constituted as human beings—the final stage so far attained by Creation—to do.

This is why, while realizing that both Christianity and, especially, Buddhism solve, each with its own position, the problem in a socially extremely useful manner, I experience no need to adhere to a religious solution. A life that is founded solely on the actual—as modern materialism would have it—makes us lose sight of our responsibility to make a spiritual ascent. On the other hand, by means of promised future ratification, religions attract those—and they are too numerous—who would allow themselves to give into the inertia of anguish. But the person who is capable of making absolute demands of himself can overcome the fear of failing to have a future life—or lives—that others find indispensable to the completion of their tasks.

Although I have oriented all my life to Beauty because I sense in it one of the forms of the qualitative aspect of being, I realize that strictness in conduct is another means of attaining a similar end. Buddhism teaches that the supreme goal of successive existences is the ninth consciousness, where it is possible to become one with the universal life, in which the individual self is engulfed.

I do not believe that my views contravene the Buddhist idea

of the universe as a great current of energy perpetuating itself. Personally, I do not foresee an end to things. And I certainly do not say that everything in the universe was made by God. I put the problem differently.

I do not believe in the Creation as a starting point. I believe in a kind of Eternity, an absolute that, ignoring our "dimensions" in time and space, escapes our understanding. The existence of the world that we know is extracted from this absolute which, for many people, is called God. I do not like using the name God because it often conceals a human—too human—concept reduced to the scale of our thought. I avoid using the word because for each believer in any given religion it corresponds to certain fixed ideas and thus assumes something too restrictive, which troubles me. But I can go for shelter to lofty authorities like Saint Thomas Aquinas, for example, who said that it is impossible to come together again with God through judgment, meaning, imagination, opinion, reason, or knowledge and who declares, in connection with Him, what he calls an "agnosticism of definition." I agree with this.

In the forefront of modern physics, behind the accessible phenomena that we call reality, the English theoretic physicist Paul A. M. Dirac (1902–) has supposed a substratum that escapes the dimensions of space and time and both our quantitative methods and our mental conceptions. Once again, I agree. Although language differs from age to age, Dirac's idea is not extremely different from that of Saint Thomas Aquinas.

Behind the matter perceptible to our senses, I feel an infinitely more vast and profound reality, of which matter is perhaps the most degraded and at the same time the most tangible state. This more profound reality comes to me through all of my deepest experiences, which I call original. Actually it comes, not from the exterior as I receive whatever I know of the world, but from an innermost source where I join with Being and Existence in an original location of lived experience where the two are one.

As it is organized, our spirit can only come into contact with the profound reality of things by means of an attempt at stripping away in order to rejoin its vital origin. The spirit is gifted with intellectual means to represent things by means of notions, which are themselves concealed in words. To organize these notions usefully, the spirit is gifted with mental structures that it tries to codify by means of something called logic. It must be understood, however, that this logic is not of one fixed kind. There is Aristotelian logic, which insists that everything must be brought together in a unity. There is in addition the logic of dialectic and contradiction, like that evolved in our age by philosophers like Stéphane Lupasco. Moreover there is a distinct mathematical logic, and so on.

The diversity of concepts, which vary according to individual, race, and period of time, and the diversity of rational systems assembling and construing these concepts seem to prove that human beings are gifted with imperative systems of understanding, I might almost say mechanisms of understanding. We can understand only according to the standards of these mechanisms. From the moment when such a mechanism is interposed between what we vaguely call reality and ourselves, we clearly become unable to pretend to understand that reality. The mechanism marking the boundary between ourselves on one side and the so-called real on the other acts like a pane of glass that, while transparent, will not permit so much as a fly to pass from the opposite side.

The only things capable of even slightly crossing this boundary are certain very profound intuitions that do not develop from intellect, logic, or conceptual notions. In many religions these intuitions animate a tendency toward mysticism in which, in culmination, they reconcile differences of dogma and differences in ways of representing God.

It is the nature of the mystical to be inexplicable. Essentially, the mystical gives a sensation of sharing: the drop that was separated from the stream falls back into the current to become water again. We return to something beyond the thinkable, but we can bring back nothing from the things that have re-entered conceptual mechanisms. Things that can be perceived—or, better, felt—shatter the mechanisms. Things that can be explained are a concession to our mental machinery, a kind of fraudulent translation. The mystical is like water which cannot be caught in a net, and we have at our disposal nothing but the net of our rational thought.

I am dissatisfied with the word God because it attempts to conceal a notion. I understand well what people look for in the notion of God but prefer not to limit it to such a framework. For some very simple believers, God is incarnate in the old man with a white beard seen in Christian iconography. People who, while going beyond such representations, nonetheless have some set notion of God, though on a much higher level than very simple believers, still seem to engage in deforming, restrictive, anthropomorphism. The only thing left is to wander in infinity by striving to avoid using images, words, or ideas.

If this is valid for the idea of God it is all the more so for the concept of Creation, in which human habits of thought have too obviously been transplanted. From daily experience, human beings know that nothing organized and truly novel can appear unless it is the fruit of concerted, voluntary action and of intelligent creation. In my opinion, the law of causality (all phenomena must have a cause), even though universal in our experience, has no meaning *outside* our world, in which matter, space, and time are one.

With his extraordinary genius, Kant sensed that the True and Being are situated far beyond such categories and are inconceivable to our mental means. Why should knowledge that is nothing but human be valuable outside humanity? This is why the very idea of the Creation seems to me not unintelligible, but too explicable as an excessive extension of our own mental limits to things that surpass them. For the world to have been called forth from nothing by a supreme intelligence who thought out and calculated its organization suggests the work of an engineer.

The concepts of infinity and eternity, actually inconceivable, cover a reality that escapes us by means of imprecise words. We can attain them only negatively by the conjectured and successive elimination of each new limit. In doing this we arbitrarily scratch out the words beginning and end without having replacements for them. They are only labels that we fabricate to hide our presentiment of something surpassing us.

As the result of a kind of concentration, from the Unknowable, that we may denominate Being, it becomes possible to find "entrances" into time and space. When, as a consequence of a tighter necessity of approach, modern physics discovered space-time, with its deformations and curves, it began to upset the dimensions of human experience. And this made it all the more possible to conjecture negatively (that is, by suspecting our own manners of understanding) the existence of something that is neither time nor space. We are sometimes troubled by the effort a dog must make to understand human thoughts that are inconceivable to him. We should imagine ourselves in the dog's place confronted with something inaccessible to us within the limits of our nature.

In the mysterious fabric of which space and time—the two dimensions to which we are accustomed—are made, it is possible to imagine the development of rents or spots that become centers of concentration, or nuclei. Thus emerge atoms at the smallest end of the scale and nebulas, stars, and astral systems at the biggest (so far as we know) end. Things that produce themselves at the level of matter renew themselves at the level of life, which supplies a coordination center for the elements constituting an organism.

On the psychic level, consciousness surges to a nucleus on which sensory material converges and forms a gravitational center that is the "I." This "I" asserts itself more and more as it rises up the rungs of the animal ladder and ultimately arrives at humanity, the most successful manifestation forthcoming up to the present time. In this process it is possible to trace an analogy with the operation of the magnifying glass, which captures diverse rays of light, collects them, and concentrates them in a focal point where an image is formed.

But the psychological coordination called the "I" may have a beginning and an end like those of astral systems. Cosmic dust gives birth to a nebula which concentrates into an astral system, which then fades and dies, returning to cosmic dust and dispersed energy. The physical body, on which the psychic manifestation is grafted, is subject to the same rhythm or organization, which makes it grow, and to dissolution, which causes it to die.

The human being appears and disappears, associating and disassociating components that, on the material plane, create a body, on the plane of life, a being endowed with existence, and on the psychic plane, a "Me." Moreover all three planes are united in a common undertaking.

Just as worlds are formed from the vagueness of cosmic dust, it would seem possible to imagine the appearance of a human being—a consciousness—created by means of phenomena resembling the concentration of what, on the basis of analogy, might be called psychic dust. But, before this psychic dust is organized around the nucleus that becomes an individual human being and after death, when the hour of that concentration has passed, there must be only something vague and indistinct.

It is in this sense that I adhere to your idea that all human life is perpetuated from an eternal past into an eternal future. But I have difficulty believing that this perpetuation takes place in the form of individual continuity.

I should like to return again to the comparison with waves and the ocean. The waves and the ocean are the same thing, yet the waves distinguish themselves from the ocean just as they distinguish themselves from each other. They occupy places in space and spread out in time. They come into being and disappear. The only thing that remains is the water from which they come into being and into which they return. The same is true of the millennia, centuries, beings, and days of Creation. Drawn from the substance of Being, they are abolished, like waves, with their changing forms, their ventures, their expansion, their foam, their crests. . . .

I see a similar ocean of energy engulfing the infinity of space and time and calling forth eddies and waves that are replaced and succeeded by others. Since energy differentiates at diverse echelons, at the lowest levels, these waves are physical things, at the highest they are thinking beings.

But the operation remains the same as in the constitution of waves. Molecules swallowed up in the infinite, collective mass of the ocean are suddenly associated with each other in a common action and an evolving form. The form is born, amplifies itself, reaches fullness and, then, relapses, degrades, and dissolves. The molecules return to their collective reserve soon to combine again with other molecules and to generate other waves.

Each wave stirs up another wave behind itself. The living being does the same thing. It engenders other waves that are not entirely the same as itself and that form groups with other molecules. Nonetheless, their mass, forms, and movements inherit some of the molecules and impetus of the preceding wave. But after a certain time, this heritage, this trace of the past, is abolished. This is true of our works too. By means of our works we hope to perpetuate the transport of the wave that we composed. Our thoughts expressed in a work of art or literature can move future waves and stimulate them to form. It is in this kind of thing, as in the case of waves, that I see extensions of ourselves that can survive after our deaths. But for how long?

From the Lesser to the Greater Self

IKEDA: As you know, the Buddhist teaching, which does posit an individual continuity of life extending from an infinite past before birth to an infinite future after death, differs from your concept of life as a wave on the ocean that comes into being and then ends. Of course, we are unaware of the continuity. The physical and spiritual functions that we perform in this life come into being at birth, reach fulfillment at adulthood and, thereafter, wane until death. But the source of physical and spiritual functions is a nucleus called the self, or the atman, which, transcending life and death, survives. While being the nucleus of the individual life, the atman embraces the universal life force, or the greater self. I consider the notion of the atman's being at once the nucleus of the individual life and embracing the universal life correct.

Our inability to recall earlier existences or to be aware of the infinite continuity of our lives does not invalidate the truth of the doctrine. Facts, whether we are aware of them or not, influence and control our lives. And, as psychoanalysis has shown, the subconscious—that is, things of which we are not actually aware—sometimes exerts stronger influences than the conscious.

There have been reports in both Europe and the United States of hypnotism used to analyze the deep levels of the subconscious. As a consequence of such studies, people have been shown to recall, subconsciously, not only their own childhoods, but also their past lives. Although I do not know the extent to which it is possible to trust such studies, from the viewpoint of Buddhist teachings the purport is possible.

Remembering past existences means that the lesser self persists consistently as an individual. Buddhist scriptures relate many stories of the training and discipline that Shakyamuni underwent in his previous existences, of which, as devout Buddhists believe, the Buddha was aware.

Except under special conditions, like hypnotic trance, ordinary people cannot recall previous existences. But whether they can be recalled or not, if it is admitted that our current selves are the results of past actions, we cannot be indifferent to the law of cause and effect. It is true that we can do nothing about the past, but we ought to strive now to create the best possible causes for good results that will manifest themselves in the future.

HUYGHE: To avoid confusion, I should like to clarify my position. I attribute the incapacity of grasping the final essence of reality to human thought. You seem to agree with this when you say that the world greatly transcends these limits. Actually, humanity is adapted functionally to space and time, but the nature of being is located outside this double dimension and we lack the means of grasping it. We can know exactly those things that are situated in reality defined by space-time. And this is why we ventured to discover and to conquer that reality by means of science which, within its own limits, is perfectly well adapted and has shown itself to be efficacious. Beyond this is where the impenetrable begins.

Science knows this and refuses to go farther. It holds suspect the philosopher who forces himself to try to go beyond the bounds of the knowable. Religions propose revelations that are actually translations from the divine to the human of the unknowable and unintelligible. This is how I view the situation of human thought in the face of the mystery of things.

Our inability to arrive at the final end of all things should not hamper us in going as far forward as we can. To my way of thinking, stating this does not imply that we must abandon the effort to approach the goal by constantly trying to make reason more supple, even if our limited means make attainment impossible. Man did not give up the idea of going to the moon merely because, for many reasons, he will never be able to set foot on the sun.

On the other hand, such a conviction by no means implies that we must limit ourselves to making the statement and then follow only our own existence, falling back on individual egoism. On the contrary, in my opinion, through the personal existence, which is known only to the person experiencing it, the individual must sense another greater existence and must allow himself to identify with it. The human being demonstrates a wonderful aptitude for going beyond his personal realm and even to risk his own happiness or his life for a great cause. History offers virtually numberless examples of individuals who have sacrificed their lives for their countries. Such instances are of the most prevalent kind. The individual has still stronger reason to be exalted by the idea of contributing to the destiny of all humanity. As we have already seen, religions encourage thinking of this kind by foreseeing punishment or reward for activities during this life.

But I believe that even the least elevated soul cannot accomplish good and escape evil out of hope for a prize or fear of punishment. It must be as a result of a conviction, which I summarize again: it is possible to trace a thrust throughout time and the thrust of time marked by a progression starting with matter, elevating itself to life, through life attaining consciousness, and, through an increasingly purified consciousness, with humanity, attaining spirituality.

We must feel ourselves participants in this movement, which we affirm without understanding its reasons (for human beings, the word reason seems to imply some kind of restraint). The movement has an imperative character like that of a natural law. As the most lucid particle in the universe, we must participate in the movement to the degree permitted by our lucidity and contribute to it since it is the orientation and destination that have grown stronger throughout time. Doing so is our responsibility. When I participate in this ascent, I feel a sense of accomplishment. I am more fully myself. Perhaps this is the goal toward which my life is directed.

Responsibility introduces the problem of cause, which you underscore. Is the cause to be found in the divine will or in our own actions? This brings up the question of grace which, posed by Christianity, assumed great importance in the split between Protestantism and Catholicism. In seventeenth-century France, with the Jansenists of Port-Royal, it provoked a conflict within Catholicism itself. And even among nonbelievers, this complex problem has rebounded with the issue of determinism and liberty.

The problem first arose with the appearance of the human personality. We have already estimated the extent to which this personality is grafted on a physical body in which all physiological causalities play a part. Not the least of the causalities is that of heredity and genetic transmission of ancestral characteristics. Genetically a character datum comes to influence our "Me." This means only that we must establish our course in connection with this character datum, no matter whether it is an encouragement or an obstacle.

Fundamentally, however, genetic transmission seems to mean the same thing as the Buddhist conviction of successive lives, each carrying a burden from the preceding life. The

Western idea, born of science, is physiological and all the more materialistic. Medical science shows that a heavy drinker who has contracted a venereal disease imposes on his children defects for which they must pay. Although it speaks its own language, this idea seems to express a conviction similar to the Buddhist notion that, through successive lives, we in a sense become our own ancestors because we transmit to posterity responsibilities for already committed acts that influence destiny. Though operative on different planes and expressed by different means, these two ideas represent a troubling connection.

In addition to causes working to determine us from within, we must add causes that act from without and that indicate the pressure of society on our character and thoughts, and the acts through which they are expressed. Education, the environment, and current ideas combine forces. Since the nineteenth century, the West has stressed social determinism; and Marxism accords a preeminent role to the structural classes of society and to the economy. Man's role is precisely to take up positions on both fronts, to use military terminology, to play the destiny of his own liberty.

The human personality approved by the lesser self is not merely the result of the forces at work on it. This personality becomes firmer as it elucidates these forces and determines its own guidance in the face of them. This is the margin of the liberty imparted to humanity. This is where our possibilities of combat and our responsibility reside.

I am in profound agreement with you in your eagerness to establish human dignity and restore a sense of it. I deeply respect and admire the way Buddhism makes this a responsibility. But, as you have come to understand, I define that responsibility in a manner corresponding to my own studies and personal experience and, perhaps, to a sense of my own responsibility acute enough to prevent my accepting an already established religion. In spite of the very profound admiration I have for the positive, elevating, and saving force of the higher religions, I wonder if they do not limit the full exercise of this responsibility in that they compel us to work out our destiny